Gendered Impacts of China's Development Initiatives in the Global South

Gendered Impacts of China's Development Initiatives in the Global South

Edited by Cai Yiping
on behalf of DAWN

BLOOMSBURY ACADEMIC
LONDON • NEW YORK • OXFORD • NEW DELHI • SYDNEY

BLOOMSBURY ACADEMIC

Bloomsbury Publishing Plc, 50 Bedford Square, London, WC1B 3DP, UK
Bloomsbury Publishing Inc, 1359 Broadway, New York, NY 10018, USA
Bloomsbury Publishing Ireland, 29 Earlsfort Terrace, Dublin 2, D02 AY28, Ireland

BLOOMSBURY, BLOOMSBURY ACADEMIC and the Diana logo are
trademarks of Bloomsbury Publishing Plc

First published in Great Britain 2026

Copyright © DAWN, 2026

DAWN has asserted their right under the Copyright, Designs and Patents Act, 1988,
to be identified as Author of this work.

For legal purposes the Acknowledgements on p. xiv constitute an extension
of this copyright page.

Cover design by Paul Smith
Cover image © Marla Rabelo, on behalf of DAWN

This work is published open access subject to a Creative Commons Attribution-NonCommercial-NoDerivatives 4.0 International licence (CC BY-NC-ND 4.0, https://creativecommons.org/licenses/by-nc-nd/4.0/). You may re-use, distribute, and reproduce this work in any medium for non-commercial purposes, provided you give attribution to the copyright holder and the publisher and provide a link to the Creative Commons licence.

No part of this publication may be used or reproduced in any way for the training, development or operation of artificial intelligence (AI) technologies, including generative AI technologies. The rights holders expressly reserve this publication from the text and data mining exception as per Article 4(3) of the Digital Single Market Directive (EU) 2019/790.

Bloomsbury Publishing Plc does not have any control over, or responsibility for, any third-party websites referred to or in this book. All internet addresses given in this book were correct at the time of going to press. The author and publisher regret any inconvenience caused if addresses have changed or sites have ceased to exist, but can accept no responsibility for any such changes.

A catalogue record for this book is available from the British Library.

Library of Congress Cataloging-in-Publication Data available

ISBN: HB: 978-1-350-55727-7
PB: 978-1-350-55728-4
ePDF: 978-1-350-55730-7
eBook: 978-1-350-55729-1

Typeset by RefineCatch Limited, Bungay, Suffolk
Printed and bound in Great Britain

For product safety related questions contact productsafety@bloomsbury.com.

To find out more about our authors and books visit www.bloomsbury.com
and sign up for our newsletters.

Contents

List of Contributors   vii
Foreword *by Kamala Chandrakirana*   xii
Acknowledgements   xiv

    Introduction: Co-production of Southern Feminist Knowledge on Global China *by Cai Yiping*   1

1   The Impact of Chinese Development Cooperation on Women in Trinidad and Tobago *by Annita Montoute, Jacqueline Laguardia Martinez, and Deborah McFee*   39

2   Gender Impacts of China's Engagement in Pacific Island Countries: Case Studies of BRI Infrastructure Projects in Tonga and Vanuatu *by Vasemaca Lutu*   63

3   Chinese Mining Projects in Ecuador and Peru: Gender Impacts and Women's Agency *by Diana Castro Salgado*   87

4   Organised Abandonment and Gendered Impacts of Extractivism in Bikita, Zimbabwe *by Hibist Wendemu Kassa and Zinzile Siphiwo Fengu*   111

5   Empowering Women in Nigerian Agriculture: Assessing the Effects of China-Nigeria Agricultural Cooperation on Female Smallholders' Livelihood, Capacity-Building, and Shifting Social Norms *by Ishola Itunu Grace*   137

6   Implications of Security Agreements on Women, Peace, and Security in Solomon Islands: A Comparative Case Study on China-Solomon Islands Bilateral Security Cooperation and the Australia-Solomon Islands Bilateral Security Treaty *by Patricia Sango Pollard*   163

7   The Gender Question in China's Soft Power Engagement in the Global South *by Govind Kelkar and Ritu Agarwal*   185

8 When Civil Society Contests Global China: Challenges and Opportunities for Gender-Related Civil Society Transnational Action on China-Backed Infrastructure Projects in the Global South *by Laura Trajber Waisbich* 207

Conclusion and Looking Forward *by Cai Yiping* 233

Index 237

Contributors

Cai Yiping is a member of the Executive Committee of Development Alternatives with Women for a New Era (DAWN). She co-leads DAWN's Sexual and Reproductive Health and Rights (SRHR) thematic analysis team together with Gita Sen. She was associate researcher at the Women's Studies Institute of China (2006-2008) and was a journalist for China Women's News (1995-2005), writing extensively on the issue of women's human rights and development. Her research focuses on the transnational feminist movement, especially in the Global South, sexual and reproductive health and rights, media, and communication. She is a PhD candidate at the Department of Global and International Studies, University of California, Irvine.

Annita Montoute is a Senior Lecturer and Acting Director at the Institute of International Relations (IIR), The University of the West Indies (UWI), St. Augustine Campus, Trinidad and Tobago. She was a research fellow at the European Centre for Development Policy Management. Her research interests include civil society and global governance, the Caribbean's external relations, and China in the Caribbean. She holds a PhD in International Relations, from The University of the West Indies. She is a trained teacher with a graduate certificate in Education from the Sir Arthur Lewis Community College.

Jacqueline Laguardia Martinez PhD, is a senior lecturer at the Institute of International Relations at The University of the West Indies. Previously, she worked as an associate professor at the University of Havana and researcher associate at the Cuban Institute for Cultural Research 'Juan Marinello'. She has participated in academic events, delivered lectures, and undertaken teaching responsibilities in North America, Latin America, and Europe. She is a member of the Cátedra de Estudios del Caribe 'Norman Girvan' at the University of Havana and the Coordinator of the CLACSO Working Group on 'Crisis, respuestas y alternativas en el Gran Caribe'.

Deborah McFee has worked at the Institute for Gender and Development Studies, the University of the West Indies, St Augustine Campus, since 2005. She has worked in the area of gender and development in Trinidad and Tobago and the wider Anglophone Caribbean since 1998. Deborah has worked on the development of three regional national gender policies and co-edited with Professor Michelle Rowley the 2017 special issue of the *Caribbean Review of Gender Studies* (CRGS) entitled 'Tool or Weapon?: The Politics of Policy Making, Gender Justice and Social Change in the Caribbean'. Her peer-reviewed publications address research on national gender policies and the politics of policy-making in the Caribbean, rethinking gender mainstreaming in the Caribbean, and women, gender, human security and the national gender policy in post-genocide Rwanda. In 2011, she was the visiting researcher at the United Nations International Criminal Tribunal for Rwanda (ICTR), conducting research in the areas of gender and human security and rape as a crime against humanity. Deborah holds a PhD from the Department of Global Governance and Human Security, University of Massachusetts Boston, McCormack Graduate School of Public Policy and Global Studies.

Vasemaca Lutu is a Fijian independent researcher. She has been engaged in several development and gender related research projects. She is also a member of the Bia i Cake Women's Co-operative, her local village women's group with a mission of 'Building alternative livelihoods through sustainable natural resource management', located in Nagigi village, Savusavu. She holds a master's degree in Leadership for Sustainability from Malmö University, Sweden and a Post-graduate Diploma in Development Studies from the University of the South Pacific. She is currently training as a commercial aircraft pilot.

Diana Castro is Deputy Director at Latinoamérica Sustentable (LAS), an Ecuadorian NGO that supports the protection of the environment and local communities within the context of Chinese investments in Latin America. Diana is a doctoral fellow in the Latin American Studies Program and holds a master's degree in international development cooperation at the Universidad Andina Simón Bolívar (UASB-Ecuador). Since 2014, Diana has studied Latin America-China relations, with a particular emphasis on Chinese financing mechanisms for development and infrastructure investment projects. Her doctoral research traces the effects that these projects have on institutional capacities of the state, the environment, and local development, delving into the Ecuadorian case. Diana has published several articles and a book on these topics. She has also worked in various Ecuadorian universities and collaborated on international research initiatives on the relevance of China in Latin America.

Hibist Wendemu Kassa is a policy interface fellow at the Institute for Environmental Futures, University of Leicester. She is also a researcher-in-residence at Thousand Currents, public foundation funding grassroots work that addresses the interdependent issues of food sovereignty, alternative economies, and climate justice in the Global South. She is an associate editor with the Agrarian South Network Research Bulletin, a tricontinental network of researchers in Africa, Latin America, and Asia. Hibist was awarded her doctorate in Sociology from University of Johannesburg. She has worked in feminist organizations and policy research institutes in Africa for over a decade and is a former DAWN Executive Committee member. She is currently working on her forthcoming book on the Political Economy of Artisanal and Small-scale Mining. She has published on academic and popular platforms on artisanal mining policy, land, social reproduction, imperialism and conflict in Africa, and the political economy of natural resources.

Zinzile Siphiwo Fengu is an avid researcher and independent consultant. She holds a BA in language and communication and a special honors degree in monitoring and evaluation from Lupane State University, and a Master of Science Degree in development studies. She has worked in the human rights sector for over 12 years and has experience in trauma healing, lobby and advocacy, and feminist movement building. She's currently studying for a PhD in development studies, and her thesis work focuses on feminist organizing in Zimbabwe. Her research interests are feminist perspectives on environmental issues, extractivism, livelihoods, disaster management, and sexual reproductive health rights.

Ishola Itunu Grace is a 2022 Yenching Scholar at Yenching Academy of Peking University's Masters of China Studies program, majoring in politics and international relations, with a research focus on China-Africa cooperation in education, human capital development, and public diplomacy. Grace obtained her bachelor's degree in Chinese language and international education from Capital Normal University, Beijing. She is fluent in Mandarin and contributes to the field of China-Africa relations through extensive field studies, observations, and interviews conducted with participants from various parts of China. Grace holds the Li Anshan Prize for Excellence in African Studies, an award for her outstanding performance in African Studies at Peking University. Additionally, she is the head of the academic planning committee of Africa Diaspora in China Network, Beijing, an affiliate of the African Union in China.

Patricia Sango Pollard is an independent researcher in gender equality, women's rights, and social inclusion in Solomon Islands. She has experience program managing the Solomon Islands Women's Rights Action Movement and sits on the boards of organizations advocating for women's rights and against commercial sexual exploitation of children. She is currently engaged with both local and regional organizations and development partners in Solomon Islands providing advice on gender equality and social inclusion. One of her recent works in 2023 was a policy paper to the Australian government on peace building and feminist foreign policy focusing on Solomon Islands, with the La Trobe University in Australia. She is currently working in the area of forestry and tourism reforms in the Solomon Island. She graduated with a master's degree in development studies from the University in the South Pacific in 2014 with a thesis on the impacts of development aid on gender equality programs in Solomon Islands.

Govind Kelkar is a feminist scholar, a PhD in the political economy of China. She is a visiting professor at the Council for Social Development and Institute for Human Development, India. She is the executive director of the GenDev Centre for Research and Innovation, India, and was a senior advisor at Landesa, Seattle, USA (May 2013–March 2020). In her concurrent assignments, Professor Kelkar was the international research coordinator of ENERGIA International, the Netherlands, and research lead on gender and energy at Swaminathan Research Foundation, Chennai. She is a distinguished adjunct faculty at the Asian Institute of Technology, Bangkok, Thailand. Professor Kelkar has the position of honorary professor at the Institute of Ethnology, Yunnan Academy of Social Sciences, China, and honorary senior fellow at the Institute of Chinese Studies, Delhi. She has authored sixteen books and numerous scholarly publications. She recently co-authored the book *Witch Hunts: Culture, Patriarchy and Structural Transformation*, Cambridge University Press, 2020.

Ritu Agarwal is an associate professor at the Centre for East Asian Studies, School of International Studies, Jawaharlal Nehru University (JNU). She holds a PhD in Chinese studies from the University of Delhi. She completed her MA in political science at JNU. Her doctoral work explored the micro-level agrarian transformation in Yunnan province, and she is currently engaged in questions of provincial transformation, especially in Yunnan. Her research interests are rural political economy, urbanization, property rights, gender studies, and provincial and Chinese politics. Dr Agarwal studied Mandarin Chinese at Beijing Language and Culture University, Beijing. She was a visiting scholar at Yunnan Academy of

Social Sciences, Kunming and visiting fellow at Yunnan Minzu University and, recently, Yunnan University. She was also affiliated with the Chinese University of Hong Kong and East Asia Institute, National University of Singapore, Singapore, to collect material for her research work.

Laura Trajber Waisbich is a South-South cooperation expert. She has fifteen years of research and policy experience in the field of development, foreign policy, and human rights, focusing on the role of Southern powers in International Development. She is a political scientist and international relations expert by training and holds a PhD in geography from the University of Cambridge. Laura is currently Deputy Program Director at the Brazil-based Igarape Institute. Previously, she worked as a departmental lecturer in Latin American studies and the director of the Brazilian Studies Programme at the Latin American Centre at the University of Oxford (UK), as well as a policy and research expert for Brazil, United States, and European think tanks and non-for profits, including the South-South Cooperation Research and Policy Centre (Articulação SUL).

Foreword

Developing analysis and engagement from a Southern feminist standpoint on China's ever-growing influence in the world – Global China, as it is framed in this book – is an undeniable imperative. Chinese investment and labor have entered communities in the Global South and impacted people's lives and natural environment. China's model of development cooperation has reshaped the way many Global South governments approach development and engage with other international development partners. China's approach to peace and security has reconfigured geopolitics in and across regions. Yet, the conversations about China in the Global South, particularly among feminists, have been much too constrained by biases, barriers and blind spots. To attain economic and gender justice and ensure sustainable and democratic development, Southern feminists need to make new breakthroughs in their relations with feminists and allies in China.

The papers in this book testify to the extent of the scope and depth of analysis and engagement necessary for a meaningful outcome. The country case studies show the vastness of Global China's geographic reach and the diversity of its fields of engagement in the Global South. They also illustrate the different ways women have responded to China's projects in their communities: some demanding better access and others calling for a total halt of operations. The book also gives us insights on new trends in China's global engagement and its gendered dimensions, on China's soft power approach and its gendered implications, and on transnational advocacy efforts directed at Chinese projects in the Global South and the absence of gender considerations.

Reading this book, it becomes crystal clear that we are just at the beginning of a long path of building a rigorous understanding of the gender dimensions and impact of Global China with all its uniqueness and complexity. We are fortunate to have such a solid beginning with this publication. The knowledge contained here does not merely provide empirical facts; its contours also equip the reader with a way of thinking about Global China that can be applied in diverse local contexts around the Global South. In this sense, we hope the book will be a reference used by future researchers and activists on Global China.

Above and beyond this book, however, the process by which this publication came to be is itself of significance and deserves special mention. Alongside publishing the research findings, this project's aim is also to build a Southern feminist knowledge community on gender in Global China. This community-building mission is crucial and has long term implications for our capacity to develop autonomous understanding and meaningful engagement on the issue. China continues to change from the inside even as its foothold in the Global South becomes increasingly entrenched. Building a foundation for a community of Southern feminist scholars actively co-producing knowledge responsive to changes inside and outside China is a significant and timely achievement. It could lead to new models of collective action and ecosystems of solidarity. But the starting point is always challenging and involves the necessary act of building bridges, given long-standing disconnects. This is reflected in Cai Yiping's description in the introductory chapter of the diverging views among scholars and the focus on creating a space for dialogue and reflection rather than pursuing consensus. Among the interesting areas of debate in this space was the binary notion of 'Western-centric' vs. 'Sino-centric' approaches. With more empirical facts from the lived realities of women in the Global South and with growing trust in this knowledge community – inside and outside China – we will be able to carry out our own autonomous analysis from a feminist perspective.

This book and the process that led to it hold the promise of overcoming a critical gap in our understanding and engagement on Global China and maybe even, as DAWN hopes, of reimagining South-South relations in ways that meaningfully address women's rights and gender equality.

Kamala Chandrakirana
DAWN General Co-Coordinator

Acknowledgements

This book is a fruit of feminist collaborative endeavor over many years. DAWN board and executive committee members – Elizabeth Cox, Fatou Sow, Lydia Alpízar Durán, Sonia Corrêa, Viviene Taylor, Kamala Chandrakirana, Claire Slatter, Corina Rodríguez Enríquez, Flora Partenio, Gita Sen, Kholoud Al-Ajarma, Kumudini Samuel, María Graciela Cuervo, Masaya Llavaneras Blanco, Vanita Mukherjee – who spearhead the project and provide the guidance throughout the research, especially their insightful comments and feedback greatly improve the project analytical framework and synthesis paper. DAWN is grateful for the commitments and enthusiasm of the authors – Annita Montoute, Jacqueline Laguardia Martinez, Deborah McFee, Vasemaca Lutu, Diana Castro Salgado, Hibist Wendemu Kassa, Zinzile Siphiwo Fengu, Ishola Itunu Grace, Patricia Sango Pollard, Govind Kelkar, Ritu Agarwal, and Laura Trajber Waisbich, and their patience in the painstaking process of revision and editing.

DAWN deeply appreciates project advisors who contributed to the development of the research framework and the review of the case studies: Peggy Antrobus, Siran Huang, T. Tu Huynh, Susie Jolly, Yingtao Li, Haifang Liu, Claire Slatter, Chuanhong Zhang.

This multi-year across-region research would not be able to be accomplished without DAWN global secretariat and info-com team working diligently behind the scenes – Sharan Sindhu, Youli Ge, Lilian Bing, Sala Weleilakeba, Kajal Matthew, Nailagovesi Vakatalai, Ana Rakacikaci, Simran Singh, Ricardo D'Aguiar, Leda Antunes, Giulia Rodrigues, Marla Rabelo, Raquel Cappelletto. Matthew Gill copyedits the manuscript of this volume. DAWN project associates Yin Yu and Lizhen (Momo) Zhang contribute to the development of the research framework and coordination of this project.

Introduction: Co-Production of Southern Feminist Knowledge on Global China

By Cai Yiping

1 Background

With China's expanded global influence on the world stage, there is heightened research and media interest on this subject, primarily focusing on China's overseas investments, especially the Belt and Road Initiative (BRI), as well as the political, socio-economic, environmental, and human rights implications in the context of rapidly shifting global geopolitics and regional dynamics (Yeh 2016, Lee 2017, Ohashi 2018, Beeson 2018, Franceschini and Loubere 2021, Amar et al. 2022, Haug et al. 2024). However, not enough attention has been paid to the gender aspect (Jolly 2016, Cai and Li 2021). Meanwhile, China's leadership has recently increased its commitment to gender equality and women's development at the global level, including providing funding to UN Women to implement the Sustainable Development Goal number five on gender equality and women's empowerment (Xi, 2015 and 2020) and mentioning gender equality and women's development for the first time in China's international cooperation policy paper, *China's International Development Cooperation in the New Era* (SCIO 2021).

To fill this knowledge gap, Development Alternatives with Women for a New Era (DAWN), in collaboration with researchers from the Global South, has conducted a research project from 2022 to 2024 to analyse the gender impact of China's engagement in the Global South. This exploratory research involves scholars with comprehensive knowledge and multiple disciplinary backgrounds from various regions of the Global South – Africa, Asia, the Pacific, Latin America, and the Caribbean. These eight case studies examine the profound and multidimensional implications of China's global engagement for women in the Global South and how various sectors such as governments, businesses, civil societies, and local communities interact with it.

This paper briefly introduces the process of this three-year collaboration and its main findings. Moreover, it reflects on what this research can contribute to overall knowledge production in the Global China field, which to date has been in urgent need of scholarship from the Global South, especially that which is grounded in the experience of women and marginalised groups in the Global South, to strengthen this field. In addition, this research sheds light on the Southern feminist re-imagination of international cooperation, South-South relations, and the integration of women's human rights into development practice in the context of the rising South and changing global geopolitics.

2 Examining trends and impacts of China's global engagement in recent times

Since this research is exploratory in nature, DAWN intentionally avoided imposing topics or modes of interpretation on the authors. We would rather leave the researchers of each case study to determine their research questions, hypotheses, and methods. As the first step, DAWN developed an analytical framework paper to guide this research (Cai and Yu, 2022). The framework paper focuses on the trajectory of China's global engagement in the past half century, especially its new trends since the 2010s to understand how gender is situated in this engagement. It reviews China's state policy and practice on gender and development, international development cooperation, and research and analysis by scholars and civil societies. It mainly explores three questions: (1) What are the new trends of China's global engagement? (2) How is the concept of gender defined in the Chinese government's official discourse and implemented in its development cooperation practice? (3) How can Southern feminist collaboration strengthen women's rights and gender equality and create new knowledge about and critiques of Global China?

Before examining new trends and the impacts of China's expansion in the past few decades, it is important to recognise China's long history of engagement with the world. China's trade relations with Asia, Africa, and Europe predate the colonisation processes in much of the Global South, which continued in the time of the Opium Wars and up through World War II, when China was controlled by European and Japanese empires. After the establishment of the People's Republic of China (PRC) in 1949, and since severing contact with its most important political ally, the Soviet Union, in 1956, China has been aligned with the former colonies and newly independent countries collectively known as the Third

World, developing countries, or the Global South (Yu 1977). This political positioning has persisted from the Bandung conference (1955) to the Non-Aligned Movement (NAM) and continues today with the Group of 77+China at the United Nations (UN). This history is significant, as it has been constantly recalled and re-narrated in contemporary China's global engagement, specifically in its relations with the Global South (Franceschini and Loubere 2021, Xi 2024).

Equally important, China's global engagement needs to be understood within the context of its longstanding and intertwined project of nation-building and worldmaking. Sharing the vision of many developing countries, Chinese leaders believe that the country's priority is to build a strong economy through modernisation and development or, more precisely, economic growth, to catch up with the developed world (Huang 2016). Meanwhile, China, along with other developing countries, has been advocating for a more equal and just world economic order, i.e. New International Economic Order (NIEO), a political agenda being sidelined by the developed countries at the UN (Prashad 2007, Getachew 2019).

Finally, China's global engagement should be examined alongside broader geopolitics from Mao's era up to now. Mao's globalism and the Three Worlds Theory responded to the reality of the Cold War and the China-Soviet Union dispute and were largely driven by an ideological and internationalist agenda (Lin 2019). As the second largest economy, China's current global engagement is a part of the 'rise of the South' phenomenon (UNDP 2013) and influenced by the US-China rivalry; it should be analysed in the context of the overhaul of global governance amid multifaceted crises faced by global capitalism.

DAWN's framework paper divides China's global engagement in the last half century into three periods: (1) 1978 to 2000: its transition from a planned to a market-oriented economy by implementing economic reform and opening-up policies; (2) 2001 to 2012: China's accelerating integration into the neoliberal global economy after joining the WTO in 2001; and (3) 2013 to now: its ongoing global expansion with the launch of the BRI and new international financial institutions, such as Asia Infrastructure Investment Bank (AIIB) and New Development Bank (NDB), or BRICS Bank, as well as its constant adaptation and adjustment in response to the resistance and competition it has been encountering from both the Global South and North.

This research primarily focuses on the latest period of China's global engagement. The DAWN analytical framework paper identifies and analyses three new trends of China's global impacts during this period: (1) defending multilateralism and China's active participation in the UN system, (2) reshaping the landscape of global development cooperation through development finance, aid, and loans, and (3) creating and strengthening new bilateral and multilateral initiatives and mechanisms with a focus on South-South cooperation, such as the BRI, the Global Development Initiative (GDI), the Forum on China-Africa Cooperation, and the China-ASEAN Free Trade Area.

2.1 Defending multilateralism and China's participation in the UN system

In 1971, General Assembly Resolution 2758 gave the Chinese seat at the UN to the PRC, replacing the Taiwan authority that had represented China (Choudhury 2020). As one of five permanent members of the UN Security Council, China has since become an active member of the most important multilateral intergovernmental platform and increasingly used its privileged position at the UN to strengthen its global power and influence global governance (Haug et al, 2024). In recent years, the Chinese government has become more vocal and proactive in defending multilateralism (Abdenur 2014, Chan 2015, Stephen 2021). Meanwhile, it has used the UN system as a platform to legitimise and amplify the benefits of the BRI framework (Liu 2021a, Haug 2024) and to integrate the BRI objectives with the seventeen Sustainable Development Goals (SDGs) through the Global Development Initiative (GDI) launched in 2021. While some researchers see China as a responsible international player in the UN system, others are suspicious about its growing influence within the organization, particularly with respect to its attitudes towards human rights (Brooks 2018, Foot 2020, Worden 2020, Oud 2020, Inboden 2021, Haug et al 2024). China regards itself as playing an active and constructive role in safeguarding world peace and stability, pursuing peaceful development, and participating in the reform of global governance, while defending its national interests, as articulated in the 'Position Paper for The Summit of the Future and the 79th Session of the UN General Assembly' (MoFA China 2024). In contrast, the policy of current Trump's administration towards the UN is guided by 'America First' approach and characterized by its retreat from the UN bodies and multilateral agreements such as Human Rights Council, World Health Organization, Paris Agreement on climate change, defunding the organization's humanitarian work, and scrutiny of UN agencies and projects alleged 'anti-American' ideologies. For example, the US denies the 2030 Agenda and SDGs, expressing that it is inconsistent with US sovereignty and adverse to the rights and interest of Americans (US mission to the UN 2025). The Trump administration's attitude and policy toward the UN leaves more room for China to play an active role in this multilateral mechanism.

2.2 Reshaping the landscape of development financing and cooperation

In 2013, China launched the Belt and Road Initiative, which expedites its overseas economic expansion to promote the five overarching goals of policy coordination, facilities connectivity, unimpeded trade, financial integration, and people-to-people bonds. Since then, China has overtaken the US and other major powers in development finance spending. According to a report by AidData, in an average year during the BRI era, China spent $85 billion on overseas development programs as compared to the US's $37 billion (Malik et al. 2021).

The key criticisms and controversies regarding Chinese development finance regard debt-trap diplomacy and a lack of transparency in trade, loan, and investment deals (Singh 2021, Kinyondo 2019, Tower 2020). Countries with political instability, low government budgets, or high levels of corruption welcome China's foreign aid and loans as they are based on the principles of non-conditionality, non-intervention, and respect for sovereignty (Condon 2012). Other criticisms stem from the negative impacts of large-scale infrastructure, mining, and energy projects on communities and the environment; opaque project agreements and excessive debt burdens; superficial environmental and social impact assessments (ESIAs) and other due diligence measures; and the danger of investments destabilizing high-conflict areas (Tower 2020).

Undoubtedly, China's development financing and cooperation have deeply influenced both practice and discourse in global development financing, which has otherwise been dominated by the Organization of Economic Cooperation and Development (OECD) countries. G7 countries announced the Build Back Better World (B3W) initiative on 12 June 2021 and launched the Partnership for Global Infrastructure and Investment on 26 June 2022. During Baiden administration, the US pledged to mobilize $200 billion in public and private capital over the next five years for this partnership in four areas – health and health security, digital connectivity, gender equality and equity, and climate and energy security (The White House 2022). All these new initiatives are expected to compete with China's BRI or China as a whole. However, since Donald Trump took the White House in 2025, the US foreign aid policy has undergone a fundamental shift. On 20 January 2025, within few hours after becoming the 47th US President, Trump issued an Executive Order 14169 pausing 90-day freeze on nearly all foreign aid, including USAID programs. In March 2025, the administration announced the plan to formally dissolve the agency by September 2025. The closure of USAID and withdrawal funding from international aid have a huge impact in the developing countries and UN agencies that rely on these fundings for delivering the basic health services like medicines, food, treatment for malnutrition, and emergency humanitarian aid. Meanwhile, China reaffirms its existing commitment on development aid and step into the aid vacuum left by the US and portrays itself as the reliable development partner on the world stage. As the China International Development Cooperation Agency (CIDCA) vice-chairman Hu Zhangliang said: "We will not behave like some countries that leave aid recipients feeling helpless, caught off guard, or unprepared for such situations" and that China would increase investment in international development. For example, China agrees to take over a 4.4 million US dollars de-mining project in Cambodia abandoned by USAID (cited in Jolly 2025). China pledges to donate 500 million US dollars to WHO in the next five years and replaces the US as the top donor of the organization (Kuo and Chiang 2025).

2.3 Creating and strengthening new multilateral mechanisms

In recent years, China has initiated and created new multilateral development institutions and funds engaging at regional levels and expanding to the global level. China has also evolved from being a co-founder and participant at these forums to acting more frequently as the initiator and host. Some researchers see this as China's attempt to affect a 'realignment of the international order through establishing parallel structures to a wide range of international institutions'; others see it as a form of 'institutional (re)balancing' of unequal global power relations dominated by US hegemony (Abdenur 2014, Stephen 2021). The latest imitative of this kind is the International Organization for Mediation (IOMed) officially launched on 30 May 2025. Headquartered in Hong Kong China, IOMed aims to fill an institutional gap in international mediation and serve as an important public good in the field of the rule of law for better global governance. Mediation by IOMed is voluntary and its result is nonbinding (Wang 2025, Sun 2025).

Platforms such as BRICS, Shanghai Cooperation Organization, the Forum on China-Africa Cooperation (FOCAC), the China-Arab States Cooperation Forum (CASCF), the China-Caribbean Economic and Trade Cooperation Forum (CCETC), Cooperation Between China and Central and Eastern European Countries, known as 17+1, and the Forum of China and Community of Latin American and Caribbean States allow China significant room to set the agenda and may belie the non-hierarchical connotations of multilateralism that China advocates. The creation of the NDB (2014) and AIIB (2015) exemplify China's expansion of its multilateralism globally and undoubtedly redistribute the power and resources held by existing organizations, diversify influence and mandates, offer more choices for service takers, and enhance China's bargaining power as they provide alternative funding for recipient countries (Stephen 2021).

Most of the new mechanisms that China has created are based on the South-South framework. The concept of Global South refers to developing and underdeveloped countries, of which many are located in the Southern Hemisphere, in Asia, the Pacific, Africa, Latin America, and the Caribbean. The Global South's lower level of economic and industrial development and dependency on the Global North is a consequence of five hundred years of European imperialism and colonialism (Mignolo 2011). However, the challenge today is to identify a common ground for compromise and collaboration in the Global South (Ramachran 2016, Weiss et al. 2016, Waisbich et al. 2021). Nevertheless, how Chinese-propelled multilateralism is distinguished from the multilateralism dominated by the Global North remains a question to be answered.

3 Probing gender in China's global engagement

3.1 Gender equality vs. equality between men and women: an ambiguous positionality

A textual analysis of Chinese official documents related to China's global engagement shows that the terms gender equality (*xìng bíe píng děng* 性别平等) and equality between men and women (*nán nǚ píng děng* 男女平等) are often used interchangeably. For instance, comparing the English and Chinese version of President Xi Jinping's remarks (Xi 2015) delivered at the Global Leaders' Meeting on Gender Equality and Women's Empowerment took place in the UN Headquarters in New York on 27 September 2015, it can be found that there are two places mentioning of *xìng bíe* (性别) in Chinese version – referring to gender perspective, and gender differences respectively. There was no reference anywhere on gender equality, or *xìng bíe píng děng* (性别平等). There were ten references of promoting, pursuing, and realizing equality between men and women, or *nán nǚ píng děng* (男女平等), and interestingly, all of which were translated into gender equality in the English version. Obviously, two terms are distinct both in Chinese and in English languages and there should be no confusions at all. However, Chinese government has been using the term gender equality at the UN without any qualifiers, nor emphasizing its binary meaning referring to the two sexes, i.e. men and women only, nor rejecting these terms all together, unlike other member states such as Russia, Iran and currently the US. US, for instance, issued a statement regarding to the Political Declaration adopted at the 59th session of the UN Commission on the Status of Women (CSW59). It said:

> In signing Executive Orders to defend Americans from unhealthy and extremist gender ideology, President Trump has made clear his Administration "will defend women's rights and protect freedom of conscience by using clear and accurate language and policies that recognize women are biologically female, and men are biologically male."
>
> US Mission to the UN 2025

For feminist advocates, the terminology matters a lot, particular in the current global context of anti-gender ideology, where gender related terms, such as gender equality, gender-based violence, and gender identities, have been weaponized to attack gender equality and women's rights language at the UN space and to roll back the Beijing Platform for Action (Murray 2022, ERC 2022, Walton 2025). Despite of Chinese state's support for the term gender equality, it is reluctant to support the language of sexual orientation and gender identity (SOGI), arguing that there is a lack of consensus on this issue among member states (Cai 2021 and 2024). The Chinese government's ambiguity on gender-related issues reflects China's longstanding and consistent adherence in diplomacy to the principle of 'seeking common ground while preserving differences' (*qiú tóng cún yì* 求同存异). It may also rise from the fact that China does not consider gender-related issues a priority and a matter of core national interest that must be defended at an international forum. China has not developed a consistent and coherent position on gender-related issues in its foreign policy compared to other more prominent areas such as trade, investment, security, human rights, counterterrorism, and climate change (Cai 2021). This positionality could also be interpreted as its attempt to maintain its progressive image of global champion for gender equality. Whatever the case might be, what matters for Chinese and transnational feminists is how to navigate and augment the political space this ambiguity possibly open for advocating women's human rights and gender equality to its full potential from local to global.

3.2 Vulnerabilities and agencies: defining women in Chinese state's development discourse and the human rights framework

The Chinese government has joined the global consensus on the commitment to promote gender equality and women's rights, including the Beijing Declaration and Platform for Action (BPfA) adopted in Beijing at the UN Fourth World Conference on Women (4WCW) in 1995, the 2030 development agenda and the SDGs adopted in 2015. In its international development cooperation programs, women are often framed as part of a vulnerable group alongside children, the elderly, and people with disabilities (SCIO 2021). Paradoxically, women's potential and agency are acknowledged at the same time. It is believed that developing women's capacity and safeguarding their health will enable women to actively contribute to building a harmonious, stable, and prosperous society and foster national economic development, which will ultimately lead to gender equality. In the Forum on China-Africa Cooperation Beijing Action Plan (2019-2021), gender equality was categorised under the youth and women's section together with women's empowerment, which was associated with health care, skill training, etc. In the renewed Action Plan (2022-2024), the discourse on gender equality and women's empowerment followed the previous path, with its emphasis on realising women's potential in the economy, politics, and security through capacity building and exchange. In a white paper *China's International Development Cooperation in the New Era* (SCIO 2021), gender equality is treated as equivalent to women's development, and safeguarding women's rights and interests is limited to health care promotion.

The state's official discourse on gender equality and women's empowerment perceives economic independence as a prerequisite for women's emancipation, which should be an inherent part of national liberation (Liu 2021b). This framing also coheres with the official Chinese position on human rights, which prioritises the right to development (RtD). The RtD holds that people's rights to subsistence and development is a fundamental human right and a prerequisite for pursuing economic, social, cultural, civil, and political rights. In contrast, the dominant Western international human rights discourse focuses on individual rights and freedom. These different approaches can be observed in Chinese development cooperation projects vis-à-vis traditional Northern donor-funded projects. China is known for its enthusiastic advocacy of the RtD at the international level and for showcasing the 'Chinese approach' to achieving human rights through economic growth and poverty alleviation as a model 'suitable for developing countries' (SCIO 2017 and 2021, Oud 2020). China claims that its investments contribute to the national economy and create jobs for locals in the host countries. However, critics highlight that these investments neglect environmental and social (gender) impacts and affect labour adversely; they also fail to promote the civil and political rights of people in the receiving countries (Osondu-Oti 2016).

3.3 Non-conditionality vs. extraterritorial obligations: the Chinese state's role in promoting gender equality in South-South cooperation

China is signatory to many international human rights treaties such as the Convention on the Elimination of All Forms of Discrimination Against Women (CEDAW), the International Covenant on Economic, Social and Cultural Rights (ICESCR), and the Convention on the Rights of Persons with Disabilities (CRPD), all of which contain the principle of gender equality. China, like all countries that signed and ratified these conventions, is obliged to report periodically on the progress made on implementing these treaties to the relevant treaty bodies. Although these obligations are primarily applied in the domestic jurisdiction, states do have extraterritorial obligations. The 'General comment No. 24 (2017) on State obligations under the International Covenant on Economic, Social and Cultural Rights in the context of business activities' states that

> the Covenant establishes specific obligations of State parties at three levels – to respect, to protect and to fulfil. These obligations apply both with respect to situations on the State's national territory, and outside the national territory in situations over which State parties may exercise control (para. 10) … Extraterritorial obligations arise when a State may influence situations located outside its territory, consistent with the limits imposed by international law, by controlling the activities of corporations domiciled in its territory and/or under its jurisdiction, and thus may contribute to the effective enjoyment of economic, social and cultural rights outside its national territory (para. 28).
>
> E/C.12/GC/24, 10 August 2017

As a signatory to this covenant, these terms apply to Chinese overseas investments and development. International financial institutions (IFIs) have developed some policies on gender-responsive investments, which set the precedents for Chinese financial institutions (Zhao et al. 2021). In recent years, Chinese government ministries collectively have issued numerous foreign investment and finance guidelines on environmental protection and social responsibilities (LAS website, n.d.). Nevertheless, the implementation of these policies on the ground remains questionable (Delfau and Yeophantong 2020, Shieh et al. 2021, The People's Map of Global China website, n. d.).

China's international development cooperation is guided by principles of non-interference, non-conditionality, and reciprocity, and is part of the South-South cooperation framework. Its efforts to promote gender equality in the Global South focus on three themes, namely health care, education, and economic empowerment. This approach is best expressed in *China's International Development Cooperation in the New Era* (SCIO 2021), which highlights China's efforts to improve maternal and child health programs in the Global South, as well as vocational and technical training to increase women's employment and their participation in the political and economic spheres. The document does not provide a comprehensive approach or strategy to mainstream gender in international development cooperation. In the same vein, health care, training, exchange, and education are the main activities in China-Africa cooperation. The FOCAC Dakar Action Plan (2022-2024) and Beijing Action Plan (2025-2027) include some more specifics such as increasing women's professional training in the infrastructure sector, creating jobs for women through Chinese manufacturing investments, enhancing reproductive health, including women in the information technology sector, training policewomen, and organising exchanges between female politicians and high-level officials. The FOCAC Beijing Action Plan (2025-2027) states

> In line with the priorities of Agenda 2063 and the AU Strategy for Gender Equality and Women's Empowerment 2018-2028, we agree to strengthen China-Africa cooperation for the promotion of gender equality and women's empowerment while respecting different traditions and cultures, particularly in the areas of employment, leadership, decent work, entrepreneurship, education and learning, agriculture, health, access to financing, prevention and response to gender-based violence.
>
> MoFA China 2021, 2024

3.4 Between rhetoric and reality: the gender impact of Chinese investments and trade in the Global South

The significant gaps between China's international commitments on gender equality and its practices of transnational trade, foreign investments, and overseas aid projects are due to inadequate knowledge about gender equality in the receiving countries and lack of strong political will on the part of China to fulfil its commitments (Lu et al. 2018). In Chinese-invested agriculture companies in Laos and Cambodia (Huang et al. 2018) and Chinese-invested textile and apparel enterprises in Vietnam, Myanmar, and Bangladesh (Liang 2019), gender awareness among managerial staff and local women workers is quite low. For example, in the Chinese-invested textile industry, Chinese managerial staff's gender stereotypes and lack of gender sensitivity led to gender wage gaps, a lack of facilities for breastfeeding and childcare, and a lack of mechanisms to prevent and manage sexual harassment in the workplace (Liang 2019).

The existing literature shows that the Chinese official discourse on gender equality and women's development is being corroborated in development practice – gender is defined as a binary concept and framed under responsible investment, in which women are computed as valuable economic assets. Both the discourse and the practice suggest that by improving women's rights and empowerment, socially responsible and sustainable investment can be realised. However, much of the current research centres on Chinese investors rather than on the affected local communities and the experiences and perspectives of women and marginalised members of these communities. Furthermore, much research is confined to the environmental, social, and governance (ESG) and corporate social responsibility (CSR) frameworks and neglects unequal multidimensional power relations between international investors, political and economic elites of the host countries, and local communities. It also rarely pays attention to the importance of an intersectional understanding of gender, class, race, age, culture, SOGI, and religion. Therefore, DAWN's collaborative research aims at filling this knowledge gap by applying a new framework and a Southern feminist critical perspective, which will be further elaborated in the following section.

4 Methodology

4.1 Global China as a concept for analysis

China's expansion into the global economy and its participation in global governance over the past two decades have had profound and multifaceted impacts at various levels. Most research about these impacts primarily applies two differentiated but interrelated frameworks. The first set of research uses a political economy framework to analyse how China's global engagement, especially its state capital, reconfigures the global capitalist system in production and consumption (So 2010, Lee 2017). The second set is embedded in the disciplines of international relations (IR) and development studies to examine China's influence on the global governance structure as well as on the international development cooperation discourse and practice (Abdenur 2014, Yeh 2016, Haug et al., 2024).

To reconcile the inherent connections among these two frameworks, Global China has emerged as a new concept in recent years. More and more researchers have been applying Global China as a concept to understand China's global engagement beyond China's territorial boundaries and to analyse the various actors involved in the process, including the burgeoning resistance to it (Lee 2017 and 2022, Franceschini and Loubere 2022). Overall, this conception abandons the assumption that China's Going Out overseas investment strategy is a state-led top-down centralised monolithic strategy. It recognises that China's global engagement takes various forms in many areas; in addition to overseas state investment, it involves, for instance, migration, global media networks, higher education, technology transfer, multilateral regional and global credit institutions, and the expansion of Chinese NGOs abroad. It allows researchers to apply an interdisciplinary and transdisciplinary lens and combine methodological approaches of ethnography, geography, cultural studies, migration studies, history, sociology, gender studies, political economy, and IR to produce more nuanced analyses on the subject (Choudhury 2020, Xu 2022, Repnikova 2022, Lu 2022, Gong 2022, Chen 2022). Thus, Global China offers a fertile ground for theoretical and methodological reorientation and requires empirical research on China's global engagement.

This DAWN research, therefore, uses Global China as an overarching concept to understand China's global engagement and its gendered implications as the result of the ongoing dynamic interactions and negotiations among various actors such as government, business, civil society, and affected communities. First, it allows the researchers to identify and interrogate the most relevant and pressing topics in their respective contexts, from Chinese investment in mining and infrastructure projects, to China's soft power, to local and transnational civic resistance. Second, it challenges the state-centric top-down approach and counters the monster vs. messiah framing (Rofel and Rojas 2022) that predominates in research on China's global engagement. Finally, it accommodates the interdisciplinary approach, as illustrated in each case study in this collection.

4.2 Southern feminist perspectives and inquiry

Southern feminist theorists argue that historically, geographically, contextually, and culturally grounded forms of knowledge should be produced, exchanged, and imagined and call for the democratisation of knowledge between the North and the South (Byrne and Imma 2019, Uchendu et al. 2019). Southern feminist scholarship criticises the dominant development discourse and practice whereby women in the Global South are instrumentalised in the neoliberal development agenda that continues widening the gap between Global North and Global South and between men and women (Sen and Grown 1987; Kabeer 2005; Bernal and Grewal 2014). Drawing from postcolonial feminist theories and Third World feminism (Mohanty et al. 1991), it recognises the importance of creating solidarity and dialogue, especially among Global South feminist and other social movements to resist ubiquitous neoliberal globalisation. Meanwhile, it problematises and rejects the idea of a utopian 'global sisterhood' (Morgan 1984 and 2003) that ignores the intersectional and structural inequalities between nations, races, genders, classes, and sexualities (Mohanty 2003).

DAWN acknowledges that the gender impact of China's engagement in the Global South is a co-production in a dynamic process of action, interaction, and contestation involving many actors; therefore, it can only be assessed in various locations simultaneously and comprehensively and is especially grounded in the realities of the South. As a Southern feminist network, DAWN strongly believes that the perspectives and experiences of women from the Global South should be at the centre of these analyses, which is only possible through dialogue, collaboration, and solidarity.

To highlight the autonomous voices of women in the Global South, this research has intentionally welcomed the collaboration of scholars from the Global South to conduct eight case studies. These case studies contribute to the knowledge about Global China by examining the different aspects of the gendered impact of China's global footprint. They are:

- 'The Impact of Chinese Development Cooperation on Women in Trinidad and Tobago', by Annita Montoute, Jacqueline Laguardia Martinez, and Deborah McFee
- 'Gender Impacts of China's Engagement in Pacific Island Countries: Case Studies of BRI Infrastructure Projects in Tonga and Vanuatu', by Vasemaca Lutu.
- 'Chinese Mining Projects in Ecuador and Perú: Gender Impacts and Women's Agency', by Diana Castro Salgado.

- 'Organised Abandonment and Gendered Impacts of Extractivism in Bikita, Zimbabwe', by Hibist Wendemu Kassa and Zinzile Siphiwo Fengu.
- 'Empowering Women in Nigerian Agriculture: Assessing the Effects of China-Nigeria Agricultural Cooperation on Female Smallholders' Livelihood, Capacity-Building, and Shifting Social Norms', by Ishola Itunu Grace.
- 'Implications of Security Agreements on Women, Peace, and Security in Solomon Islands: A Comparative Case Study on China-Solomon Islands Bilateral Security Cooperation and the Australia-Solomon Islands Bilateral Security Treaty', by Patricia Sango Pollard.
- 'The Gender Question in China's Soft Power Engagement in the Global South', by Govind Kelkar and Ritu Agarwal.
- 'When Civil Society Contests Global China: Challenges and Opportunities for Gender-related Civil Society Transnational Action on China-backed Infrastructure Projects in the Global South', by Laura Trajber Waisbich.

Each case study explores one or more of the following questions in a regional or national context:

(1) What role does gender play in China's global engagement?
(2) How do Chinese investments and aid projects influence gender equality and women's lives and human rights in local communities?
(3) As a new actor, do China's overseas investments and development programs differ from those of traditional donors and investors in terms of gender policies and gender-related impact assessments? If so, how? If not, why?
(4) How do Southern feminist and social movements strengthen women's rights and gender equality and achieve social and environmental justice in the face of potentially adverse impacts of Chinese foreign aid and investment?

The aim of this collaboration is to challenge the narrow framing of China's global engagement defined by a state-led top-down approach and thus shake off Western racism and totalitarian control of knowledge production. This work also aims to hold states and corporate sectors, from both the South and North, accountable for safeguarding the human rights and well-being of women and people of the South.

4.3 Co-production of knowledge

Southern feminist collaboration is nothing new, but it has never been easy. As Byrne and Imma (2019) remind us, the Global South is multiple and flexible.

That requires Southern feminist scholarship and activism to decentralise and decolonialise the knowledge production. DAWN considers this research project an exemplary Southern feminist collaborative knowledge production as it provides the space for dialogue, critique, debate on the subject, and reflection on each other's positions, rather than pursuing consensus. DAWN convened the research advisory group that is comprised of the DAWN board and executive committee members, DAWN partners, and other experts who have given invaluable support throughout this research, including brainstorming on the analytical framework, identifying the possible researchers, peer-reviewing the draft case studies, and attending the authors' meeting, webinars, and advocacy events as commentators to disseminate the research findings. In alignment with the analytical framework, researchers for case studies determined their own topics, research questions, and appropriate methods based on their interest, expertise, and resources. Meanwhile, to facilitate this collaborative research, DAWN created the shared folders that contain useful references for researchers. DAWN convened two gatherings, one online and one in-person, where researchers and advisory group members could exchange ideas, raise difficult questions, and have candid conversations. For example, scholars often diverge over the issues of 'Western-centric' vs. 'Sino-centric' approaches, how to assess actual impacts when some Chinese projects are withdrawn and are not being implemented, and whether some concepts and categories, such as neocolonialism, state capitalism, state feminism, neo-imperialism, and the Beijing Consensus, can be applied to this research without appropriate contextualisation and problematisation. These dialogues, debates, and self-reflection have deepened the understanding of not only the issues that each case study tackles but also the positionality of the researchers and, therefore, have contributed to the strengthening of solidarity and collective vision that this research aims at advancing, to develop a Southern feminist knowledge community and network on gender and Global China.

4.4 Challenges and limitations of the research

This research was conducted during the COVID-19 pandemic, which made it extremely difficult to do field research to collect first-hand empirical data due to the lockdowns and financial constraints. Some researchers expressed their frustrations about getting responses from key informants and about a lack of data and communication from the actors they intended to investigate. Moreover, current geopolitics and the deeper ideological divide between China and the

West could make any meaningful dialogue impossible and even irrelevant. The researchers identified these as common challenges.

In addition, the subject of this research, Global China, is constantly developing and thus requires sustained feminist collective analyses to understand its complex dynamics. This includes the rapid and ever-changing global geopolitical context and environment, such as Trump's administration's 'American First' foreign policy and intensifying tariff war against China and other global trade partners, as well as the defunding of the UN and resolving USAID that has shaken the international development cooperation landscape. From China side, the Chinese government and enterprises are also constantly adjusting and improving their global strategies, further enhancing their influence and role in global governance, and responding to criticism and calls from local communities. Regrettably, the results of this study may not accurately and timely reflect these changing dynamics. Nevertheless, DAWN hopes that this study will preserve a historical documentation of China's overseas development projects or provide a baseline report for future in-depth research on the related subjects.

Finally, regarding the title of this book 'Gendered Impact of China's Development Initiatives in the Global South', DAWN recognizes the paradox between broader scope of the subject and limited aspects that this research could possibly tackle. As mentioned earlier, in Chinese official documents and position papers, 'gender equality' and 'equality between men and women' are often used interchangeably. The researchers in this project acknowledge that women and gender are different concepts, and one cannot be substituted for the other. The latter is understood as a more complex social construct. Nonetheless, while the case studies must narrow down their focuses on women, they also note the diversity among women and try to contextualize the historical, cultural, religious, and political constructions of gender roles and norms in their analyses. Overall, these studies dived into the concrete case and project or issues without overlooking the large picture and broader and intersectional perspectives. Another important aspect in the field of Global China studies that this research did not touch upon is sexuality. Some scholars (Rofel and Liu 2021) have already provided more pioneering and nuanced perspective on the sexuality impacts of China's international engagements, beyond its relation to abuse, exploitation, and inequality and laid the solid ground on the further intellectual interrogation on the intersectional and multi-dimensional gender and sexuality impacts of China's development cooperation.

In the following section, I introduce the main findings of the eight case studies and what can be drawn from them to assess the China-Global South relation from a gender perspective and reimagine the Southern feminist vision on gender and development.

5 Main findings and reflections

The eight case studies come from different regions of the Global South – Asia, the Pacific, Africa, Latin America, and the Caribbean – and cover a wide range of issues related to China's global engagement, such as soft power, investment in mining and infrastructure projects, and the role of civil societies. The broad scope of this research project was by design. DAWN left it to the researchers' discretion to identify the topic that was most relevant and important to them. It also depended on the resources at their disposal and their availability as regards the process and methods of data collection, and their own personal connection with the relevant stakeholders. Despite the resultant diversity, the research findings all respond to the key guiding questions, and some common issues have emerged from this research that are worth further exploration.

5.1 Main findings

5.1.1 *In terms of whether the gendered impact of China's engagement in the Global South is positive or negative, the eight case studies show mixed results. They vary depending on the nature of the project, who the main actors are, and how they engage with the local communities*

From the Pacific to the Caribbean to Africa, women benefit directly and indirectly from Chinese state funded infrastructure projects, such as the construction of roads and health facilities and agricultural cooperation projects. Tonga and Vanuatu both are important partners in China's BRI in the Pacific. China quickly responded to the cyclone, volcanic eruption, and tsunami that severely damaged the infrastructure in those countries, helping rebuild houses, buildings, roads, bridges, and communication lines. In addition, China provided medical supplies, food, other necessities, water tanks, and tents and deployed medical staff (Lutu in this volume). Improved infrastructure and humanitarian projects provide vast benefits through employment and business opportunities and address the practical needs of women, therefore creating the environment for achieving gender equality goals and women's economic empowerment. However, it remains questionable whether this 'trickle down' strategy would bring transformative change towards gender equality in society, especially when lacking the meaningful participation of civil society and women's organizations.

Similarly, in Trinidad and Tobago, the Chinese presence has been largely seen within the male dominated construction sector. In the case of the Couva Hospital project, women benefit tremendously from the various services offered, many of which are in high demand by women and their children. The nursing training facility housed at the hospital is disproportionately accessed by women, as the nursing profession is female dominated. But in the case of the e TecK industrial park, the project doesn't consider facilitating women's employment or promoting women-owned business or women's entrepreneurship (Montoute et al. in this volume).

The case study on China-Nigeria agriculture cooperation assesses the benefits for female smallholder farmers from Chinese-led agricultural trainings. On the one hand, female smallholders experience less improvement in income and livelihood opportunities after the training due to institutional barriers, credit access, and occupational segregation. On the other hand, despite the limited direct economic impact, the training increased female smallholders' willingness to adopt modern agricultural technologies and techniques, fostering food security and rural development (Ishola in this volume). In contrast, the case studies on Chinese investment in the mining industry in Africa and Latin America found that these projects, like their predecessors, brought more negative impacts than positive to the communities and environment, which were disproportionally borne by women (Castro in this volume, Kassa and Fengu in this volume). In addition, each case study analyses the factors that lead to these impacts and what should to be done to improve them.

5.1.2 These case studies indicate that even though women's development and gender equality have been included in China's latest state policy paper on international cooperation as a priority, on the operational level, Chinese actors have not put gender or women's issues at the forefront in their global engagement strategies, nor do they have any concrete action plan or guidelines for implementing this policy (Montoute al et. in this volume, Lutu in this volume, Ishola in this volume)

The case study examining China-Solomon Island bilateral security cooperation points out that China does not have a national action plan on the women, peace, and security (WPS) agenda even though China has become the biggest funder for the UN peacekeeping operation (Pollard in this volume). In Tonga and Vanuatu, the author has not witnessed any BRI projects that support gender equality at the community level apart from the construction of vital infrastructure such as school buildings, roads, and bridges. China-based companies under the BRI do not have much engagement with women and girls (Lutu in this volume).

All the case studies reaffirm one critical issue that the analytical framework has identified, the gap between the rhetoric of official state policy and the lack of operational guidelines and implementation strategies in practice. Nevertheless, a critical question yet to be addressed is whether efforts to close this gap would lead to tension between those efforts and China's stated non-interference policy. I will further discuss this question in the next section on rethinking South-South relations and conditionality. Furthermore, after examining the gender question in China's soft power, Kelkar and Agarwal suggest that without a fundamental transformation of gendered power relations within the family and society in China, the structural patriarchy will remain and any attempt at building and narrating a 'good China story' is likely to remain inconclusive (Kelkar and Agarwal in this volume).

5.1.3 *These case studies put women and their agency at the centre of the analyses. The case studies disclose that women are often at the forefront of the struggle against Chinese mining companies and hydropower dam projects, and, in some cases, they managed to stop projects completely with local activism and transnational advocacy*

Most of these case studies interviewed women, women's organizations, and women activists and amplify women's voices. The case study by Castro (in this volume) on two mining projects in Peru and Ecuador shows that women are representative at the local level, and there are women leaders with great popular legitimacy; however, their work is still incipient, and their participation is very limited and sometimes invisible. Waisbich (in this volume) notes that in the successful campaigns against the Chinese-invested power plant in Kenya and a hydropower dam in Southeast Asia, gender issues were not consistently brought up, discussed, or given priority by the leaders of the transnational campaigns.

The authors point out that the reasons for this are complex. The persistency of patriarchy and discriminatory gender norms, the strategic prioritisation of other issues such as environmental impact, the downplay of gender concerns in the campaigns, and the lack of gender awareness and related policy guidelines are some of the factors leading to gender blindness.

5.1.4 Grounded in the reality and experience of women in the Global South countries, these case studies reorient the focus from Chinese actors to the actors in the host countries that receive Chinese development finance and investment and, therefore, the studies hold all duty bearers accountable for women's rights and gender equality

It is important to build the capacity of the receiving countries and the affected communities so that they can better engage and negotiate with China and make investors and national and local governments more accountable for the environment and human rights (Montoute et al in this volume, Lutu in this volume, Kassa and Fengu in this volume). Community-based activists, national actors, and institutions in the host countries played the pivotal role in contesting socially and environmentally controversial and risky projects and forcing governmental and business actors, some of them Chinese, to reconsider investment plans and policy priorities. The Lamu case in Kenya also features greater engagement of multilateral actors, including co-financing institutions, the African Development Bank, and specialised UN agencies. Their involvement provided Kenyan groups with additional pressure points for transnational activism besides China-related ones (Waisbich in this volume).

Moreover, Global South countries should strengthen their partnership and collaboration with local communities, civil society organizations, and women's rights organizations to ensure their commitment to gender equality and that women's development is implemented and fulfilled in the process of international development cooperation to meet national development needs. There is a clear call for transnational activism and South-South feminist alliance and solidarity (Castro in this volume, Kelkar and Agarwal in this volume).

5.2 Reflection on the findings

Since its inception, DAWN has intentionally avoided putting forward hypotheses that we did not have enough evidence to support. Instead, we left the researchers in each case study to determine their research questions, hypotheses, overall concepts, and methods. As the project has evolved and is now concluding, we now certainly have more evidence to discuss some key issues emerging from this research and in the larger context of China's role in the changing world from a gender perspective.

5.2.1 Rethinking South-South relations and engendering South-South cooperation

China is not the only emerging player in global development financing, but it is undoubtedly the most important. China claims that 'as the largest developing country in the world, China is a natural member of the Global South' (CIDCA 2023). Meanwhile, it avoids being perceived as a donor country. China's foreign policy is based on the longstanding Five Principles of Peaceful Co-existence. These are mutual respect for sovereignty and territorial integrity, mutual non-aggression, non-interference in each other's internal affairs, equality and mutual benefit, and peaceful coexistence. This policy was initiated by Premier Zhou Enlai in the negotiations between China and India in 1953 and then was extended in the Ten Principles of Bandung, adopted at the Asian-African Conference (known as the Bandung Conference) in 1955. China's international development cooperation is also guided by the principles of non-interference, non-conditionality, and reciprocity within the South-South cooperation framework (SCIO 2021a). Originating in the Cold War politics in 1960s and 1970s, South-South Cooperation (SSC) refers to cooperation among developing countries to collaborate and share knowledge, skills, and initiatives in specific areas based on mutual needs, such as agriculture, urbanisation, and health for their individual and/or mutual benefits. It has evolved since the first High-level United Nations Conference on SSC and the adoption of the Buenos Aires Plan of Action (BAPA) in 1978. In the current context, especially since the second High-level UN Conference on SSC (BAPA+40) held in March 2019, it has been further invigorated as an important framework to implement SDGs to complement traditional North-South cooperation (Mawdsley 2014, Gray and Gills 2016, UN 2019, Haug 2022, Waisbich and Mawdsley 2022). The purpose of SSC is to contribute to the national well-being of peoples and countries of the South. Its practice is guided by fundamental principles, such as partnership and solidarity, mutual respect and mutual benefit, respect for national sovereignty, equality, non-conditionality, non-interference, and strengthening multilateralism (G77 and China 2019, UN 2019). Induced by the significant changes taking place in international political and economic relations, SSC practice has evolved into a new phase, manifested in new trends, such as engaging multiple stakeholders and various actors beyond the state and invigorating SSC for the implementation of SDGs. These current trends raise some important questions: What are the implications for the role of human rights within SSC, as human rights are essential to achieving SDGs? How can SSC concretely and meaningfully engage communities and civil society organizations, including women's rights and feminist organizations, in all stages of the development process, as it emphasises the importance of inclusiveness and multi-stakeholder partnership?

The outcome document of the BAPA+40 conference recognises the contribution of South-South and triangular cooperation in promoting gender equality and the empowerment of women and girls in sustainable development and encourages further efforts to mainstream gender perspectives in these modalities of cooperation (UN 2019). Unfortunately, it does not provide a step-by-step manual on how to mainstream gender perspectives in SSC; this knowledge can only come from extensive practice.

These case studies examine China's practice in SSC and impel us to rethink SSC from a gender perspective. First, a gender perspective helps to transform SSC from state-centric to people-centric development cooperation. Since its emergence, SSC has been remarkably state-centric. Most of the Bandung Principles refer to the states (except 'promotion of mutual interests and cooperation', which can be interpreted in different ways). In 1978, BAPA took a similar approach, mostly focusing on state-to-state cooperation. DAWN's research indicates the shortfalls and limitations of this approach. As these case studies have shown, China prioritises the state-to-state connection, but on the ground, the impact of SSC goes far beyond the states' relations. Second, bringing a gender perspective to SSC can enhance the holistic rights-based approach by mitigating the false divide between needs and rights, and development and rights. As some Global South scholars have noted, China's investment and financing in developing countries may help to improve social and economic rights but potentially hinder civil and political rights due to the lack of transparency in the negotiations and the participation of the local communities (Osondu-Oti 2016, Kamga 2018). A gender perspective and a human rights approach can reinforce each other. As Waisbich's case study suggests, while rights-based advocacy might not necessarily find an easy and immediate way into policy advocacy efforts in China, it can certainly help build a space for gender issues to be more present and visible in the years to come (Waisbich in this volume). Third, a gender perspective in SSC can enhance accountability, the mechanism for which would not be possible without the efforts and collaboration of women and feminist movements in those countries. It requires more participation of civil society groups and people of the affected communities and monitoring not only the governments, which so far are the mainstay of SSC, but also the other actors, such as the commercial sector. In the case study on China-Nigeria agriculture cooperation, the main component of the project – training for smallholder farmers – is implemented by a Chinese enterprise. Overall,

DAWN's project contends that more and better South-South connections among civil society groups, including women's rights groups and the feminist movement, are important. Civic South-South relations can allow Chinese organizations to hear from groups in developing countries about their experiences in dealing with Chinese stakeholders overseas.

5.2.2 Challenging the gender issue as a conditionality in international development cooperation and problematising feminist foreign policy

The landscape of international development cooperation has changed substantially over the last decade, marked by the Fourth High-Level Forum on Aid Effectiveness in Busan in 2011 and the presence of actors from rising power countries such as China. China's development financing helps to fill the funding gap faced by developing countries to achieve their SDGs, which is estimated to be between $2.5 trillion and $4 trillion annually (UN 2024). China's development financing is concentrated in infrastructure, food security, climate change, health, and education to meet the most urgent needs of developing countries; these are the areas that DAWN's analyses focus on.

There is little research exploring the gender impact of China's aid projects compared to that of traditional donors' projects. Zhang and Huang's (2023) research compares the World Bank's (WB) and China's aid projects in Africa and concludes that WB aid increases local support for gender equality and the results differ between sectors and genders. Foreign aid to gender-sensitive sectors has the most significant impact on women's attitudes toward gender equality and therefore helps diffuse gender norms to local populations. In contrast, Chinese aid shows no similar effects.

Compared to traditional aid, China's development assistance is often considered more attractive by recipient countries because it does not come with policy conditionality like that of other donor countries or the international financial institutions such as the WB and the International Monetary Fund (IMF) (Li 2017). Conditionality refers to the requirements and conditions of the donor countries or institutions for their recipients to change or introduce certain policies or structural adjustments in order to receive funding. Proponents of conditionality, such as the IMF, argue that it helps to ensure that the recipient country adopts strong and effective policies, which often means fiscal stringency and austerity policies, or to contribute to democratisation in recipient countries (IMF n.d.). However, empirical evidence suggests that the relationship between conditional aid and democratisation in Africa and elsewhere is contingent upon the historical context (Kentikelenis et al. 2016, Li 2017, Zhang and Huang 2023).

Furthermore, Global South feminist scholars contend that conditionality imposed by donors has not resulted in gender equality and the improvement of women's status. Instead, it exacerbates the conditions of women and the most marginalised populations. Because conditionalities usually involve austerity measures and the cutting of public financing of health care, social services, and education, they severely diminish national policy options and capacity (Alemany and Dede 2008, Muchhala 2024). When it comes to conditionalities regarding human rights and gender issues, the reform of gender discriminatory customary law, and gay rights, for example, they become more complicated and controversial and encounter the resistance of recipient governments (Lange and Tjomsland 2014, Provost 2023).

Why do many Southern governments move away from being compliant development partners to take a more self-assured stand? This new self-confidence is partly because of the economic and political rise of the South and partly because of new financial resources available from new donors, such as China. This of course is welcomed by the governments of Global South countries, but is it good news for women in the Global South? This research is particularly interested in assessing what China's non-conditionality policy means for women in the Global South and exploring whether and how gender issues could potentially be situated in this policy.

Since 1990s, a gender mainstreaming strategy has been widely adopted by traditional donors, multilateral development agencies, and international development NGOs. Gender mainstreaming is defined as the 'process of assessing the implications for women and men for any planned action, including legislation, policies, or programmes, in all areas and at all levels' (UN 1997). It is worth noting that extant evidence demonstrates that the implementation of gender mainstreaming policy and strategy primarily relies on the cooperation of recipient country governments and the strong support of NGOs and civil societies.

DAWN's case studies have shown that Chinese actors do not apply a gender mainstreaming approach and have little interaction with local communities or women's NGOs (Castro, Lutu, Pollard, Waisbich, Ishola, in this volume) compared to traditional development partners. For example, Solomon Islanders are not aware of what the China-Solomon Island security agreement fully entails as the document was never disclosed, unlike the 2017 Solomon Islands-Australia security treaty (Pollard in this volume). In Tonga, a women's group of the Civil Society Forum of Tonga initiated gender equality awareness programmes in their communities with the support of development partners; however, they were not aware of China's BRI projects and its focus on women's development in Tonga (Lutu in this volume).

In this context, is there any way to impel China to take gender equality into consideration in its foreign policy and international development cooperation without conflicting with its non-conditionality and non-interference principles? To examine this question, it might be useful to begin by examining the emerging trend of 'feminist foreign policy'.

In recent years, several countries have re-labelled their foreign policy as feminist, pioneered by Sweden in 2014 and followed by Canada (2017), France (2019), Mexico (2020), Luxemburg (2021), Spain (2021), Chile (2022), Liberia (2022), Colombia (2022), and Germany (2022), declaring that the countries' diplomacy will place girls and women at the centre of their work and ensure that a feminist perspective will be central to policy. Some women's NGOs, such as the International Women's Development Agency (IWDA) and the International Centre for Research on Women (ICRW), brought together feminist scholars, activists, and political scientists and organised a discussion on this topic. Although it varies in terms of naming and strategies (Partis-Jennings and Eroukhmanoff 2024), feminist foreign policy is guided by the four Rs: rights, representation, resources, and reality. This means examining whether girls and women have the same human rights as boys and men, whether women are represented throughout local and federal government, and whether the national budget addresses gender matters and has enough resources allocated to address girls' and women's issues, while also recognising that policy isn't going to change things instantly (Government Offices of Sweden n.d., ICRW n.d., Köhler 2022, Foteini 2023, Ridge et al. 2019, Conley 2022, UNWomen n.d., Thompson 2020). Each country takes its own approach as to how such a policy works. Overall, in the past decade, the implementation of feminist foreign policy has been very reductive, selective, and unsystematic; that is, it was not reflected in the actions, strategies, policies, or even the bulk of the financing related to foreign policy. Also, feminist foreign policy does not address overarching macroeconomic issues such as austerity policies and conditionalities that frame the context for gender and other policies and directly impact women's wellbeing.

Using ideology to guide foreign policy is not new. It can be observed in the anti-imperialism and anti-hegemony that were the priority of Chinese foreign policy in 1960s and 1970s (Choudhury 2020) and in the integration of the concept of human rights into US foreign policy by President Jimmy Carter in late 1970s (Moyn 2010, Donnelly and Whelan 2020). Feminist foreign policy should be transformative of entrenched and asymmetrical political, economic, and societal power hierarchies, advocating economic well-being, honouring planetary boundaries, and ensuring peace. This needs to be the objective of each country's foreign policies while taking a holistic and intersectional approach to diplomacy. Unfortunately, this is far from how it is interpreted and implemented in real-world politics. The feminist agenda is weaponised in an increasingly polarised and divided world and used to impose sanctions on certain countries, while sometimes being traded off for other political interests. Feminist foreign policy, therefore, at its best, is mistakenly equivalent to gender awareness raising; at its worst, it is instrumentalised to maintain hegemony and superpower status. For instance, in an article on advancing a feminist US foreign policy, the author asks: 'Can the United States use its progress in areas such as the Women, Peace and Security (WPS) Agenda to emerge as a gender superpower?' (Graham and Corrado 2021). The US and its allies' policies on Afghanistan, Gaza, and Ukraine make a sham of their feminist foreign policy advocacy.

5.2.3 Towards Southern feminist collaboration and solidarity for gender equality and just development

We reiterate that gender equality does not mean being a conditionality, as many researchers and advocates have already pointed out. To problematise the current trend of feminist foreign policy does not mean to defy the feminist principles and feminist politics that are deeply rooted in the struggles and activism against patriarchy and injustice experienced by women, gender-nonconforming people, and oppressed and marginalised groups. From the above analyses and evidence from DAWN's research, we conclude that neither conditionalities nor feminist foreign policy are viable routes to integrate gender issues into China's engagement in the Global South. If this is the case, then what is the alternative? DAWN's research project intends to provide new ideas and innovative activism with Global South experience and perspectives.

A clear message that can be drawn from all the case studies is that achieving gender equality and fulfilling women's human rights is not a conditionality, but a goal to be integrated into each country's development agenda. It is also a commitment made by the government through its national laws and policies and the international policy framework, such as CEDAW, BPfA, and SDGs. Undoubtedly, international development cooperation should contribute to achieving this goal as well. Therefore, each actor involved in this process must take responsibility. Although Chinese government authorities, regulators, and business associations have issued a growing number of guidelines to promote good performance by companies operating abroad, gender related issues are largely absent. Two case studies on Chinese-invested mining projects show that Chinese companies are unprepared to address the demands of local communities regarding aspects of transparency, accountability, and human rights, and they lack effective mechanisms for due diligence, comprehensive risk assessment, dialogue, and compensation (Castro, Kassa and Fengu in this volume). Montoute et al. (in this volume) stress that while China should assume its responsibility, Caribbean governments should be treated 'as active agents in their relationships as sovereign independent states with the capacity to shape and influence the nature and substance of development projects executed with China'.

This study reminds China and the Global South countries that they all have their own responsibilities in promoting gender equality and women's development, aligned with their national and international commitments. On the 30th anniversary of the 4WCW and today, it is necessary to revisit those commitments.

China is currently at a critical moment to consider how to position gender in its international development cooperation. For example, on 29 April 2024, the China International Development Cooperation Agency (CIDCA), in collaboration with the All-China Women's Federation (ACWF), launched the Exchange and Training Base for Global Women's Development Cooperation. CIDCA has committed to increase support for women's international development cooperation through providing trainings, financing resources for women's employment and entrepreneurship, supporting UNWomen, and promoting global women's cooperation and exchange (CIDCA 2024). Chinese feminist scholars regard this newly established institution as a good platform for exchange and advocacy to integrate gender into China's international development cooperation.

Another mechanism that Chinese and Global Southern feminists have long utilised to strengthen South-South feminist solidarity and advocacy is the CEDAW review. Women's organizations Acción Ecológica and CooperAcción submitted a shadow report to the CEDAW committee in April 2023. This report drew the attention of the CEDAW committee to the Chinese government's failure to comply with its extraterritorial obligations and its commitments to CEDAW to protect women's human rights outside its national territory, specifically in mining projects operated by Chinese state-owned companies Las Bambas in Peru and Rio Blanco in Ecuador (Acción Ecológica and CooperAcción 2023). It calls on the Chinese government to establish oversight mechanisms to monitor, investigate, and stop violations of women's rights caused by the mining activities of Chinese state-owned companies operating outside their territory. It is encouraging to see that there are two paragraphs in the CEDAW committee's concluding observations on the 9th periodic report about China responding to this call. It mentions '*China's International Development Cooperation in the New Era*, which identifies eight areas of cooperation, including gender equality, in 2021' and calls upon the Chinese government to 'ensure that the *White Paper on China's International Development Cooperation in the New Era* mandates the fundamental guarantees of the Convention' (UN CEDAW Committee 2023). The two local NGOs translated the CEDAW committee's concluding observations and disseminated them to their communities as a tool for the further advocacy. This is just one example of South-South feminist collaboration that combines research and activism, as well as links the local with the national and global.

References

Abdenur, Adriana Erthal (2014), China and the BRICS Development Bank: Legitimacy and Multilateralism in South-South Cooperation. *IDS Bulletin* 45 (4): 85–101. https://doi.org/10.1111/1759-5436.12095

Acción Ecológica and CooperAcción (2023), *Shadow report to the 85th Session of CEDAW review of China*. Available online at UN Treaty Body Database: https://tbinternet.ohchr.org/_layouts/15/treatybodyexternal/Download.aspx?symbolno=INT%2FCEDAW%2FCSS%2FCHN%2F52211&Lang=en (Accessed 2 October 2024)

Alemany, Cecilia and Graciela Dede (2008), *Conditionalities undermine the Right to Development: an analysis based on a Women's and Human Rights perspective*. Published by WIDE, AWID, DAWN, IGTN.

Amar, Paul, Lisa Rofel, Maria Amelia Viteri, Consuelo Fernandez-Salvador, and Fernando Brancoli (2022), *The Tropical Silk Road: The Future of China in South America*. Stanford University Press.

Beeson, Mark (2018), Geoeconomics with Chinese characteristics: the BRI and China's evolving grand strategy, *Economic and Political Studies*, 6:3, 240–256, https://doi.org/10.1080/20954816.2018.1498988

Bernal, Victoria and Inderpal Grewal (eds) (2014), *Theorizing NGOs: States, Feminisms, and Neoliberalism*. Durham: Duke University Press.

Brooks, Sarah M. (2018), Will the Future of Human Rights Be 'Made in China'? In *Made in China Journal* (blog). July 7, 2018. Available online: https://madeinchinajournal.com/2018/07/07/will-the-future-of-human-rights-be-made-in-china/ (Accessed 30 September 2024)

Byrne, Deirdre C. and Z'étoile Imma (2019), Why 'Southern Feminisms'?, *Agenda*, 33:3, 2–7. https://doi.org/10.1080/10130950.2019.1697043

Cai, Yiping (2021), What Do Gender Equality and Women's Rights Have to Do with China's Global Engagement? *Feminist Studies*. 47; No. 2. 450–462.

Cai, Yiping (2024), Between cooptation and emancipation: Chinese women's NGOs and power shifts at the United Nations, *Global Policy*, 15(Suppl. 2), 148–159. https://doi.org/10.1111/1758-5899.13369

Cai, Yiping and Li Yingtao (2021), Global China from a Gender Lens, *IDEES*. No. 52. "*China before a World in crisis*". Available online: https://revistaidees.cat/en/global-china-from-a-gender-lens/ (Accessed 30 September 2024)

Cai, Yiping and Yin Yu (2022), *An Analytical Framework on the Gender Impact of China's Global Engagement in the Global South*. Suva: DAWN. Available online: https://dawnnet.org/wp-content/uploads/2023/02/20230202-China-Analytical-Framework.pdf (Accessed 30 September 2024)

Chan, Gerald (2015), China Eyes ASEAN. *Journal of Asian Security and International Affairs* 2 (1): 75–91.

Chen, Weiwei (2022), China and Africa: Ethiopia Case Study Debunks Investment Myths. *The Conversation*. 2022. Available online: http://theconversation.com/china-and-africa-ethiopia-case-study-debunks-investment-myths-177098 (Accessed 1 October 2024)

Choudhury, Golam Wahed (2020), *China in World Affairs: The Foreign Policy of The PRC Since 1970*. Routledge.

CIDCA (China International Development Cooperation Agency) (2023), *Wang Yi: China naturally member of Global South*. Available online: http://en.cidca.gov.cn/2023-07/12/c_902381.htm (Accessed 2 October 2024)

CIDCA (China International Development Cooperation Agency) (2024), "全球妇女发展合作交流培训基地"揭牌仪式暨全球妇女发展与合作研讨会在京举办. Available online: http://www.cidca.gov.cn/20240429/84700be0b2694f20bace5e7acb1fc094/c.html (Accessed 9 August 2024)

Condon, Madison (2012), China in Africa: What the Policy of Nonintervention Adds to the Western Development Dilemma. *The Fletcher Journal of Human Security*. Vol. 27. 5–25.

Conley, Mikaela (2022), Feminist Foreign Policies Increase in Number. Do They Matter? *PassBlue* 14 February 2022. Available online: https://us4.campaign-archive.com/?e=cc2f9fa8a0&u=5d5693a8f1af2d4b6cb3160e8&id=b43bc511b7 (Accessed 11 February 2022)

Delfau, Karen, and Pichamon Yeophantong (2020), *State of Knowledge: Women and Rivers in the Mekong Region*. Oakland, USA: International Rivers.

Donnelly, Jack, and Daniel J. Whelan (2020), *International Human Rights*, Sixth Edition, Routledge.

ERC (The Equal Rights Coalition) (2022), *Anti-Gender Movement Background Paper*, 8 September 2022. Available online: https://equalrightscoalition.org/documents/anti-gender-movement-background-paper/ (Accessed 29 June 2025)

Foot, Rosemary (2020), Shaping from within: A UN with Chinese Characteristics? *East Asia Forum*. August 3, 2020. Available online: https://www.eastasiaforum.org/2020/08/03/shaping-from-within-a-un-with-chinese-characteristics/ (Accessed 30 September 2024)

Foteini, Papagioti (2023), *Feminist Foreign Policy Index: A Qualitative Evaluation of Feminist Commitments*. Washington DC: International Centre for Research on Women.

Franceschini, Ivan, and Nicholas Loubere (eds) (2022), *Global China as Method*. 1st edition. Cambridge University Press. https://doi.org/10.1017/9781108999472

Franceschini, Ivan, and Nicholas Loubere (eds) (2021), Archaeologies of the Belt and Road Initiative. *Made in China Journal*. Volume 6, Issue 2.

Getachew, Adom (2019), *Worldmaking after Empire*. Princeton University Press.

Government Offices of Sweden, Ministry for Foreign Affairs. n.d. *Handbook: Sweden's feminist foreign policy.*

Graham, Shirley, and Megan E. Corrado (2021), *How to Advance a Feminist U.S. Foreign Policy*. Available online: https://www.usip.org/publications/2021/03/how-advance-feminist-us-foreign-policy (Accessed 23 January 2023)

Gray, Kevin, and Barry K. Gills. (2016), South–South cooperation and the rise of the Global South. *Third World Quarterly*, 37:4, 557–574.

Group 77 and China (2019), *Statement on behalf of the Group 77 and China by the State of Palestine, Chair of G77 and China, at the Second UN High-Level Conference on South-South Cooperation.* Buenos Aires, Argentina, 20 March 2019.

Haug, Sebastian (2022), Beyond Mainstreaming? Past, Present and Future of UN Support for South-South and Triangular Cooperation. *Asian Journal of Peacebuilding*. Vol. 10 No. 1. 15–44.

Haug, Sebastian (2024), Mutual legitimation attempts: the United Nations and China's Belt and Road Initiative. *International Affairs* 100:3 (2024) 1207–1230. https://doi.org/10.1093/ia/iiae020

Haug, Sebastian, Rosemary Foot and Max-Otto Baumann (2024), Power shifts in international organizations: China at the United Nations. *Global Policy*, 15 (Suppl. 2), 5–17. https://doi.org/10.1111/1758-5899.13568

Huang, Siran, Liu Haoxue, Zhou Xuan, and Zhang Hongfu (2018), 中国农业海外投资性别影响调研报告 ——以中国农业企业投资老挝、柬埔寨为例. 商道纵横 (Syntao). Available online: http://syntao.cn/newsinfo/2110671.html (Accessed 1 October 2024)

Huang, Yiping (2016), Understanding China's Belt & Road Initiative: Motivation, Framework and Assessment. *China Economic Review* 40 (September): 314–321. https://doi.org/10.1016/j.chieco.2016.07.007

Inboden, Rana Siu (2021), China at the UN: Choking Civil Society. *Journal of Democracy*, Vol. 32, No. 3, 124–135.

International Centre for Research on Women (ICRW). n.d. Coalition for a Feminist Foreign Policy in the United States. Available online: https://www.icrw.org/publications/toward-a-feminist-foreign-policy-in-the-united-states/ (Accessed 23 January 2023)

International Monetary Fund (IMF). n.d. *IMF Conditionality*. Available online: https://www.imf.org/en/About/Factsheets/Sheets/2023/IMF-Conditionality (Accessed 2 October 2024)

Jolly, Susie (2016), Why Gender and Sexuality are Central to China's Relationships with the Global South, *Just Matters*, Ford Foundation. Available online: https://www.fordfoundation.org/news-and-stories/stories/posts/why-gender-and-sexuality-are-central-to-china-s-relationships-with-the-global-south/ (Accessed on 30 September 2024)

Jolly, Susie (2025), USAID crashed – Can China help? *China Development Brief*, 14 March 2025. Available online: https://mp.weixin.qq.com/s/0ENokZN8it6XGHD7poCsPQ (Accessed on 29 June 2025)

Kabeer, Naila (2005), Gender equality and women's empowerment: A critical analysis of the third millennium development goal 1, *Gender & Development*, 13:1, 13–24.

Kamga, Serges Djoyou (2018), Realizing the right to development: Some reflections. *History Compass*. https://doi.org/10.1111/hic3.12460

Kentikelenis, Alexander E., Thomas H. Stubbs and Lawrence P. King (2016), IMF conditionality and development policy space, 1985–2014, *Review of International Political Economy*, 23:4, 543–582 https://doi.org/10.1080/09692290.2016.1174953

Kinyondo, Abel (2019), Is China Recolonizing Africa? Some Views from Tanzania. *World Affairs* 182 (2): 128–64. https://doi.org/10.1177/0043820019839331

Köhler, Gabriele (2022), *Feminist foreign policy?* Available online: https://www.icrw.org/publications/toward-a-feminist-foreign-policy-in-the-united-states/ (Accessed 20 July 2022)

Kuo, Lily, and Vic Chiang (2025), China to donate $500 million to WHO, stepping into gap left by U.S. *The Washington Post*. 21 May 2025. Available online: https://www.washingtonpost.com/world/2025/05/21/china-who-donation-500-million/ (Accessed 29 June 2025)

LatinoAmérica Sustentable (LAS). n.d. *Chinese Guidelines*. Available online: https://latsustentable.org

Lee, Ching Kwan (2017), *The Specter of Global China: Politics, Labor, and Foreign Investment in Africa*. University of Chicago Press.

Lee, Ching Kwan (2022), Global China at 20: Why, How and So What? *The China Quarterly* 250 (June): 313–331. https://doi.org/10.1017/S0305741022000686

Li, Xiaojun (2017), Does Conditionality Still Work? China's Development Assistance and Democracy in Africa. *Chinese Political Science Review*. Vol. 2, 201–220. https://doi.org/10.1007/s41111-017-0050-6

Liang, Xiaohui (2019), Gender Equality in China's Overseas Investment: Case Studies on Chinese Textile and Apparel Enterprises in Vietnam, Myanmar, and Bangladesh. *Frontiers of Law in China* 14 (4): 478–499.

Lin, Chun (2019), China's New Globalism. In Leo Panitch and Greg Albo (eds.) *Socialist Register Vol. 55: The World Turned Upside Down?* New Yor University Press, Monthly Review Press. 150–172.

Liu, Le (2021a), The Role of the United Nations in Promoting the Belt and Road Initiative. *International Forum*, Vol. 4, 27–48.

Liu, Petrus (2021b), Thinking Gender in the Age of the Beijing Consensus. *Feminist Studies* 47 (2): 341–371.

Lu, Haina, Xiaohui Liang, and Chenping Wang (2018), *Improving Gender Equality Through China's Belt and Road Initiative*. Cultural and Education Section of the British Embassy in China.

Malik, Ammar A., Bradley Parks, Brook Russell, Joyce Jiahui Lin, Katherine Walsh, Kyra Solomon, Sheng Zhang, Thai-Binh Elston, and Seth Goodman (2021), *Banking on the Belt and Road: Insights from a new global dataset of 13,427 Chinese development projects*. AidData.

Mawdsley, Emma (2014), Human Rights and South-South Development Cooperation: Reflections on the "Rising Powers" as International Development Actors. *Human Rights Quarterly*. August 2014, Vol. 36, No. 3, 630–652.

Mohanty, Chandra (2003), *Feminism without borders: Decolonizing theory, practicing solidarity*. Duke University Press.

Mohanty, Chandra, Ann Russo, and Lourdes Torres (ed.) (1991), *Third World Women and the Politics of Feminism*. Indiana University Press.

Morgan, Robin (ed.) (1984), *Sisterhood is global: The international women's movement anthology*. Anchor Books.

Morgan, Robin (ed.) (2003), *Sisterhood is Forever: The Women's anthology for a new millennium*. Washington Square Press.

Moyn, Samuel (2010), *The Last Utopia: Human Rights in History*. The Belknap Press of Harvard University Press.

Mignolo, Walter (2011), The Global South and World Dis/order. *Journal of Anthropological Research*. Vol. 67, No. 2, 165–188.

Ministry of Foreign Affairs (MoFA) the People's Republic of China (2021), *Forum on China-Africa Cooperation Dakar Action Plan (2022–2024)*. Available online: http://www.focac.org/eng/zywx_1/zywj/202201/t20220124_10632444.htm (Accessed 1 October 2024)

Ministry of Foreign Affairs (MoFA) the People's Republic of China (2024), *Forum on China-Africa Cooperation Beijing Action Plan (2025–2027)*. Available online: http://www.focac.org/eng/zywx_1/zywj/202409/t20240926_11497783.htm (Access 1 October 2024)

Ministry of Foreign Affairs (MoFA) the People's Republic of China (2024), *Position Paper of the People's Republic of China for The Summit of the Future and the 79th Session of The United Nations General Assembly*. Available online: https://www.fmprc.gov.cn/eng/zy/wjzc/202409/t20240920_11493896.html (Accessed 23 September 2024)

Muchhala, Bhumika (2024), *A Feminist Political Economy Lens Towards Equity and Justice in the Global South*. Third World Network.

Murray, Laura (2022), 'Missing the point': A conversation with Sonia Corrêa about the emergence and complexities of anti-gender politics at the intersections of human rights and health, *Global Public Health*, 17:11, 3243–3253, https://doi.org/10.1080/17441692.2022.2135751

Ohashi, Hideo (2018), The Belt and Road Initiative (BRI) in the context of China's opening-up policy, *Journal of Contemporary East Asia Studies*, 7:2, 85–103, https://doi.org/10.1080/24761028.2018.1564615

Osondu-Oti, Adaora (2016), China and Africa: Human Rights Perspective. *Africa Development/Afrique et Développement*. Vol. 41, No.1, 49–80.

Oud, Malin (2020), Harmonic Convergence: China and the Right to Development. Nadège Rolland (ed.) *An emerging China-centric order – China's Vision for a New World Order in Practice*. The National Bureau of Asian Research, Special Report #87.

Partis-Jennings, Hannah, and Clara Eroukhamnoff (ed.) (2024). *Feminist Policymaking in Turbulent Times: Critical Perspectives*. Routledge Studies in Gender and Global Politics. London and New York: Routledge.

Prashad, Vijay (2007), *The Darker Nations: A People's History of the Third World*. The New Press.

Provost, Claire (2023), *Progressive cash for the anti-LGBTQI backlash? How aid donors and 'feminist' governments have funded backers of Uganda's deadly Anti-Homosexuality Bill*. The Institute for Journalism and Social Change.

Ramacharan, Bertrand G. (2016), Normative human rights cascades, North and South. *Third World Quarterly*, 37:7, 1234–1251. https://doi.org/10.1080/01436597.2016.1154438

Repnikova, Maria (2022), Rethinking China's Soft Power: 'Pragmatic Enticement' of Confucius Institutes in Ethiopia. *The China Quarterly* 250 (June): 440–463. https://doi.org/10.1017/S0305741022000340

Ridge, Alice, Caroline Lambert, Joanne Crawford, Rachel Clement, Lyric Thompson, Sarah Gammage, and Anne Marie Goetz (2019), *Feminist Foreign Policy Key Principles & Accountability Mechanisms*. IWDA, ICRW, NYU.

Rofel, Lisa, and Carols Rojas (eds.) (2022), *New World Ordering: China and the Global South*. Duke University Press.

Rofel, Lisa, and Petrius Liu (eds.) (2021), Global Intimacies: China and/in the Global South. *Feminist Studies*, Vol. 47; No.2.

Sen, Gita and Caren Grown (1987), *Development, Crises, and Alternative Visions: Third World Women's Perspectives*. New Feminist Library.

Shieh, Shawn, Lowell Chow, Zhong Huang, and Jinfei Yue (2021), Understanding and Mitigating Social Risks to Sustainable Development in China's BRI: Evidence from Nepal and Zambia. *ODI: Think Change*. April 1, 2021. Available online: https://odi.org/en/publications/understanding-and-mitigating-social-risks-to-sustainable-development-in-chinas-bri-evidence-from-nepal-and-zambia/ (Accessed 2 March 2025)

Singh, Ajit (2021), The Myth of 'Debt-Trap Diplomacy' and Realities of Chinese Development Finance. *Third World Quarterly* 42 (2): 239–253. https://doi.org/10.1080/01436597.2020.1807318

So, Alvin Y. (2010), Globalization and China: From Neoliberal Capitalism to State Developmentalism in East Asia. In Berch Berberoglu (ed.) *Globalization in the 21st*

Century, 133–154. New York: Palgrave Macmillan. https://doi.org/10.1057/9780230106390_7

State Council Information Office of the People's Republic of China (SCIO) (2017), *Full Text of Beijing Declaration Adopted by the First South-South Human Rights Forum*. December 11, 2017. Available online: http://english.scio.gov.cn/scionews/2017-12/11/content_50096884.htm (Accessed 1 October 2024)

State Council Information Office of the People's Republic of China (SCIO) (2021), *China's International Development Cooperation in the New Era*. Available online: https://english.www.gov.cn/archive/whitepaper/202101/10/content_WS5ffa6bbbc6d0f72576943922.html (Accessed 30 September 2024)

Stephen, Matthew D. (2021), China's New Multilateral Institutions: A Framework and Research Agenda. *International Studies Review* 23 (3): 807–834. https://doi.org/10.1093/isr/viaa076

Sun, Yun (2025), *The purpose and promise of China's International Organization for Mediation*. 6 June 2025. Available online: https://www.brookings.edu/articles/the-purpose-and-promise-of-chinas-international-organization-for-mediation/ (Accessed 29 June 2025)

The People's Map of Global China. n.d. https://thepeoplesmap.net

The White House (2022), *Fact Sheet: President Biden and G7 Leaders Formally Launch the Partnership for Global Infrastructure and Investment*. 26 June 2022. Available online: https://www.presidency.ucsb.edu/documents/fact-sheet-president-biden-and-g7-leaders-formally-launch-the-partnership-for-global (Accessed 29 June 2025)

Thompson, Lyric (2020), *Feminist Foreign Policy: A Framework*. Washington, DC: International Center for Research on Women. Available online: https://www.icrw.org/wp-content/uploads/2021/07/FFP_Framework_EN_June2021update.pdf (Accessed 2 October 2024)

Tower, Jason G. (2020), Conflict Dynamics and the Belt and Road Initiative Ignoring Conflict on the Road to Peace. *Analysis* 97. Berlin, Germany: Brot für die Welt.

Uchendu, Uchechukwu, Griet Roets and Michel vandenbroeck (2019), Mapping constructs of gender in research on Igbo women in Nigeria: embracing a southern feminist theoretical perspective. *Gender and Education*, Vol. 31, No. 4, 580–524.

UNWomen. n.d. *Feminist Foreign Policies: An Introduction*.

United Nations (UN) (1997), *Official Records of the General Assembly, Fifty-second Session, Supplement No. 3* (A/52/3/Rev.1)

United Nations (UN) (2019), A/RES/73/291. *Buenos Aires outcome document of the second High-level United Nations Conference on South-South Cooperation*. 15 April 2019. Available online: https://www.unsouthsouth.org/wp-content/uploads/2019/10/N1911172.pdf (Accessed 2 October 2024)

United Nations (UN) (2024), *Financing for Sustainable Development Report 2024*.

United Nations (UN) CEDAW Committee (2023) *CEDAW committee concluding observation on the ninth periodic report of China*. CEDAW/C/CHN/CO/9. 31 May 2023.

United Nations Development Programme (UNDP) (2013), *Human Development Report 2013 – The Rise of the South: Human Progress in a Diverse World*. UNDP.

United States Mission to the United Nations (2025), *Explanation of Position on the Commission on the Status of Women (CSW) Political Declaration*. 10 March 2025. Available online: https://usun.usmission.gov/explanation-of-position-on-the-commission-on-the-status-of-women-csw-political-declaration-location-of-remarks/ (Accessed 29 June 2025)

Waisbich, Laura Trajber, and Emma Mawdsley (2022), South-South Cooperation. Kearrin Sims et al., (eds). *Handbook of Global Development*. London: Routledge. 82–92.

Waisbich, Laura Trajber; Supriya Roychoudhury and Sebastian Haug (2021), Beyond the single story: 'Global South' polyphonies. *Third World Quarterly*, 42:9, 2086–2095.

Walton, Kate (2025), *Opposition to gender equality around the world is connected, well funded and spreading. Here is what you need to know about the anti-gender movement*. Available online: https://www.cnn.com/interactive/asequals/anti-gender-equality-threat-explained-as-equals-intl-cmd/# (Accessed 29 June 2025)

Wang, Yi (2025), *Reconciliation, Cooperation and Harmony Through Extensive Consultation, by Joint Contribution, for Shared Benefit — Jointly Writing a New Chapter on the Rule of Law in Global Governance*, Remarks by H.E. Wang Yi at the Signing Ceremony of the Convention on the Establishment of the International Organization for Mediation. 30 May 2025. Available online: https://www.fmprc.gov.cn/eng/wjbzhd/202505/t20250530_11637277.html (Accessed 29 June 2025)

Weiss, Thomas G. and Pallavi Roy (2016), The UN and the Global South, 1945 and 2015: past as prelude? *Third World Quarterly*, 37:7, 1147–1155.

Worden, Andréa (2020), China at the UN Human Rights Council: Conjuring a "Community of Shared Future for Humankind? Nadège Rolland (ed.) *An emerging China-centric order – China's Vision for a New World Order in Practice*. The National Bureau of Asian Research, Special Report #87.

Xi, Jinping (2015), *Promoting Women's All-around Development and Building a Better World for All*. Remarks by H. E. Xi Jinping President of the People's Republic of China at the Global Leaders' Meeting on Gender Equality and Women's Empowerment. 30 May 2024. Available online: https://www.fmprc.gov.cn/eng/xw/zyjh/202405/t20240530_11340950.html (Accessed 30 September 2024)

Xi, Jinping (2020), *Statement by H. E. Xi Jinping President of the People's Republic of China at the High-level Meeting on the Twenty-fifth Anniversary of the Fourth World Conference on Women*. Available online: https://www.fmprc.gov.cn/eng/xw/zyjh/202405/t20240530_11341460.html (Accessed 30 September 2024)

Xi, Jinping (2024), *Address by Chinese President Xi Jinping at conference marking 70th anniversary of Five Principles of Peaceful Coexistence*. 28 June 2024. Available online: https://english.www.gov.cn/news/202406/28/content_WS667e6d1dc6d0868f4e8e8a82.html (Accessed 30 September 2024)

Xu, Liang (2022), Engendering China–Africa Encounters: Chinese Family Firms, Black Women Workers and the Gendered Politics of Production in South Africa. *The China Quarterly* 250 (June): 356–75. https://doi.org/10.1017/S0305741022000431

Yeh, Emily T. (2016), Introduction: The geoeconomics and geopolitics of Chinese development and investment in Asia. *Eurasian Geography and Economics*, 57:3, 275–285.

Yu, George T. (1977), China and the Third World. *Asian Survey* 17 (11): 1036–1048. https://doi.org/10.2307/2643352

Zhang, Chuanhong and Zhenqian Huang (2023), Foreign Aid, Norm Diffusion, and Local Support for Gender Equality: Comparing Evidence from the World Bank and China's Aid Projects in Africa. *Studies in Comparative International Development*. Vol. 58, 584–615. Available online: https://link.springer.com/article/10.1007/s12116-023-09381-4 (Accessed 2 March 2025)

Zhao, Zhiqian, Hongyu Guo, and Yunwen Bai (eds) (2021), *Promoting Gender-Responsive Investments A Reference Framework for Financial Institutions*. Beijing: Greenovation Hub.

1

The Impact of Chinese Development Cooperation on Women in Trinidad and Tobago

by Annita Montoute, Jacqueline Laguardia Martinez, and Deborah McFee

Introduction

As a result of growing interest in the People's Republic of China's (hereafter, as PRC or China) relations with the Caribbean, there has been an abundance of academic literature and opinion articles on the subject. It is noteworthy that much of the research and many reports place the analysis of China's trade and economic relations within the broader Latin American and the Caribbean (LAC) framework (Gachúz Maya and Urdinez 2022; Piccone 2020; Dussel Peters 2019; Gil Barragán and Aguilera Castillo 2017; Niu 2015; Domínguez et al. 2006). When focusing on the English-speaking Caribbean, the tendency is to analyze the region as a single unit, with emphasis on Jamaica and Trinidad and Tobago, the largest economies in the Caribbean Community (CARICOM) (Gonzalez Vicente 2021; Gonzalez Vicente and Montoute 2020; Minto 2019; Bernal 2016). These studies also prioritize economic and trade relations; women and gender issues seem absent from the literature. There is therefore, to a large extent, gender blindness and bias in the scholarly literature and by extension in policy debates and practice relating to China-Caribbean engagement.

This study attempts to fill this gap by examining women in Chinese development cooperation in the Caribbean via the cases of the e TecK Phoenix Park Industrial Estate and the Couva Hospital in Trinidad and Tobago. Another gap this paper fills is that it conducts micro level analysis in contrast to other predominantly macro level analyses. To undertake this exploration, we pose the guiding question: What are the impacts of Chinese development cooperation projects on women, i.e., how does Chinese development cooperation empower or disempower women in the Caribbean context? By examining specific projects and focusing on communities and women, the paper favours a bottom-up rather than the typical top-down approach to Chinese development cooperation.

1. China's Approach to Development Cooperation in the Caribbean

China's development cooperation is conceptualized as South-South cooperation and it is said to be based on shared interests, the needs of participating countries, and for the mutual benefit of China and the country in question, assisting developing countries to achieve Sustainable Development Goals (SDGs) (State Council Information Office of the People's Republic of China 2021). China states that its development cooperation is aimed at reducing poverty and improving people's lives to reduce the North-South divide and foster more just and equitable international relations.

For China, 'international development cooperation' refers to bilateral and multilateral actions to promote economic and social development within the framework of South-South cooperation. China understands cooperation as a multidimensional process that includes traditional practices, such as the provision of technical assistance and human resource training, financing through non-concessional loans, trade promotion, investment in strategic areas, and participation in infrastructure projects. Cooperation initiatives are often supported by government-to-government agreements (Laguardia Martínez 2022). Chinese development cooperation challenges traditional models by promoting its own perspective on South-South cooperation that includes loans, credits, investment, trade, professional training, and technological transfer, all in one project. China's vision and practice of development cooperation overlaps with investment projects carried out in the developing countries. Therefore, disaggregating data related to investments and development cooperation initiatives in the case of China's engagement with partners in the global South proves to be difficult since data is not clearly differentiated.

The parameters for China's relations with the Caribbean have been laid out in two Chinese policy papers on Latin America and the Caribbean in 2008 and 2016. China has also used the Caribbean-China Economic and Trade Cooperation Forum as a platform to promote its relationship with the Caribbean. Another instrument is the consultations between the Ministry of Foreign Affairs of China and the Ministries of Foreign Affairs of the Caribbean countries that have diplomatic relations with China.

Chinese development cooperation faces many criticisms. The Chinese articulation of its development cooperation model and agenda is often vastly different from that of civil society and other critical voices. Journalist Afra Raymond points out the disconnect between the rhetoric and reality of China's development cooperation in Trinidad and Tobago. In his critique of an affordable public housing project constructed by a Chinese company on government-provided land, he reported that the cost of the houses was beyond the reach of the low-income population for which they are intended (Raymond 2019).

Another critique of Chinese economic engagement in the Caribbean region is that Chinese firms are undercutting national contractors, not because of their inherent competitiveness but due to the various privileges they possess. These include access to inexpensive credit, tax breaks and duty-free concessions on equipment and materials, and exclusive access to cheap Chinese labour (Gonzalez Vicente and Montoute 2020).

On a wider level, it has also been found that the nature of the trade relationship between the Caribbean and China poses a threat to the long-term development of the region; the large trade deficit, as well as the importation of manufactured products from China and the exportation of raw materials from the Caribbean are repeating historical patterns of economic dependency (Montoute 2013; Girvan 2006). The One China Policy which facilitates the exclusion of Caribbean countries with diplomatic relations with Taiwan from development cooperation and the largely bilateral nature of the Caribbean–China relationship facilitate competition between countries and undermine rather than strengthen regional integration. Additionally, the employment of mainly Chinese labour is not conducive to facilitating technology transfer (Montoute 2013).

2. China's Position on Gender

According to the report *'Equality, Development and Sharing: Progress of Women's Cause in 70 Years Since New China's Founding'*, the development of women and gender equality have been articulated as important elements of China's socialist system and have been identified as having played a significant role in Chinese reform, opening, and modernization. Evidence of this can be found in several policy initiatives: Chinese Communist Party (CCP) guidelines on women's work, women's rights protection legislation by the National People's

Congress, mechanisms to promote the cause of women by the Chinese People's Political Consultative Conference (CPPCC), government systems for the implementation of national gender equality policies, and enhancing the role of the Women's Federation as a bridge between the CCP, the government, and women (State Council Information Office of the People's Republic of China 2019).

In China, gender refers to man and woman, reflecting a binary interpretation. Gender equality, as well as its related work, tends to focus on structural, material mechanisms regarding women's equal participation in development (Cai and Li 2021). The Chinese position is that 'equality of opportunity for development is a prerogative both of nations and of individuals who make up nations,' as articulated in the United Nations (UN) Declaration on the Right to Development. For China, 'equal access to development opportunities and development benefits are the ideals of human society wherein each and every citizen can achieve well-rounded development and enjoy full right to development.' (State Council Information Office of the People's Republic of China 2016). In 1980, China signed and ratified the UN Convention on the Elimination of All Forms of Discrimination against Women (CEDAW).

In January 2021, the State Council Information Office released the white paper '*China's International Development Cooperation in the New Era*' where for the first time, gender equality was outlined as an area of priority for China's future international development cooperation (State Council Information Office of the People's Republic of China 2021).

While China has articulated a public position that welcomes women's participation in the development process on the whole (State Council Information Office of the People's Republic of China 2016), there may be a need to examine those gaps that may exist between documented policy papers, the levels of implementation, and the ideological gender norms which are fundamental to gender inequities in any society. Additionally, the extent to which principles of gender equality and equity are central to overseas development cooperation is not evident. It is therefore not clear whether Chinese projects have specific elements to ensure that the empowerment of women is not left to chance and the extent to which projects are deliberately designed to enable and facilitate women's participation and empowerment in the development process at the national and community levels.

It is within this context that this essay examines the case of Trinidad and Tobago, a Caribbean small island developing state (SIDS) and one of the founding members of CARICOM, with an established history of diplomatic relations with the PRC since 1974. For this paper, the Phoenix Industrial Park and Couva Hospital are identified as development cooperation projects because the loans for both projects were provided on concessional terms by China. The analysis focusing on these two projects of Chinese development cooperation in Trinidad and Tobago is informed by the sex disaggregated policy data of the region. Such data affords us a reading of the socio-economic impact of policy along lines of sex. Therefore, our analysis centres on the impact of policy on the lived realities of women.

3. Conceptual Framework: Framing Gender and Women's Agency in the Context of China's Development Cooperation in the Caribbean

For the purpose of this paper, it is recognized that women's rights are human rights. The human rights of women are an inalienable, integral, and indivisible part of universal human rights. The protection of such rights requires specific and targeted approaches to economic development that make room for the particularity of women's economic, political, and social positionings. We recognize that women and gender are not interchangeable; one cannot be substituted for the other. 'Woman' is used to represent those persons who are female, being mindful of the ways in which being a woman is shaped by diverse social, historical, and economic contexts (Andermahr et al. 2000). The engagement with those who are sexed female is informed by the fact that the inquiry is largely shaped by data compiled and disaggregated by sex and not gender. It is important to note that gender is understood as a more complex social construct. Ultimately, this essay seeks to use facets of our postcolonial gendered reality to expand the boundaries of our understanding of the Chinese presence in the Caribbean.

The construction of gender and the process through which we seek to analyze the place of women is largely informed by Caribbean post-modernist theorizing and is a form of Third World feminism focused on the Caribbean. Third World feminism is not focused exclusively on the idea that all women are oppressed by men (Alexander and Mohanty 1997). Men are seen as possible allies, imperialism and global inequities are essential drivers of the oppression faced by women, and lastly, complex interplays of masculinities and femininities undergird systems of gendered inequities (Barriteau 2012; Hooper 2000). Third World feminism is not a reaction to gaps in Western feminist theorizing but rather argues for a comparative, relational theorizing that is transnational in its response to global forms of old and emerging imperialisms (Alexander and Mohanty 1997). The Caribbean-based post-modernist work of Eudine Barriteau (2003) defines gender, providing a more culturally relevant frame for investigating how Caribbean feminist organizing converses with the Caribbean state, its people, and structures of global investment patterns in the region.

Barriteau constructs gender as a system with two principal dimensions, one ideological and one material:

- The ideological dimension of gender demonstrates how, within a given society, notions of femininity and masculinity are constructed and maintained.
- It is from these notions of masculinity and femininity that men and women gain different access and are unequally allocated status, power, and resources within a society, thereby bringing to life the material dimension of the social relations of gender (Barriteau 2003).

In her use of gender as a social construct, Barriteau does not conflate women with gender, and she recognizes the construction of masculinities within the gender system and the role of the Caribbean post-colonial state as an enforcer of inequality (Barriteau 2003: 9). These are the institutionalized inequalities that Caribbean feminists have advocated to change over the years.

This definition provides a lens through which one can undertake a necessary analysis of gender as articulated in structures, in public policy, and global investment patterns. Such analysis interfaces with gender on multiple fronts: firstly, as gender is used to establish a constituency in the development language: that is, men, women, masculinities, and/or femininities and its intersections with power, race, class, colour, religion, hierarchies, and gendered relations of power among groups of men and groups of women, within global governance structures. It also allows for an understanding of gender as an ideological framer of underlying assumptions that establish a policy space and its particular attending practices.

As it relates to the Chinese presence in the region, the high level of female-headed households, the sustained higher levels of unemployment among women, and the gender disaggregation and clustering patterns are foundational to how we understand and map the impact of the Chinese presence on women in the region (Seguino 2003; Seguino and Grown 2006).

Caribbean feminist activists in the international women's movement have a long history of investigating the unequal terms of global trade, enhancing the visibility of Caribbean women in the economy and the need for more gender-sensitive readings of the political economy of the small-island states such as those in the Caribbean (Rowley and Antrobus 2007). As early as the 1980s, the work of the Women in the Caribbean Project (WICP)[1], led by Joycelin Massiah[2] from The University of West Indies at Cave Hill, showed that the place of Caribbean women as characterized by a dual work role, both within the household and outside the household, as an economic necessity and existing beyond narrow Western constructs of the male breadwinner, is not applicable to this region (Anderson 1986). From the 1980s to the present, the role of feminist activists and scholars in the region has been to articulate the place of women in the economy, the impact of increasingly liberal trade regimes and modes of development, and the place of gender-blind and gender-neutral-oriented policies in exacerbating inequities throughout the region.

While the region recognizes the opportunity presented to some men and women by globalization-enhanced free movement, planning and public policymaking is increasingly called upon to simultaneously weigh the possible loss of livelihood, employment, and business to others (Massiah 1990; French 1994). The voices of regional activists were loudest in the 1980s and early 1990s regarding the impact of structural adjustment and similar liberal economic movements. Activists called for investment and economic activity to be informed by goals of gender equity and equality and commitment to gender-sensitive implementation. They surmised that the movement of Chinese capital into the region would only result in increased economic inequality with a wide cross section of regional women bearing the brunt of the social and economic fallout (Wedderburn 2006).

As Chinese investment has increased significantly into the 21st century with the internationalization of the Chinese presence, the extent to which we can frame its impact on women's lives depends heavily on the extent to which data facilitates an inquiry into the place of women in the economy.

In Trinidad and Tobago, the Chinese presence has been predominantly within the construction sector. A largely male dominated sector, the movement of Chinese men into Trinidad and Tobago as workers does not afford a clear correlation between the employment of women and the movement of Chinese capital into the country. It must be noted that although some women have operated in management in many of these companies, the sector remains largely dominated by males. Contexts that more obviously locate Caribbean women in the Caribbean-China Economic and Trade Cooperation Forum are those donations that afford training opportunities, specifically higher education degrees for Caribbean nationals, and the gender analysis of the impact of infrastructure projects as a means of improving women's lived realities through the expanded provision of basic needs.

Of significance to this research is the place of industrial parks in the enhancement of entrepreneurial opportunities nationally. Industrial Park projects are linked to economic diversification strategies to promote manufacturing, logistics, and emerging industries. They tend to rely on factories and manufacturing industries.

As regards women in these parks, there tends to be a reinforcement of existing economic patterns of segregation within the labour market. Outside of where women can be employed as factory workers, there is a limited space for small and micro enterprises, which are largely owned and operated by women. That is, besides those women who provide food and similar services to the largely male workforce within the estates, the labour force participation in such spaces tends to mirror traditional sex disaggregation in the Caribbean workforce. Women tend to cluster in service and men in technical occupations. Of some importance may be the ability of such spaces to provide a catchment area for the work of migrant women.

4. Methodology

As the broad research objective is to understand Chinese development cooperation in the Caribbean, using a gender lens, an interpretivist paradigm has been selected. An interpretivist philosophy assumes that the world is socially constructed and inherently subjective. The research method therefore has a relativist ontology and subjectivist epistemology. This approach is therefore suitable for exploratory research undertakings, i.e., those whose aims are to interpret social reality. Naturally, a qualitative research design is aligned to this research paradigm. There are five types of qualitative research: ethnography, narrative research, phenomenology, grounded theory, and case study.

Case studies are suitable for research problems that require an in-depth understanding of a phenomenon (Ebneyamini and Sadeghi Moghadam 2018; Creswell 2007). This research consists of in-depth description and analysis of two cases – the Phoenix Park Industrial Estate and Couva Hospital.

In keeping with the definition of a case study and to obtain an in-depth understanding of phenomenon, we utilize a variety of data collection tools for triangulation, including desk review and semi-structured interviews. Purposive and snowballing sampling is utilized. To ascertain the perspectives of women, a women's rights-based organization was examined by way of document review and focus group discussion which took place as part of the group's monthly meeting on 25 February 2023. Additionally, an interview was conducted with the organization's director of fundraising on 3 March 2023.

It is important to note that the organization grounds its work in the critical need for civil society organizations to challenge structures of governance to ensure that representation and transparency are core drivers of governance processes.

5. Analysis of the Case Studies: Couva Hospital and e TecK Phoenix Industrial Park

5.1 Couva Hospital

The Couva hospital (originally the Couva Children's Hospital, currently operating as the Couva Medical Multi-Training Facility) is a project developed by the governments of the PRC and the Republic of Trinidad and Tobago. It was financed by the Export-Import Bank of China (CEXIM) via a loan on concessional terms to the government of Trinidad and Tobago. The Couva hospital was constructed by Shanghai Construction (Caribbean) Group (SCG)[3]. The Trinidad and Tobago government agency charged with building the facility was the Urban Development Corporation of Trinidad and Tobago (UDeCOTT)[4]. The project began in 2012 and was completed in 2015, but it was not commissioned. In 2019, it was renamed the Couva Medical and Multi-Training Facility Ltd and became jointly owned by the government of Trinidad and Tobago and The University of the West Indies (UWI) with 300 UWI students being trained at the facility. The hospital became the only paying facility in the public health sector (Braxton-Benjamin 2018).

The Couva Children's Hospital was completed in March 2015 under the previous People's Partnership administration and commissioned by former Prime Minister Kamla Persad-Bissessar on 14 August, three weeks before the 2015 general election. However, the opening was ceremonial as the facility was not actually used. With the change to the People's National Movement administration in September 2015, the Minister of Health announced that there were insufficient funds for opening the hospital given the government's financial constraints. As such, they reported that the hospital could not be used as the construction was still ongoing, rendering it unfit and unsafe for use by medical personnel and the citizenry. The rationale for the conversion of the children's hospital to a medical and multi-training facility was to broaden the hospital's use and function, including research, and to upgrade it to attract an international clientele (Loubon 2019).

With the onset of the COVID-19 pandemic, based on a public health asset assessment, the Ministry of Health decided to use the hospital as a parallel health facility to treat COVID-19 patients (UDeCOTT, email correspondence, March 3, 2023). During the COVID-19 period, the SCG provided the maintenance of the hospital (Shanghai Construction Caribbean Group Ltd. 2023).

Among the departments and services offered by the Couva Hospital are diagnostic and imaging, surgery, burn and plastics programme, critical care, mother and child care, birthing, paediatric outpatient clinic, adult outpatient clinic, paediatric rehabilitation, a pharmacy and laboratory, and a helipad to provide helicopter access for emergency patients (Shanghai Construction Caribbean Group Ltd, email correspondence, February 27, 2023; UDeCOTT, email correspondence, March 3, 2023).

In the development of this project, two public consultations were held in May 2012 in Couva at the Preysal Community Centre to provide information to and receive feedback from the community and stakeholders. During these exercises, UDeCOTT spoke about the construction, design, and infrastructure development elements of the project. The Ministry of Health hosted discussions with its various other stakeholders to determine the end user brief - the scope of services that would be offered - the estimated number of patients to be seen, and the materials needed to care for each possible case expected to access the services among other areas (UDeCOTT, email correspondence, March 3, 2023).

According to the SCG, all segments of society are considered beneficiaries of the hospital. Apart from the burn victims' ward, which was intended to serve the energy sector, the hospital caters to the general population, with many services and facilities specifically for women. Some of these include a breast cancer machine, which was the first in the Caribbean region, and a training facility for Trinidadian nurses, most of whom are women. Going forward, digital construction technology promises to give women the opportunity to work in the construction sector without having to engage in heavy physical tasks on the construction site (Shanghai Construction Caribbean Group Ltd. 2023.).

5.2 Phoenix Industrial Park

The origin of the Phoenix Industrial Park lies in the broad vision of the government of Trinidad and Tobago that consistent high quality foreign direct investment (FDI) and domestic investment is key to sustained growth. One of the key channels for attracting such investment is through strategic spaces where investors can operate and collaborate. This view is based on the observation that special economic zones and industrial parks are used to attract FDI flows in top investment destinations globally. The government took the position that it was necessary to sell industrial lands and economic spaces in the pursuit of competitiveness and prosperity. Based on projections from the Beijing Construction Engineering Group (BCEG), the ten Chinese factories that are guaranteed to operate in the park will generate approximately USD $200 million annually. The park will house a total of sixty to eighty factory shells, directly employ over 4,500 people, and contribute about $1.6 billion annually to GDP.

The park is a government-to-government project financed through a $104,295,000 loan by CEXIM. The project was developed through a memorandum of understanding (MOU) between the state enterprise and e TecK and is constructed by the BCEG. It covers 133 acres and contains five factory shells of 5,000 square metres each.

Two consultations were held in 2019 as requested by the Environmental Management Authority (EMA) prior to construction in the form of focus groups. The first was with members of the fence-line community, specifically, residents whose abode is located between one and five kilometres from the park. Only communities close to the park were consulted because it was felt that they would be the most severely impacted by its construction and operations (Ministry of Trade and Industry, email correspondence, August 29, 2023).

The objectives of the community consultations were to address their concerns and to determine their needs and demands (Beijing Construction Engineering Group 2023). Residents were concerned about land tenure for those who were occupying state lands illegally, health, safety, security and environment (HSSE) risks such as dust during construction, and employment opportunities on the project. In terms of impact, from a positive standpoint, there has been an increase in construction jobs, retail business (food, construction materials, etc.) and sales. On the other hand, surrounding communities have been negatively affected by noise and dust (e TecK, email correspondence, March 9, 2023).

The other consultation was with the general public, including major stakeholders on the project as well as the fence-line community. Stakeholders on the project included contractors, government ministries, regulatory bodies, state agencies, and the regional corporation (e TecK, email correspondence, March 9, 2023). Other stakeholders engaged were the EMA and the Occupational Safety and Health Agency (OSHA) to address environmental protection and health and safety issues, respectively. The consultations did not target women's or men's groups specifically (e TecK, email correspondence, March 9, 2023; Beijing Construction Engineering Group 2023).

BCEG stated that during this process, some women indicated interest in establishing businesses in the industrial estate. As the project is still ongoing, some of the outcomes of the consultations have not been implemented (Beijing Construction Engineering Group 2023).

A feasibility study was also conducted for the project, the objective of which was to understand the viability of the project towards development of Trinidad and Tobago's physical infrastructure in the non-energy sector (e TecK, email correspondence, March 9, 2023).

There is a clause in the contract between the contractor (BCEG) and the employer (e TecK) on local content which states that the contractor guarantees the usage of 60 per cent local labour and the purchase of at least 50 per cent of materials from local manufacturers and local suppliers in Trinidad and Tobago, and BCEG has complied with both. Local labour was of all levels from unskilled to professional. The average local labour utilized fluctuated from 70 to 90 per cent (Ministry of Trade and Industry, email correspondence, August 29, 2023).

In February 2023, Trade and Industry Minister Paula Gopee-Scoon announced that four Chinese companies and eight local companies signed agreements to operate at e TecK's Phoenix Park Industrial Estate. The local businesses are Pillai's Tools Company Ltd (logistics and distribution); Ali's Hardware and Metal Fabricators (manufacturing); Southern Reflection Glass (manufacturing); Global Tobacco (manufacturing); Valcom EMI Ltd (distribution); Pour Me One Brewery (food and beverage); Centaur Construction and Services (manufacturing); Ramps Logistics TT (logistics); and Pricesmart TT Ltd (logistics and distribution). The Chinese companies are Hygiene Product Company Ltd (manufacturing); Summit Luggage Company Ltd (manufacturing); MSK Seafood (logistics and distribution); and First Caribbean Marketing Company (logistics and distribution) (Lindo 2023).

Thus far, the project has generated employment opportunities for both men and women in administration, engineering, and construction. Once businesses begin their operations at the park there will be further employment opportunities for residents in the fence line and wider communities. E TecK states that they are in support of any project which provides an environment for women's empowerment and equal opportunity (e TecK, email correspondence, March 9, 2023). The Ministry of Trade and Industry stated that many technical personnel were women (Ministry of Trade and Industry, email correspondence, August 29, 2023).

BCEG envisaged that women will be able to benefit from the industrial park itself via employment from investments which will come to the park. Ten Chinese investors are already confirmed and/or operating in the industrial estate. One is already producing luggage. According to the BCEG, this company is being encouraged to employ women. Another firm will be producing women's sanitary products; this business is likely to employ female workers. Other businesses in line to set up business there include SMJ and Pricesmart, both of which have a significant number of women employees (Beijing Construction Engineering Group 2023).

Additionally, BCEG asserts that although there are no concessions for women, this sector of the population is welcome to invest either by buying land or leasing factory shells for their business. Women who own small businesses may benefit from the smaller lots which are available. Women will be encouraged to work in operations as well as be trained in the manufacturing companies in the industrial estate (Beijing Construction Engineering Group 2023).

E TecK's Phoenix Park Industrial Estate, designed to provide technological infrastructure and real estate for businesses operating in the manufacturing and assembly sectors, is somewhat removed from the activism of civil society organizations involved with women's issues. Although a gender audit of persons administering and working in the service delivery of park services shows a significant number of women, the business focus of the park is not in sectors in which women traditionally operate.

6. Conclusions and Policy Recommendations

The analysis of the impacts of two Chinese development cooperation projects on women in Trinidad and Tobago shows limited involvement of civil society organizations and activism dealing with women's issues. In the case of the e TecK industrial park, no business focus was identified in sectors in which women traditionally operate. They did not make a gender needs or impact analysis or think about the specific needs of women in designing the project. The gendered needs as they relate to the dual roles of care and work for Caribbean women within the workplace were not part of the planning in these two cases.

The research does not establish a clear correlation between the employment of women and the movement of Chinese capital into the country, particularly in the case of the industrial park. This project has not targeted women's employment specifically. While there are spaces for small and micro enterprises, they did not emerge out of a deliberate strategy. It was not part of the procurement process to attract businesses owned and operated by women or to create possibilities for women's entrepreneurship. It was reported that the employer (e TecK) and the contractor (BCEG) followed the procurement regulations and laws of Trinidad and Tobago, as well as their individual contractual obligations – which did not specifically reference the promotion of women's entrepreneurship in the venture.

In the case of the Couva Hospital, it is clear, however, that women benefit tremendously from the various services offered, many of which are in high demand by women and their children. The nursing training facility housed at the hospital is accessed by women disproportionately because the nursing profession is female dominated.

Based on the research results, we consider that beyond China's policy positions in favour of gender equity, women empowerment and agency, there is a need to transfer this to its international development cooperation strategy.

A first suggestion is that China practice gender mainstreaming in its development cooperation engagements as a strategic approach for attaining gender equality and women's empowerment. China may promote gender mainstreaming more decisively by assessing development needs and ensuring a favourable impact on gender equality through project formulation, implementation, monitoring, and evaluation in the framework of their development cooperation initiatives. We suggest improving gender mainstreaming by:

1. Conducting research to understand women's situations in recipient countries and communities.
2. Considering sex disaggregated data and gender indicators for a better understanding of gender related issues.
3. Giving highest priority to projects with the capacity to promote gender equality and the agency of women and girls.
4. Giving highest priority to projects in the area of reproductive health and gynaecology.
5. Giving highest priority to projects that involve the deliveries of gender-sensitive goods and materials.

6. Conducting gender-aware and gender-sensitive dialogue with partners involved in development cooperation projects.
7. Considering, for each development cooperation initiative, how it will address the specific needs and interests of women and girls.
8. Emphasizing the gender approach in development cooperation initiatives related to human resources development, vocational training, and technical cooperation.
9. Giving highest priority to projects that enhance women's employability and women's skills needed to adapt to changes in technology and labour demand.
10. Including a gender-driven approach in people-to-people exchanges and cultural cooperation, making sure that in the projects designed to improve the lives of local people the interests of women and girls are taken into consideration and that women actively participate in the decision-making and implementation processes.
11. Dialoguing with women's organizations in recipient countries to ensure the inclusion of local women's perspectives in the monitoring of, evaluation of, and feedback on the development cooperation initiatives. It is important to ensure that the experience of diverse groups of women become part of the discussion.
12. Consulting with women who are working in and utilizing spaces developed by cooperation projects to ensure that their perspectives are included and ascertaining how their working conditions might be tailored to meet their specific needs.

A major role in China's international development cooperation policy corresponds to the Belt and Road Initiative (BRI). On the occasion of the Third Belt and Road Forum held in 2023 and the 10th anniversary of the BRI, it could be a good momentum for China to accentuate the importance of gender mainstreaming as a key component of the BRI.

China has launched projects that address housing, water supply, health care, education, the provision of basic public services, and building infrastructure in rural areas, among others. The findings showed that the workers in the two projects were predominantly male. As such, general services such as safe, clean washroom facilities were provided for everyone, from which women also benefited. There are no provisions for equity in pay between men and women or day care facilities for working mothers on site to enhance the working conditions of female workers.

Women, as one of the most vulnerable groups in developing countries, need to be considered when assessing the results and impacts associated with these projects. In the execution of these initiatives, the enforcement of security measures has to be considered as well to ensure women access without risking their physical and psychological integrity. For instance, it is key that the projects allow women to gain safer access to sanitary facilities, install sidewalks and streetlights, and facilitate access to credit and childcare services. The practice of gender mainstreaming in development cooperation promoted by China has to be present as soon as negotiation processes with recipient countries begin. All parties should be involved in the promotion of gender equality and women's and girls' empowerment whilst considering national and local contexts. Chinese cooperation authorities and facilitators should encourage the participation of women as counterparts in the political dialogue and the adoption of a gender perspective in negotiations related to development cooperation, making sure that gender mainstreaming is present at all stages from planning to monitoring and evaluation of cooperation projects.

Whilst China should assume this responsibility, Caribbean governments should not be relegated to being passive agents in the process, with China doing all or most of the acting. This stance simply reinforces the donor-recipient dependent syndrome which has traditionally plagued the Caribbean's relations (and indeed those of the rest of the global South) in development partnerships. We suggest that recipient countries also take responsibility for promoting their own gender agenda in development cooperation projects. We therefore position the Caribbean as active agents in their relationships as sovereign independent states, having the capacity to shape and influence the nature and substance of development projects executed with China or any other country. This means that how women's needs are to be accommodated in and impacted by various initiatives must be reconciled and settled in development processes at the national level, first and foremost. National gender policies need to include the links between gender and economic justice, gender and trade, and gender and investment, and this should be clearly articulated in development strategies.

Projects designed in a framework of development cooperation with a partner (such as the PRC) must adopt an approach more sensitive to issues of equality and inclusion and include innovations that illustrate best practices. Fundamental to these are policies and services that help women balance responsibilities to family and work outside the household. Specifically, they should provide opportunities for consultations with women who represent those who work in these facilities – e.g., unions and professional nurses' associations. And this needs to be emphasized in case studies of actual practice.

Only when this is done can women's needs be meaningfully integrated and reflected in development cooperation initiatives with China, from conceptualization to implementation.

Notes

1. The WICP was a research project conducted between 1979 and 1982. Led by Dr Joycelin Messiah, the project undertook the most extensive in-depth study of women in the Caribbean (Barriteau, 2003).
2. Professor Joycelin Massiah is the first female director of the Institute of Social and Economic Research (Eastern Caribbean), The University of the West Indies at Cave Hill, now SALISES. Also, she is former regional director of the UNIFEM, Caribbean Office.
3. S.C.G. Caribbean Group Ltd. is a subsidiary of Shanghai Construction Group. Shanghai Construction Group is one of the world leaders in construction industry, is a public company with majority shares owned by the government of China. In 2022, it was ranked 8th among the 250 largest engineering contractors in the world by the US Engineering News Record and ranked 321 among the world's top 500 enterprises (Interview, Shanghai Construction Caribbean Group Ltd, 27 February 2023).
4. The Urban Development Corporation of Trinidad and Tobago (UDeCOTT) is a state-owned company.

References

Alexander, M. J. and Mohanty, C. T. (1997), *Feminist Genealogies, Colonial Legacies, Democratic Futures*, New York: Routledge.

Andermahr, S., Lovell, T. and Wolkowitz, C. (2000), *A Glossary of Feminist Theory*, London: Arnold Publishers.

Anderson, P. (1986), 'Conclusion: Women in the Caribbean,' *Social and Economic Studies* 35 (2): 291-324.

Barriteau, E. (2003), 'Theorizing the Shift from "Women to Gender" in Caribbean Feminist Discourse: The Power Relations of Creating Knowledge', in Eudine Barriteau (ed), *Confronting Power, Theorizing Gender: Interdisciplinary Perspectives in the Caribbean*, 27-45, Kingston, Jamaica: University of the West Indies Press.

Barriteau, E. (2012), *Love and Power: Caribbean Discourses on Gender*. University of the West Indies Press.

Beijing Construction Engineering Group (2023), Interview conducted by author, February 27, Trinidad and Tobago.

Bernal, Richard. L. (2016), *Dragon in the Caribbean. China's Global Re-Dimensioning – Challenges and Opportunities for the Caribbean*, Ian Randle Publishers.

Braxton-Benjamin, Nikita (2018), 'Name Change for Couva Children's Hospital', *Trinidad and Tobago Daily Express*, 1 October. Available online: https://trinidadexpress.com/news/local/name-change-for-couva-childrens-hospital/article_fb6a5c96-c5b0-11e8-b75c-d31651c3b058.html

Cai, Y. and Li, Y. (2021), 'Global China from a Gender Lens', *China before a World in Crisis, IDEES*, 24 July: 52. Available online: https://revistaidees.cat/en/global-china-from-a-gender-lens/#note-01 (accessed 14 March 2023).

Creswell, J. W. (2007), *Qualitative inquiry and research design: Choosing among five approaches*, California: Sage Publications.

Domínguez, Jorge I., Amy Catalinac, Sergio Cesarin, Javier Corrales, Stephanie R. Golob, Andrew Kennedy, Alexander Liebman, Marusia Musacchio-Farias, João Resende-Santos, Roberto Russell, and Yongwook Ryu (2006), 'China's Relations With Latin America: Shared Gains, Asymmetric Hopes', Working Paper, June. Available online: https://www.wcfia.harvard.edu/files/wcfia/files/dominguez_chinas.pdf

Dussel Peters, Enrique (ed) (2019), '*China's Foreign Direct Investment in Latin America and the Caribbean: Conditions and Challenges*', Academic Network of Latin America and the Caribbean on China.

Ebneyamini, S. and M. R. Sadeghi Moghadam (2018), 'Toward Developing a Framework for Conducting Case Study Research', *International Journal of Qualitative Methods*, 17: 1-11. Available online: https://journals.sagepub.com/doi/pdf/10.1177/1609406918817954 (accessed 14 March 2023).

French, J. (1994), 'Hitting Where it Hurts: Jamaican Women's Livelihood in Crisis', in Pamela Sparr (ed), *Mortgaging Women's Lives: Feminist Critiques of Structural Adjustment*, 165-179, London: Zed Books.

Gachúz Maya, J. C., and Urdinez, F. (2022), 'Geopolitics and geoeconomics in the China-Latin American relations in the context of the US-China trade war and the COVID-19 pandemic', *Journal of Current Chinese Affairs*, 51 (1): 3-12. Available online: https://doi.org/10.1177/18681026221098770

Gil-Barragán, Juan M. and Andres Aguilera Castillo, (2017), 'China and Latin America: Strategic partners or competitors?', *Revista Escuela de Administración de Negocios*, July: 2-23. DOI: 10.21158/01208160.n82.2017.1642

Girvan, N. (2006), 'Caribbean Dependency Thought Revisited'. *Canadian Journal of Development Studies/Revue Canadienne d'études Du Développement*, 27 (3): 328–352. Available online: https://doi.org/10.1080/02255189.2006.9669151

Gonzalez Vicente, R. and A. Montoute (2020), 'A Caribbean perspective on China-Caribbean relations: global IR, dependency and the postcolonial condition', *Third World Quarterly*, 42 (2): 219-238. Available Online: https://doi.org/10.1080/01436597.2020.1834841

Gonzalez Vicente, R. (2021), 'Over Hills and Valleys Too. China's Belt and Road Initiative in the Caribbean,' in Florian Schneider (ed), *Global Perspectives on China's Belt and Road Initiative. Asserting Agency through Regional Connectivity*, 171-194, Amsterdam: Amsterdam University Press.

Hooper, C. (2000), 'Masculinities in Transition: The Case of Globalization', in Marianne H Marchand and A. Runyan (eds), *Gender in Global Restructuring*, 59-73, Oxon: Routledge.

Laguardia Martínez, J. (2022), 'La presencia china en Trinidad y Tobago (1950-2020)', in Mukien Adriana Sang Ben (ed), *La presencia china en el Gran Caribe: Ayer y hoy*, 681-745, Santo Domingo, República Dominicana: Centro de Estudios Caribeños (PUCMM).

Lindo, Paula (2023), '12 tenants secured for Phoenix Park Industrial Estate', *Trinidad and Tobago Newsday*, 11 February. Available online: https://newsday.co.tt/2023/02/11/12-tenants-secured-for-phoenix-park-industrial-estate/ (accessed 14 March 2023).

Loubon, Michelle (2019), 'No Longer the 'Children's Hospital', *Trinidad and Tobago Daily Express*, 16 May. Available online: https://trinidadexpress.com/news/local/no-longer-the-childrens-hospital/article_a5dc0a80-77db-11e9-a4ed-9bae94acc035.html

Massiah, J. (1990), *Making the Invisible Visible: Indicators for Planning for Women in Caribbean Development*. UNESCO Project, Cave Hill, Barbados: Institute for Social and Economic Research (Eastern Caribbean).

Minto, J. (2019), 'Examining the Lending Practices of Chinese Policy Banks in the Caribbean (2000-2018)', in Enrique Dussel Peters (ed), *China's Financing in Latin America and the Caribbean*, 153-176, Boulder, Colorado: Lynne Rienner Publishers.

Montoute, A. (2013), 'Caribbean-China Economic Relations: what are the Implications?', *Caribbean Journal of International Relations & Diplomacy*, 1 (1): 110-126. Available online: https://journals.sta.uwi.edu/ojs/index.php/iir/article/view/344/304 (accessed 14 March 2023).

Niu, Haibin (2015), 'A New Era of China-Latin America Relations', *Anuario de Integración, 11, CRIES*, 39-51. Available online: https://www.cries.org/wp-content/uploads/2016/02/03-Niu.pdf

Piccone, Ted (2020), 'China and Latin America: A Pragmatic Embrace', *Global China Assessing China's Growing Role in the World*, July. Available online: https://www.brookings.edu/articles/china-and-latin-america-a-pragmatic-embrace/

Raymond, Afra. (2019), 'Property Matters – New Public Housing', *A Thinking Man's Weblog*, 29 May. Available online: https://afraraymond.net/2019/05/29/property-matters-new-public-housing/

Rowley, M. and P. Antrobus (2007), 'Feminist Visions for Women in a New Era: An Interview with Peggy Antrobus', *Feminist Studies*, 33 (1): 64-87.

Seguino, S. (2003), Why are Women in the Caribbean So much More Likely than Men to Be Unemployed? *Social and Economic Studies*. 552 (4): 83-120. Mona: University of the West Indies.

Seguino, S. and Grown, C. (2006), Gender Equality and Globalization: Macroeconomic Policy for Developing Countries. *Journal of International Development*, 18(8): 1081-1104.

Shanghai Construction Caribbean Group Ltd. (2023), Interview by author, February 27, Trinidad and Tobago.

State Council Information Office of the People's Republic of China (2016), '*The Right to Development: China's Philosophy, Practice and Contribution*', White Paper. Available online: http://english.www.gov.cn/archive/white_paper/2016/12/01/content_281475505407672.htm#:~:text=China%20values%20the%20articulation%20in,development%20on%20an%20equal%20basis (accessed 14 March 2023).

State Council Information Office of the People's Republic of China (2019), '*Equality, Development and Sharing: Progress of Women's Cause in 70 Years Since New China's Founding*', White Paper, 19 September. Available online: http://english.scio.gov.cn/2019-09/20/content_75226098_2.htm (accessed 14 March 2023).

State Council Information Office of the People's Republic of China (2021), '*China's International Development Cooperation in the New Era*', January. Available online: http://zw.china-embassy.gov.cn/eng/zgjj/202112/t20211216_10470559.htm (accessed 14 March 2023).

Wedderburn, J. (2006), 'Gender, Trade Liberalization and the CARICOM Single Market and Economy: Challenges and Options for Civil Society', *Caribbean Quarterly* 52 (2-3): 138-155.

Appendix 1.1 – Interview Schedule

State/Company Actors

1. Were there consultations **in general** and with **women and women's groups** in particular, on the establishment of the Phoenix Industrial Park and the Couva Hospital? Were impact assessments and needs analyses conducted for this project?
   If no to question 1, why not?
   If yes to question 1:
   (i) What were the objectives of these exercises?
   (ii) Which groups were targeted for these exercises?
   (iii) Were women's needs and the potential impact on women considered or are being considered? If yes, in what way?
   (iv) What were the outcomes of consultation/participation, needs analyses and impact assessments?
   (v) Were the findings of needs analyses/impact assessments implemented? If yes, to what extent, and how were they implemented or are being implemented?
2. Which groups have been or are being impacted (positively or negatively) by this project?). Explain how they have been or are being impacted.
3. How have/are specific groups of women been/being impacted (positively or negatively) by the two projects under study?
4. What opportunities/avenues are being provided for various societal groups to take advantage of, and benefit from the Phoenix Industrial Park and the Couva Hospital?
5. What opportunities/avenues are being provided for women specifically, to take advantage of, and benefit from the Phoenix Industrial Park and the Couva Hospital?
6. How could the participation of women be facilitated, promoted and/or enhanced through the two projects under study and in Chinese development cooperation projects in Trinidad and Tobago, in general?
7. What considerations could have been/should be given in the establishment of the two projects and in Chinese development cooperation projects in general, to ensure that women are not negatively impacted and are empowered?

Women's Organizations/ Social Movements/Activist Groups

1. To what extent are women and gender issues are/ being considered in the conceptualisation and implementation of Chinese development cooperation projects?
2. Were you and/or your organization consulted at any stage in the design, development and implementation of the Phoenix Park Industrial Estate and the Cova Hospital projects?
3. If yes to question 2
    (i) Do you know what the objectives of these exercises were?
    (ii) What views did you express?
    (iii) Do you know what the outcome of needs analyses and impact assessments were?
    (iv) Do you know the findings of needs analyses/impact assessments implemented and if yes, do you know if they were implemented?
    (v) What is the outcome of these consultations?
    (vi) Do you know if needs analyses and impact assessments were conducted for the design and development of these two projects?
4. What are the women and gender impacts of Chinese development cooperation projects, i.e., how do they empower or disempower women? How have/are specific groups of women been/being impacted (positively or negatively by these projects?) What opportunities/avenues are/were being provided for women to take advantage of and benefit from the two projects in question?
5. How do women perceive the impact of the two projects under study on their lives? What are your views on the design/development of the two projects in question? Have/how are specific groups of women been impacted (negatively/positively) by the Phoenix Park Industrial Estate and the Cova Hospital? If yes, in what way? What are your views on Chinese development cooperation projects in general?
6. How can Chinese development cooperation be designed and executed to promote women and gender empowerment and agency? How can the participation of women be facilitated, promoted and/or enhanced in the design and development of Chinese development cooperation projects? What considerations should be given in the design, development, and implementation of Chinese development cooperation projects to ensure that women are empowered?

Appendix 1.2 – List of Interviewees

- Ministry of Trade and Industry, Trinidad and Tobago
- Evolving Tecknologies and Enterprise Development Company Limited
- Urban Development Corporation of Trinidad and Tobago
- Beijing Construction Engineering Group
- Shanghai Construction Caribbean Group Ltd

2

Gender Impacts of China's Engagement in Pacific Island Countries

Case Studies of BRI Infrastructure Projects in Tonga and Vanuatu

by Vasemaca Lutu

Introduction

Looking at Pacific geopolitics of infrastructure, there seem to be two approaches: first, a developmental interest linked to the United Nations sustainable development goals (SDGs) and, second, a security-related focus on competition between powerful global and regional players vying for access to possible bases for their naval vessels and military aircraft as well as for resources. Bilateral and multilateral diplomacy, aid, technical assistance, and loans for major infrastructural development feature in both approaches (PANG, 2022). Globally, the United States has been the dominant power and remains predominant in the Pacific. The security alliances of Australia, New Zealand, and the US during the Cold War actively engaged in the policy of 'strategic denial' to keep the Soviet Union away from the Pacific region through colonialism in the 1970s, followed by diplomacy, regional organizations, economic control, and cheque book diplomacy (Crocombe, 2007). The latter strategies were techniques employed by Australia, New Zealand, the US, Japan, and France until the early 2000s with multilateral institutions such as the Asia Development Bank (ADB) and the World Bank, bankrolled by powerful countries that supported their control of development in Pacific Island Countries (PICs), particularly in infrastructure and utilities[1].

In 2013, China introduced a major global initiative, the Belt and Road Initiative (BRI), and later the Maritime Silk Road Initiative, both of which have provided China a framework for financial and technical cooperation throughout the global South. Now, with the BRI, cooperation between China and PICs has deepened and expanded. As a result, the US and Australia have become increasingly concerned with China's influence in the Pacific region. Adding fuel to these concerns, the Solomon Islands signed a security accord with China in early 2022, causing fears in New Zealand and Australia of the possibility of a Chinese military base in the region[2].

Although funding and technical assistance by China is welcomed, the gender implications of these infrastructure projects remain underexplored. Therefore, this paper seeks to provide a comprehensive analysis of China's engagements in infrastructure projects in two PICs, namely, Tonga and Vanuatu, with a view to particularly highlighting the gender impacts of these projects based on two main research questions:

(1) Do China's infrastructure investments and projects assist Tonga and Vanuatu in implementing their own programs supporting gender equality, women's rights, and development? Do gender equality goals feature at all in these investments? Or rather do they only serve China's own interests or benefit local elites in the two countries?

(2) How does gender play a role in development financing in PICs? Are there any differences between China and other major donors' investment policies regarding gender equality in Tonga and Vanuatu? If so, how do they differ? If not, why not?

To provide answers to these questions, the paper is organised as follows: first, a methodology for the research will be discussed. Second, a context will be provided on PICs and international development cooperation. Third, China's development cooperation in the region will be discussed. Fourth, the status of gender equality in PICs and China's international cooperation will be highlighted. Fifth, a discussion and analysis of the case study findings will be outlined. Finally, some concluding remarks and recommendations will be made.

1. Methodology and Data Collection Methods

This paper supports the views of Cai (2021) and Lu (2019) that human rights and gender are incorporated in China's BRI and global engagements and should be aligned to its commitments on gender equality (Cai and Yu, 2022). The case study examines the approaches used in promoting gender equality and women's empowerment pursued at country programme levels as well as discusses what these initiatives have achieved and identifies key challenges and recommendations.

With China's global reach, there is interest in whether its commitments to gender equality and its policies and frameworks align with BRI projects and investments overseas. There is also a need to identify whether China's gender policies and operational guidelines in these infrastructure projects help PICs in promoting their own efforts to advance women's development. Hence, the paper focuses on Tonga and Vanuatu and proceeds from the assumption that because of their heavy reliance on China, the gender implications of both PICs' infrastructure projects will be similar.

Mixed data collection methods were used for the research and included primary and secondary data sources. Primary data collection involved key observer interviews, reviewers' feedback, and an authors' meeting workshop. Personnel from Tongan and Vanuatu government authorities, women's and disability groups, civil society organizations (CSOs), and two independent gender equality, disability, and social inclusion consultants participated in the research. Interviews were carried out through email correspondence, phone calls, and online Zoom calls as the researcher could not travel to the two PICs to conduct the study. If the key observers were unavailable for the online interviews via Zoom, the option of filling in one or more questionnaires was provided to them.

A total of fourteen persons and organizations were contacted to participate in the research as key observers, of which only seven provided feedback[3]. Secondary data included a desk review of academic articles, journals, online news, and reports by non-governmental and regional organizations, CSOs, and local governments. All information collated from both primary and secondary sources are cited in the paper in ways that protect trust and maintain the ethical standards of confidentiality adopted throughout the study.

2. PICs and International Development Cooperation

PICs are vulnerable to many economic, social, and environmental impacts including characteristics such as their small size, geographical remoteness from major islands and markets, narrow resource supplies in terms of access to water, energy, agriculture, mineral, infrastructure and technological resources, and high risks from climate change effects. Additionally, another development challenge is meeting the SDGs. Therefore, PICs look to bigger development partners for assistance in the aforementioned areas.

The US, Australia, and New Zealand have predominantly been the PICs' traditional partners. The US withdrew from the Pacific after the Cold War ended, resulting in the closure of its embassy in Solomon Islands in 1992, the closure of the United States Agency for International Development (USAID) office, and the withdrawal of Peace Corps volunteers (Beck, 2020). Australia and New Zealand then stepped in to fill the role left by the US. Due to the political disturbances such as ethnic conflicts in Solomon Islands (1998 to 2000) and various coups in Fiji, Australia viewed the Pacific from a security lens, less as a region to do business in than one in which it had to uphold 'stability'. Since the 2006 Fiji coup, the geopolitics of the region has been disturbed by more assertiveness from PICs and the increasing influence of China.

Due to growing concerns about the rise of China and intensifying geopolitics in the region, the US returned to the South Pacific, resuming its USAID programmes. Australia put forward its 'Pacific Step Up' initiative and New Zealand its 'Pacific Reset' strategy. These three countries have also divided their focus on their respective spheres of influence in Melanesia, Polynesia, and Micronesia by increasing bilateral aid and relationships, as well as via regional organizations such as the Pacific Islands Forum Secretariat (PIFS) and Pacific Community (SPC)[4]. It is clear that in their aim to reduce China's influence, these three Western countries have resumed or made new commitments to improving and increasing aid in the Pacific.

3. China's Development Cooperation in the Pacific

China's relationship with PICs is formed with mutual understanding and assistance through South-South cooperation in its bid to promote joint efforts for enhanced development. Since the 1970s, Beijing has funded more than 100 aid projects in the Pacific region including in-kind assistance such as providing expertise in the areas of health, agriculture, education, and environmental conservation[5], trained about 10,000 local professionals, and established embassies in Tonga and Fiji[6]. From 1992 to 2021, trade between China and PICs saw an average increase of thirteen per cent, with more than $20 billion being invested by Chinese businesses in PICs[7]. China has continued to finance projects with attractive loans to Pacific governments under the ambitious BRI development campaign and has carried out almost 500 complete plant projects and provided concessional loans, technical support, and in-kind assistance to help build important infrastructure[8].

During the second conference of the China-Pacific Economic Development and Cooperation Forum in November 2013, China's vice-premier Wang Yang announced that Chinese aid to the Pacific had reached a total of $1.48 billion (USD) from 1970 to November 2013, and approximately $1 billion in commercial loans from the China Development Bank would be disbursed to support infrastructure development (Zhang, 2018). China has also shifted towards grant financing in the Pacific in the hope of remaining a major financier in the region.

However, China's growing presence in the Pacific has not come without scepticism. Issues concerning debt sustainability and allegations of China pursuing 'debt trap' diplomacy in the region have ensued. For example, in 2019, the Solomon Islands and Kiribati switched diplomatic ties from Taiwan to China. Beijing was subsequently accused of attempting to bribe members of parliament of the Solomon Islands by offering development funding as an incentive for the switch[9]. In April 2022, Solomon Islands signed a security agreement with China giving their security forces access to uphold social order at Honiara's[10] request, much to the dismay of the people of Malaita[11], who resisted the change in allegiance from Taipei to Beijing. Local communities have been reported as saying that Chinese state-owned enterprises pursue investment deals with national leaders while neglecting the concerns and interests of the common man[12].

Similar concerns have been raised by Federated States of Micronesia's (FSM) former president, David Panuelo, who accused China of political warfare and capturing the elite (in the form of gifts and cash to members of government). Today, the Marshall Islands, Nauru, Palau, and Tuvalu are the only PICs that still maintain diplomatic relations with Taipei[13]. These smaller PICs have chosen to remain allied to Taiwan given the many allegations and debates on China's economic and political interests in the region; hence, a more transparent partner such as Taiwan is preferred.

Another critique of China's economic engagement regards its low-quality infrastructure and debt-creating loans that seem to suggest a 'beggars cannot be choosers' attitude. China is perceived as having strategically invoked the South-South discourse with PICs in hopes that they will view each other as 'developing countries' who share the same experiences of Western colonialism[14]. China is scrutinised for using debt rather than aid to hold a dominant position in the international development finance market, leaving low-income and middle-income countries to suffer the brunt of repayment of loans which in turn creates major public financial management issues.

Moreover, in May 2022, China's foreign minister, Wang Yi, began a ten-day Pacific tour in hopes of securing a multilateral agreement that would strengthen security and economic ties with the region[15]. However, Yi's efforts proved futile due to a lack of support from PICs regarding China's security pact. Despite the setback, China is still working closely with PICs to address issues such as climate change, sustainable development, disaster management, health, agriculture, trade, tourism, technological advancement, and civil aviation[16].

China's relations with PICs are heavily influenced by internal politics within these countries and growing geopolitical competition, particularly from the US, Australia, and New Zealand. PICs still view China as a highly valued development partner that can deliver benefits, despite the criticisms. PICs' engagement with China seems to be more economic and diplomatic, although there has been a rise in cultural exchange and 'soft power' applications with the establishment of Confucius Institutes, scholarships, and training programme opportunities over the years.

4. Gender Equality in PICs and in China's International Cooperation

PICs adopted the first regional instrument promoting gender equality known as the Pacific Platform for Action (PPA) on the Advancement of Women and Gender Equality in 1994. The PPA was first reviewed in 2004, then again in 2013, and is now the Pacific Platform for Action for Gender Equality and Women's Human Rights 2018-2030[17]. The new framework incorporates existing regional and international instruments for promoting gender equality, such as the 2012 Pacific Leaders Gender Equality Declaration (PLGED) and the 2030 Agenda for Sustainable Development. A goal of the PLGED was to increase women's political participation.

Also, PIFS announced the 2050 Strategy for the Blue Pacific Continent, which seeks to promote women's empowerment and their active participation in economic, social, and political areas.[18] Despite various challenges, the past twenty-five years have seen significant advancements in gender equality policies and legislation in the region.

The Convention on the Elimination of All Forms of Discrimination against Women (CEDAW), the Beijing Platform for Action (BPfA), and the SDGs as well as regional agreements have established standards and indicators that are facilitating progress. However, progress on the impacts and implementation of these policies on the ground has been quite slow; for instance, political representation of Pacific women has increased by only four per cent in the past two decades[19]. A common theme arising from the Pacific Islands Forum women leaders meeting held in June 2022 was the call for the Pacific to move from rhetoric to action.

Given China's overall strong position on gender equality, it is still unclear whether its gender equality and women's development policies are actually implemented in overseas development programmes. The white paper *'China's International Development Cooperation in the New Era'* (SCIO, 2021) states that in promoting women's development, China has empowered women and protected women's rights and interests through the implementation of various maternal and childcare programmes, for example, through the provision of medical supplies, medical staff, and training programmes to improve clinical services in developing countries. Assistance has also been provided through capacity development and technical training programmes aimed at increasing women's employment and participation in political and economic activities (SCIO, 2021).

In support of the aforementioned, China has invited women's institutions and organizations from PICs to take part in events such as the Conference on Commemorating the Tenth Anniversary of the Fourth World Conference on Women and the International Forum on Women and Sustainable Development. In October 2019, the Tongan Women's Economic Capacity Building Workshop was successfully held in China, and, in May 2021, the All-China Women's Federation organised the China-Solomon Islands Video Dialogue on Women and Poverty Reduction[20].

5. Gender Analysis of China's BRI Infrastructure in PICs – Two Case Studies

The following section highlights China's ties with the two PICs, the status of gender equality and women's issues, the importance of infrastructure to women's development, and why Tonga and Vanuatu were chosen as the two case study countries for this research, as well as main findings.

5.1 China's Relationship with Tonga and Vanuatu

China has had diplomatic relations with Tonga since 1998 with the provision of assistance in key areas of trade, politics, commerce, infrastructure, fisheries, healthcare, education, agriculture, and tourism. Infrastructure projects that have been heavily supported by China in recent years have mainly focused on water and sanitation, transportation, renewable energy, telecommunications, and information and communications technology. The Ministry of Commerce, People's Republic of China (MOFCOM) has funded a number of grant-based infrastructure projects in Tonga over the years, for example, the construction of a stadium for the 2019 Pacific Games[21].

Tonga is ranked third in the world for disaster risk due to its high susceptibility and exposure to natural hazards such as cyclones and tsunamis (World Risk Report, 2021). Its most notable disaster occurred in January 2022 with a massive volcanic eruption that triggered a tsunami destroying houses, roads, and infrastructure in various parts of the country. China stepped in by providing logistics support, prefabricated houses, tractors, and other necessary equipment.

China and Vanuatu have had diplomatic ties since 1982, and, over the years, development, trade, and humanitarian assistance, including for COVID-19 impacts, have increased. Beijing has provided millions of dollars in loans and grants, with more than ten cooperation documents in infrastructure, technology, civil aviation, maritime affairs, and fisheries signed between the two countries[22]. Most of the Chinese projects are grant funded, including the prime minister's office and Korman Stadium[23].

In late February and early March 2023, Vanuatu suffered two consecutive cyclones (Judy and Kevin), followed by an earthquake that resulted in the destruction of many public facilities and residential buildings and property losses. China responded by providing humanitarian relief assistance worth approximately 100 million Vanuatu Vatu (VUV)[24]. Disaster relief materials included first aid kits, tents, and folding beds. Additionally, the Chinese government and Red Cross Society of China (RCSC) provided cash aid worth $500,000 and $100,000 respectively to Vanuatu[25]. The Vanuatu government received the grants with the hopes of assisting all those adversely affected by the cyclones[26].

Both Pacific governments view infrastructural development as pivotal to a sustainable and prosperous society as it enhances economic and social activities and improves access and interconnections for people in rural and urban areas. Hence, China has been the go-to partner given its lucrative offers and quick responses with aid and development.

5.2 Gender Equality and Women's Issues in Tonga and Vanuatu

Tonga signed the BPfA in 1995 and participated in the Beijing+25 review process in 2020 incorporating gender components into major resilience and disaster risk reduction projects. Regionally, the PLGED was adopted by Tonga in 2012. Some of the main national commitments to gender include the Tonga Strategic Development Framework (II) 2015 to 2025 and National Women's Empowerment and Gender Equality Tonga (WEGET) Policy and Strategic Plan of Action 2019 to 2025[27]. The Women's Affairs and Gender Equality Division (WAGED) under the Ministry of Internal Affairs is the national agency for women and oversees the monitoring, evaluation, and implementation of the WEGET policy.

However, in March 2015, public opposition to Tonga's ratification of CEDAW was mobilized by women in some church groups who raised concerns that the treaty may disrupt social norms. Many protests and petitions were carried out led by the Catholic Women's League opposing CEDAW's ratification claiming that it would promote same sex marriages and abortion[28]. A key Tongan observer stated that the government needs to separate itself from religious affiliations and not allow the Church to dictate to or mislead the people – the government should focus on its agenda and commitments to protecting women and other affected groups under CEDAW (Interview, 11 March 2023).

In 2018, the labour force participation rates were 38.4 per cent for women and 56.2 per cent for men while unemployment rates were 3.6 per cent for women and 5.7 per cent for men (Tonga Statistics Department, 2018). The gender disparity is quite evident, and the same holds for employment in economic sectors. Although women's participation in the agriculture, fisheries, and forestry sectors were reportedly low, women are known to play a significant role in the subsistence agricultural workforce in Tonga.

In 2021, a total of 22.1 per cent of households were led by women as men moved abroad to work under the seasonal worker schemes in Australia, New Zealand, and the US[29]. Women have traditionally held high social status within communities due to the *fahu*[30] system, which has the eldest or another chosen sister take up a position of respect and authority within the family.

However, in reality, it is evident that most Tongans still view men as the key decision makers who take leadership roles. In the November 2021 election results, twelve of the seventy-five candidates (sixteen per cent) were women; however, none were elected. There was one female non-elected member of the twenty-six-seat legislature, resulting in a 3.7 per cent representation of women in legislature[31]. The last four elections have unfortunately not resulted in more than eight per cent female representation in parliament[32].

Vanuatu's commitment to advancing gender equality resulted in its signing of the BPfA in 1995 and producing its Beijing +25 national review report in 2019, which identified key areas to address such as quality education and training for women's development. At the regional level, Vanuatu signed the PLGED in 2012, and its regional review published by PIFS in 2016 indicated some progress in the participation of women in the political space and in the collection of gender equality and disabilities data.

Some of Vanuatu's national commitments to gender include the National Sustainable Development Plan 2016 to 2030, National Gender Equity Policy 2020 to 2030, and Implementation Plan and Monitoring and Evaluation Strategy 2020 to 2025, which is aimed at promoting equality, respect, opportunities, and responsibilities among women and men of all ages and abilities. The Department of Women's Affairs (DWA) under the Ministry of Justice and Community Services (MJCS) is the national agency for women and is responsible for the monitoring and evaluation of its national gender policies.

Some critical factors affecting gender relations in Vanuatu include patriarchal values introduced through religion and traditional power structures and *Kastam*[33]. As of March 2022, there are no female Member of Parliament (with none in parliament since 2012) due to lack of finances and resources to contest seats[34]. The Vanuatu DWA in 2011 proposed an amendment to the Municipalities Act to ensure that some seats be reserved for women on the municipal councils, establishing a quota system for women to contest local government elections.

Vanuatu has the highest disaster risk rating in the world (World Risk Report, 2021). This rating is caused by high vulnerability to natural disasters such as cyclones and tsunamis. Such disasters affect vulnerable groups such as women and lower socio-economic classes. Women are also the main caregivers for children and the elderly; hence, when a disaster occurs, their workload is likely to increase.

5.3 Infrastructure Matters to Women's Development

While poor infrastructure affects both men and women, there is a disproportionate impact on women due to the level of access to services, financial difficulties, and gender inequality. In the Pacific, women spend the majority of their time carrying out household chores and taking care of family members. For instance, in Tonga, it was estimated that more than fifty per cent of women were working longer every week on non-economic activities, such as household chores – cooking, looking after children and the elderly, when compared to men (Pacific Region Infrastructure Facility, 2016).

Local norms and restrictions coupled with inaccessible infrastructure can deepen inequalities already faced by many women and other marginalised groups, thus leaving them more susceptible to risks during disasters (Morgan et.al, 2020). Natural disasters have adverse negative impacts on women and girls that affect their food security, safety, health, and livelihoods. In Vanuatu, women are usually responsible for putting food on the table for their families and carry out 63.6 per cent of unpaid reproductive labour (Williams, 2020).

Improving infrastructure connectivity and design, particularly for rural or poor communities, can assist women in gaining better access to health and transportation services. For example, better road access allows women to reach health centres more easily than they would with poor road conditions. In some rural Pacific communities, women (as well as girls, boys, and men) have to walk long distances or cross rivers in order to catch a bus or truck. When walking in the early hours of the morning or at dusk, women are more prone to safety and security risks. Hence, infrastructure design and implementation incorporating the needs of women and other vulnerable groups must be taken into consideration in order to reduce these adversities and ensure benefits for women.

Tonga and Vanuatu were chosen as case studies since they have both accumulated large debts, with the former owing more than sixty per cent and the latter owing almost fifty per cent of its overseas debt to China[35]. Since 2008, The Export-Import Bank of China (CEXIM) has provided two major concessional loans to Tonga which commenced in November 2008 and March 2010 respectively. The first loan was about $72 million while the second loan was approximately $48 million (Dornan and Brant, 2014). The loans were to be provided for a period of twenty years with a five-year grace period at an interest rate of two per cent (ibid). Vanuatu's debt to CEXIM totalled about $137 million at the end of 2022 with authorities having made repayments since 2018 amounting to 2 billion VUV in 2021 based on less concessional loans from China (IMF Staff Report Vanuatu, 2023). The borrowing terms of the loan were a two per cent interest rate and twenty-year maturity with a five-year grace period[36].

5.4 Main Findings from the Gender Analysis of the Case Studies in Tonga and Vanuatu

This section discusses the impacts of some infrastructure projects on local communities, women, and other marginalised groups and how they have assisted Tonga and Vanuatu in promoting gender equality. The cases will also shed some light on the role gender plays in development financing with reference to China and other development partners.

5.4.1 Tonga

China has funded many infrastructure projects in Tonga, including sidewalk construction in Nukua'lofa (the capital) in 2018 worth about $5.5 million and the construction of the St. George government building in 2015 worth about $13.3 million in grants[37]. The former project was facilitated by the Ministry of Infrastructure in partnership with China and Dongguan city, while the latter was led by the Shanghai Construction Group. The completion of both projects allowed locals to have better access to roads and safe building conditions. Over the years, Dongguan city has provided Tonga with various donations and other in-kind assistance including twenty boat engines (March 2023)[38], tractors, computers (January 2022), and 500 water tanks (September 2021) to vulnerable families facing water shortages[39].

A key observer stated that 'beggars cannot be choosers', and although China has helped a lot in terms of infrastructure development and the dissemination of aid relief, technical equipment, and much more, the St. George building which houses various ministries still has major plumbing issues, and the donation of computers to schools and other educational institutions lasted less than a year. Furthermore, the observer added that 'most of the BRI projects in Tonga bring in their own Chinese workers and materials, [and] if locals were to be employed, it would be mainly as security guards at their work sites' (Interview, 16 March 2023). Bozzato (2017) states that Chinese foreign aid is tied, conditional, or both; for instance, contractors for CEXIM's concessional loans must be local Chinese companies with approximately fifty per cent of materials procured from China. Female employment in these projects is rare in Tonga in terms of actual involvement in the construction phase of buildings, roads, etc. Women tend to have an indirect role in the form of support services such as cooking for workers at project sites (Interview, 20 March 2023).

Additionally, China has assisted greatly in disaster relief aid. After the volcanic eruption in 2021, China responded within seventy-two hours with the provision of medical supplies, medical staff deployment, and the donation of containers as make-shift temporary housing. The observer stated that whether these containers reached the most vulnerable is another cause for concern – not regarding China but rather the Tongan governing agency responsible for the allocation of these resources (Interview, 24 February 2023).

Moreover, funding from China, including the BRI, is in the framework of a government-to-government network. It is directed towards the various ministries and departments, who then inform the public (CSOs, NGOs, women's and disability groups, etc.) of the funding and programmes that are available.

However, financial assistance or requests by CSOs and other parties can be made (based on their priority areas of interest) directly to the Chinese embassy in Tonga. As a result, office supplies such as tables and printers were provided to the organization upon request. The observer also states that China's assistance and operational guidelines are unclear: 'they do not specify what areas they prioritise when we want to apply for assistance'. Besides China, funding and assistance is also provided by Australia's Department of Foreign Affairs and Trade (DFAT) and the New Zealand Ministry of Foreign Affairs and Trade (MFAT) (Interview, 20 March 2023).

Women's groups under the Civil Society Forum of Tonga (CSFT) initiate gender equality awareness programmes in their communities with the help of funding from either WAGED or development partners such as DFAT; however, the observer is not aware of the status of BRI projects and its focus on women's development in Tonga (Interview, 20 March, 2023). This statement could indicate the missing link or lack of collaboration between CSOs, Chinese companies, and affiliates.

With regards to marginalised groups, about sixty per cent of the Lavame'a Tae'iloa Disabled Peoples Association members are women. The observer has expressed concerns that persons with disabilities (PwD) are still being ignored. There is a wide disconnect between the relevant governing bodies and disability groups in terms of inclusivity: funding and programmes do not directly benefit PwD as they are not involved in the decision-making process. Moreover, 'in 2016, there were 10,100 PwD registered under the Ministry of Internal Affairs; of this number only 2,520 PwD were assisted after the volcanic eruption in early 2022.' (Interview, 21 June 2023). The observer is uncertain how many of the unassisted PwD were women but reiterated the lack of support or a survey to update statistics and find out whether those affected actually received the necessary support. Also, some of the buildings constructed either under the BRI or by other contracted companies are not always 'disability friendly': for example, they do not have ramps (Interview, 24 February 2023).

Another important part of the BRI is fostering educational and cultural exchange opportunities for Pacific Island students and adults through scholarships for study in China and work exchange programmes. According to the observer, China has donated thirty laptops to the WAGED to help assist the department with its community training for women's groups in the communities and outer islands. Additionally, China invited twenty-five government staff members to China for a six-week training in 2018, 2019, and 2020. As a result, women's groups are able to learn how to write reports and apply for grant funding. Capacity building of government staff members and cultural exchange is also enhanced. China's support to the WAGED aligns with Tonga's WEGET policy outcome three: 'equitable access to economic assets and employment' and also to two of China's BRI goals, namely, people-to-people connectivity and infrastructure connectivity. Through China's support, women are given the opportunity to enhance their technological and writing skills, experience new environments, and learn new skills, thereby strengthening gender inclusion, economic prospects, and women's empowerment in terms of access to resources. However, there is an evident gap of women's participation in leadership roles in the infrastructure sector and therefore in infrastructure decision-making processes (email response, 6 April 2023).

5.4.2 Vanuatu

The Tanna and Malakula Road Rehabilitation Project was funded by China through concessional loans worth approximately $52 million[40]. The project was led by the China Civil Engineering Construction Corporation and facilitated by Vanuatu's Ministry of Finance and Economic Management. The project has connected local villages and communities and is often referred to as the 'road of hope' by locals. A story shared by *China Daily Online* noted that a vegetable grower on Tanna Island who used to travel seven to eight hours every day to sell his produce now reaches the market in just forty-five minutes. Additionally, the project employed around 400 local workers during the first two phases of the road project[41].

Ni-Vanuatu people living on Tanna and Malaka islands have benefited a lot since the completion of the road project. Accessibility to markets and other public services have improved their economic, health, safety and security, food, and nutrition status. The creation of jobs for locals has certainly boosted their income security and their ability to take care of their families, and they have learned new technical construction skills. However, some setbacks are the lack of data available on the number of employed local women workers and insufficient information on the gender policies of these Chinese companies, if any. Another cause for concern was the allegations made by civil servants claiming that the late minister for infrastructure made an informal agreement on the project without advice from the civil service (Dornan and Brant, 2014).

In support of the people-to-people connectivity goals under the BRI, China offers around twenty government scholarships and hundreds of training opportunities each year to Vanuatu[42]. The benefits of China's assistance are in alignment with Vanuatu's National Sustainable Development Plan (NSDP) 2030 under all three pillars of society (quality education, social inclusion), environment (food and nutrition security), and economy (improved infrastructure, strengthening rural communities, and creating jobs and business opportunities)[43]. Efforts to align the Global Development Initiative, a China-led initiative launched in 2021 aiming at steering global development toward SDGs, with the NSDP 2016 to 2030 are still in progress.

However, some BRI projects have come under scrutiny and criticism. In June 2017, Ni-Vanuatu workers renovating the Malapoa College in Port Vila (the capital of Vanuatu) claimed that their Chinese employer, Yanjan Group, had violated Vanuatu's labour laws. They claimed that they were overworked and paid in cash without pay slips. An added concern was the language barrier between them and Chinese managers and their inability to effectively voice their grievances[44]. This suggests a need to monitor and compel adherence by Chinese contractors to Vanuatu labour laws by the Vanuatu government to ensure protection of the rights, safety, security, and well-being of local workers. It is crucial that no workers, including women workers, are exploited.

Furthermore, according to an observer, 'Chinese funding has very little to do with women; NGOs and CSOs programmes are not directly funded by China but come through the responsible government agency and/or development partner organizations – government to government'. The observer has not witnessed any BRI projects that support gender equality at the community level apart from the construction of vital infrastructure such as school buildings, roads, and bridges. China-based companies under the BRI do not have much engagement with women and girls (Interview, 21 March 2023).

China has assisted Vanuatu immensely in terms of infrastructural development and accessibility to support services such as hospitals, particularly in remote areas and villages. However, women are not directly involved in the BRI projects given their lack of technical expertise, but they do assist in the provision of food and catering services in some of the project sites (Interview, 19 April 2023). This is reiterated by another key observer who states that women are usually offered lesser roles in infrastructure projects involving waste services, cleaning, and cooking support services (Interview, 9 May 2023).

When asked about China's role in gender equality, particularly under the BRI projects in both case studies, one Tongan observer noted that 'China has greatly assisted in terms of infrastructure development and employment for some of the local people. . . . better access to roads, interconnectivity between outer islands has improved due to port/wharves upgrade and construction; however, to my knowledge, women and girls do not appear to be at the forefront in these BRI projects' (Interview, 21 June 2023). Similar sentiments were reiterated by a Ni-Vanuatu observer who indicated that 'China's strength lies in infrastructural support to Vanuatu; however, promoting and implementing its gender equality policies may be its weakness' (Interview, 28 June 2023).

In contrast, both observers stated that they have worked in collaboration with Australia's DFAT regarding gender equality awareness and implementation in their communities. Both gender development policies of DFAT and the Tongan and Vanuatu governments are aligned to bring more awareness to the local communities. However, a Tongan observer noted that although awareness campaigns and trainings have been carried out in some communities, follow-up sessions or engagement with the locals by donor organizations are rare (Interview, 28 June 2023). Another key observer mentioned that 'financial institutions such as ADB and World Bank on development projects appear to have surface level analysis and not directly impacting the local communities – have they engaged with the local women and sought feedback from them? . . . . it appears that these organizations are not good with facilitative dialogue' (Interview, 9 May 2023). There is a lot of interest in gender equality; however, people do not see the value on the ground. More work is still needed to assess the impacts of these projects and whether they are actually reaching and benefiting women in the long run. (Interview, 12 May 2023).

6. Conclusion and Recommendations

Infrastructural development plays a pivotal role in Pacific Island communities and contributes to social, economic, and environmental development. The introduction of China's BRI projects has been a major catalyst in this endeavour throughout the region. They also provide rapid economic benefits with no questions asked; hence, it is no surprise that Pacific Island governments prefer China as their aid donor despite wide scepticism from other major donors such as Australia, the US, and New Zealand.

China has also reaffirmed its commitments to the pursuit of gender equality on the global stage and perceives that strengthening women's capacity and protecting their health will ultimately lead to building a prosperous and stable environment for economic and political development. In the white paper *China's International Development Cooperation in the New Era*, released in January 2021, the UN SDGs are highlighted as one of its core initiatives to help developing countries achieve the goals, most importantly, SDG five on gender equality.

However, despite China's global commitment to gender equality, a common theme arose from both case study countries indicating that China does not appear to have incorporated these policies in its BRI projects. The lack of collaboration, understanding, and communication between China and local CSOs, NGOs, and other minority groups such as disabled persons is also evident from the two case studies although it should be noted that China's 'soft power' practices are eminent through the provision of capacity building initiatives and educational opportunities such as scholarships and grants. China clearly is characterised by infrastructure and views this as more crucial for both Tonga and Vanuatu in terms of achieving interconnectivity via roads, bridges, ports, etc., which are prioritised over gender equality issues in the two PICs.

In comparison, development partners and donors such as DFAT and ADB have incorporated gender frameworks and policies in alignment with SDG five for their investment projects in PICs. The ADB has a policy on gender and development that acts as the framework for gender and development activities. The policy takes into account gender mainstreaming as the key focus for promoting gender equality and women's empowerment in its operations. Also, DFAT's leadership training in mainstreaming gender equality in infrastructure programmes seeks to actively engage women and girls during the project's implementation process.

Observers (non-state actors) in both PICs reiterate that donor coordination and arrangements exist only through 'government-to-government' cooperation. Some note that assistance and implementation of Chinese aid and investments do not reach the intended beneficiaries at the community level. Thus, national governments and responsible agencies such as the Ministries of Finance have indeed impacted the effectiveness and implementation of China's assistance on the ground. Given their close ties to political leaders, their capacity to provide a broader assessment of the impacts of a project is vital (Dornan and Brant, 2014). Although the key observers are reluctant to specify explicitly who the 'local elites' are that actually benefit from Chinese infrastructure investments, they do recognise that this phenomenon does exist.

From the interviews, it is evident that China still has a lot to learn in terms of creating more transparent processes regarding the implementation of its gender equality policies in its infrastructure projects. While DFAT and ADB have gender development frameworks in place, a similarity to China is that they too still have setbacks in the implementation phases of their gender equality programmes and their long-term impacts on women, more so for the latter country. It is also noteworthy that poor alignment between provincial and national planning and sectors working independently hinders gender equality progress in Vanuatu (MJCS, 2019).

In terms of progress that China could make in its BRI gender equality policies and implementation on the ground are these measures:

- Allowing for open communication and dialogue with local non-state actors such as CSOs, NGOs, women's groups, and other marginalised groups. These actors are the key players in reaching out to women at the community and grassroots level.
- Revisiting the urgent need to include women's agency and development in its projects.
- Putting more emphasis and action on SDG five, particularly towards Chinese firms contracted under the BRI and making sure that projects comply and align with national gender equality policies and strategies.
- Accessibility and transparency in its gender equality operational guidelines and implementation, for example, the translation of official Chinese documents to English for easier understanding and accessibility.
- More media awareness and campaigns to encourage local women and girls to gain access to opportunities, possibly in technical aspects of the construction phase of its projects.
- More awareness regarding the specification of priority areas for Chinese assistance such as gender development so that it is clear to potential local organizations and women's groups who may wish to apply.
- Feasibility studies to understand where and how women can be assisted, for example, targeting women groups in a local community where the implementation phases of the project occur. This can be carried out in collaboration with the local governing agency.
- Addressing language barriers and considering employing more local workers, particularly women.
- Creating a framework on direct and indirect impacts on women with intentional outcomes and to identify the strengths, weaknesses, opportunities, and threats (SWOT analysis) of the projects.
- Regular follow-ups with governing bodies regarding the dissemination and provision of financial, medical, and technical assistance to assess whether or not it is actually benefiting women.
- Considering the reasonable accommodation for women and marginalised groups such as PwD when constructing buildings etc., for instance, the inclusion of ramps.

It is also vital that PICs actively participate in bringing gender equality to the forefront of its infrastructural development needs and work closely with China and other development donors in facilitating the much-needed progress in this priority area. Governing agencies need to be more transparent in the monitoring, evaluation, and coordination of China's BRI infrastructure projects involving contracted private Chinese companies. Moreover, enhancing the capacity of the women's affairs and infrastructure divisions' personnel in both countries to enable them to advise on and monitor the inclusion of gender mainstreaming in all donor-funded infrastructure projects is pivotal. Additionally, progress and annual reports on the gender impacts of China's BRI projects should be produced by recipient Pacific governments, shared with national women's groups, CSOs, government agencies, and other target groups, and made publicly available online. Independent research and awareness campaigns by women's groups could help to promote gender equality and women's development initiatives in the infrastructure sector. And finally, there is a need for the effective coordination of a steering committee of national authorities and women's groups and CSOs to create a framework that will help assess the direct and indirect impacts of BRI projects on gender equality.

Notes

1 Naidu, V., Lutu, V. and Asi, C. (2022). *Regional Report on Pacific geopolitics and infrastructure development: a four-country study for PANG (Pacific Network on Globalisation)*, Suva (Not yet publicly released).

2 Westcott, B. (2023). *Why US and China Compete for Influence with PI Nations*. Available online: https://www.washingtonpost.com/business/2023/07/11/how-us-china-seek-influence-with-solomons-and-other-pacific-island-nations/42e9279e-1fa9-11ee-8994-4b2d0b694a34_story.html (Accessed on 15 July 2023)

3 Key observers who participated are: the Civil Society Forum of Tonga (Executive Director), Department of Women's Affairs and Gender Equality Division – Tonga (M&E Officer), Lavame'a Tae'iloa Disabled Peoples Association Tonga (President), Vanuatu National Council of Women (Executive Director), the Director of Vanuatu Internet Governance Forum (part of the 'Smart Sistas Initiative' Programme aimed at empowering girls to take up employment in the Information Communication Technology (ICT) sector in Vanuatu) and two independent GEDSI consultants.

4 Naidu, V., Lutu, V. and Asi, C. (2022). *Regional Report on Pacific geopolitics and infrastructure development: a four-country study for PANG (Pacific Network on Globalisation)*, Suva (Not yet publicly released).

5 Bozatto, F. (2017). 'Gifts That Bind: China's Aid to the Pacific Island Nations', *Asia Japan Journal* 12, p. 19
6 Zhang, D. (2022). *China's influence as a Pacific donor,* Lowy Institute. Available online: https://www.lowyinstitute.org/the-interpreter/china-s-influence-pacific-donor (Accessed on 22 January 2023)
7 Yi, W. (2022). *China stands ready to build six new platforms for cooperation with PICs*. Ministry of Foreign Affairs, People's Republic of China. Available online: https://www.fmprc.gov.cn/mfa_eng/wjdt_665385/wshd_665389/202205/t20220531_10695001.html (Accessed on 1 March 2023)
8 ibid
9 Petersson, L. (2022). 'China's growing influence in the South Pacific'. *Uttryck Magazine*. Available online: https://www.uttryckmagazine.com/chinas-growing-influence-in-the-south-pacific/ (Accessed on 25 February 2023)
10 Capital of Solomon Islands.
11 Solomon Islands' most populous province.
12 Kemish, I. (2022). *Great powers and small islands: An update from the Pacific and its engagement with Australia,* Observer Research Institute. Available online: https://www.orfonline.org/expert-speak/great-powers-and-small-islands-an-update-from-the-pacific-and-its-engagement-with-australia/ (Accessed on 1 March 2023)
13 Pohle-Anderson, C. and Staats, J. (2023). *Pro-Taiwan Pacific Island Leaders Show Cracks in China's Appeal: Some local and national leaders are calling for greater scrutiny of China's activities*. United States Institute of Peace. Available online: https://www.usip.org/publications/2023/05/pro-taiwan-pacific-island-leaders-show-cracks-chinas-appeal (Accessed on 20 May 2023)
14 Ratuva, S. (2022). *Pacific Agency: A Devalued Political Capital?* Australian Institute of International Affairs. Available online: https://www.internationalaffairs.org.au/australianoutlook/pacific-agency-a-devalued-political-capital/ (Accessed on 11 May 2023)
15 Staats, J. (2022). *Four Takeaways from China's Tour of the Pacific Islands*. United States Institute of Peace. Available online: https://www.usip.org/publications/2022/06/four-takeaways-chinas-tour-pacific-islands (Accessed on 8 May 2023)
16 Kinabalu, K. (2022). *Visit to Pacific Island countries practice of China's equality-based diplomacy, boosts common development*, Chinese FM. Xinhua. Available online: http://www.chinaview.cn/20220606/66b2bd3a6b874384b8f1aa1a034b9b81/c.html (Accessed on 15 May 2023)
17 The Pacific Community (SPC), 2018. *Pacific Platform for Action on Gender Equality and Women's Human Rights 2018-2030.* Available online: https://www.spc.int/sites/default/files/wordpresscontent/wp-content/uploads/2017/09/PPA-2018-Part-I-EN2.pdf (Accessed on 19 February 2023)

18 Bester, E. (2022). *Wrong balance of power in the Pacific,* Lowy Institute. Available online: https://www.lowyinstitute.org/the-interpreter/wrong-balance-power-pacific (Accessed on 1 March 2023)
19 ibid
20 Ministry of Foreign Affairs, People's Republic of China. (2022). *Fact sheet: cooperation between China and PICs.* Available online: https://www.fmprc.gov.cn/mfa_eng/wjdt_665385/2649_665393/202205/t20220524_10691917.html (Accessed on 11 February 2023)
21 Hughes, L. (2019). *Tonga: Between an Irresistible Force and an Immovable Object.* Future Directions International. Available online: https://www.futuredirections.org.au/publication/tonga-between-an-irresistible-force-and-an-immovable-object/#:~:text=A%20report%20published%20in%202017,aid%20to%20the%20Pacific%20Islands. (Accessed on 13 February 2023).
22 Ati, M. and Haicheng, Z. (2022). 'China, Vanuatu embark on new journey together', *China Daily Global.* Available online: https://www.chinadaily.com.cn/a/202203/22/WS6239227da310fd2b29e5265d.html (Accessed on 15 February 2023)
23 XinhuaNet. (2018), *China's aid contributes to Vanuatu's development: ambassador.* Available online: http://www.xinhuanet.com/english/2018-04/23/c_137131384.htm (Accessed on 16 November 2022)
24 Embassy of People's Republic of China in Vanuatu. (2023). *Ambassador Li Minggang Published a Signed Article "New Start, New Opportunities" on the Occasion of 41st Anniversary of the Establishment of Diplomatic Relations between China and Vanuatu.* Available online: http://vu.china-embassy.gov.cn/eng/sgdt/202303/t20230326_11049250.htm. (Accessed on 27 March 2023)
25 ibid
26 Vanuatu Daily Post. (2023). *VT59M Grant from China for Emergency Humanitarian Assistance.* 15 April 2023. Available online: https://www.dailypost.vu/news/vt59m-grant-from-china-for-emergency-humanitarian-assistance/article_83feb4b5-9a0a-5165-9084-bd3f9c2ac240.html (Accessed on 25 May 2023)
27 Ministry of Internal Affairs Tonga. (2019). *National Women's Empowerment and Gender Equality Tonga Policy 2019-2025,* SPC. Available online: https://hrsd.spc.int/sites/default/files/2021-07/WEDGET_STRATEGIC_PLAN_OF_ACTION_2019_2025_Final.pdf (Accessed on 20 February 2023)
28 Radio NZ Pacific. (2015). *Tonga government steps away from CEDAW ratification.* Available online: https://www.rnz.co.nz/international/pacific-news/283057/tonga-government-steps-away-from-cedaw-ratification (Accessed on 25 May 2023)
29 Tonga Statistics Department. (2021). *Tonga Population and Housing Census 2021.* Available online: https://microdata.pacificdata.org/index.php/catalog/861 (Accessed on 19 March 2025)

30 The '*Fahu*' system grants the power of decision-making within families, and in some contexts, it ranks sisters above brothers.
31 Guttenbeil-Likiliki, 'O. November (2021). *No women elected in Tonga: time to change the story,* DevPolicyBlog, 19 November 2021. Available online: https://devpolicy.org/no-women-elected-in-tonga-time-to-change-the-story-20211119/ (Accessed on 5 March 2023)
32 ibid
33 *Kastam* practices embody concepts of community and tradition and are not uniform throughout Vanuatu but vary depending on the location and culture of specific Ni-Vanuatu groups.
34 UN Women. (2022). *Gender Equality Brief for Vanuatu.* Available online: https://asiapacific.unwomen.org/sites/default/files/2022-12/UN_WOMEN_VANUATU.pdf (Accessed on 14 February 2023)
35 Greenfield, C. and Barrett, J. (2018). *Payment due: Pacific Islands in the red as debts to China mount.* Available online: https://www.reuters.com/article/us-pacific-debt-china-insight-idUSKBN1KK2J4 (Accessed on 14 February 2023)
36 AID Data. Available online: https://china.aiddata.org/projects/37748/ (Accessed on 20 June 2023).
37 Li, C. (2022). *The BRI in Oceania,* University of Hawai'I at Mania, Department of Asian Studies. Available online: https://www.cfe-dmha.org/LinkClick.aspx?fileticket =FaplgGeo2ps%3D&portalid=0 (Accessed on 5 March 2023)
38 Matangi Tonga Online. (2023). *Tonga receives 20 boat engines from Dongguan City.* Available online: https://matangitonga.to/2023/03/31/tonga-receives-20%20 boat%20engines%20from%20China (Accessed on 28 April 2023)
39 Matangi Tonga Online. (2023). *China donates 500 water tanks for families vulnerable to water shortage.* Available online:https://matangitonga.to/2021/09/23/china-donates-500-water-tanks-tonga (Accessed on 28 April 2023)
40 Li, C. (2022). *The BRI in Oceania,* University of Hawai'I at Mania, Department of Asian Studies. Available online: https://www.cfe-dmha.org/LinkClick.aspx?fileticket =FaplgGeo2ps%3D&portalid=0 (Accessed on 30 March 2023)
41 China International Development Cooperation Agency. (2023). *China-aided road project builds hope in Vanuatu.* Available online: http://en.cidca.gov.cn/2023-03/02/c_865431.htm (Accessed on 5 March 2023)
42 Ati, M. and Haicheng, Z. (2023) *China, Vanuatu embark on new journey together.* Available online: https://www.chinadaily.com.cn/a/202203/22/WS6239227da310fd2b29e5265d.html (Accessed on 28 March 2023)
43 Vanuatu National Review Report. (2019). *Review on the 2030 Agenda for Sustainable Development.* Available online: https://sustainabledevelopment.un.org/content/documents/23336Republic_of_Vanuatu_VNR_2019.pdf (Accessed on 12 April 2023)

44 Radio New Zealand. (2017), *Vanuatu workers claim mistreatment by Chinese firm*, 30 June 2017. Available online: https://www.rnz.co.nz/international/pacific-news/334191/vanuatu-workers-claim-mistreatment-by-chinese-firm (Accessed on 24 February 2023)

References

Beck, C. (2020). 'Security Challenges', *Special Issue: How does the 'Pacific' fit into the 'Indo-Pacific'?* Vol. 16, No. 1, pp. 11-16. Institute for Regional Security

Bozzato, F. (2017). 'Gifts that Bind: China's Aid to the Pacific Island Nations'. *Asia Japan Journal 12.*

Cai, Y. and Yu, Y. (2022). *An Analytical Framework on Gender Impact of China's Global Engagement in the global South.* DAWN Discussion Paper #47, Suva Fiji.

Crocombe, R. G. (2007). *'Asia in the Pacific islands: Replacing the West'*, IPS, USP, Suva.

Dornan, M. and Brant, P. (2014). 'Chinese Assistance in the Pacific: Agency, Effectiveness and the Role of Pacific Island Governments'. *Asia and the Pacific Policy Studies,* Wiley Publishing Asia Pty Ltd. Available online: https://www.lowyinstitute.org/sites/default/files/chinese_assistance_in_the_pacific.pdf (Accessed on 18 May 2023)

International Monetary Fund Staff Report Vanuatu. (2023). *Staff Report for the 2023 Article IV Consultation — Debt Sustainability Analysis.* 27 February 2023. Available online: https://www.imf.org/en/Publications/CR/Issues/2023/03/20/Vanuatu-2023-Article-IV-Consultation-Press-Release-Staff-Report-and-Statement-by-the-531181 (Accessed on 21 May 2023)

Li, C. (2022). *The Belt and Road Initiative in Oceania: Understanding the People's Republic of China's Strategic Interests and Engagement in the Pacific,* University of Hawai'i at Manoa, Department of Asian Studies. Available online: https://www.cfe-dmha.org/LinkClick.aspx?fileticket=FaplgGeo2ps%3D&portalid=0 (Accessed on 15 February 2023)

Government of Tonga. (2013). *'Tonga NIIP 2013-2023'.* PRIF. Available online: https://www.theprif.org/sites/default/files/documents/Tonga-National-Infrastructure-Investment-Plan-2013-2023.pdf (Accessed on 23 February 2023)

Ministry of Justice and Community Services. (2019). *Beijing +25 National Review Report Government of Vanuatu.* Available online: https://www.asiapacificgender.org/sites/default/files/2024-03/Vanuatu%27s%20National%20Review%20for%20Implementation%20of%20the%20Beijing%20Platform%20for%20Action%20%282019%29.pdf (Accessed on 27 February 2023)

Morgan, G., Bajpai, A., Ceppi, P., Al-Hinai, A., Christensen, T., Kumar, S., Crosskey, S., and O'Regan, N. (2020). 'Infrastructure for gender equality and the empowerment of women'. *UNOPS,* Copenhagen, Denmark. Available online: https://content.unops.org/publications/UNOPS-Infrastructure-for-Gender-Equality-and-the-Empowerment-of-women.pdf (Accessed on 10 May 2023)

Pacific Region Infrastructure Facility. (2016). *Review of Gender and Infrastructure*, PRIF Coordination Office, NSW, Australia.

PANG. (2022). *Regional Report on Pacific geopolitics and infrastructure development: a four-country study for PANG (Pacific Network on Globalisation)*, Suva. https://static1.squarespace.com/static/631e7e482f2ed14cbe31c1ac/t/635602eaa667d879afab4b3a/1666581232162/All+That+Blue+Briefing+Paper.pdf (Accessed on 13 May 2023)

State Council Information Office of the People's Republic of China (SCIO). (2021). *China's International Development Cooperation in the New Era*, Available online: http://english.scio.gov.cn/node_8021417.html (Accessed on 15 May 2023)

Tonga Statistics Department (TSD). (2018). *Tonga Labour Force Survey 2018*. Available online: https://tongastats.gov.to/survey/labour-force-survey/ (Accessed on 20 February 2023)

Zhang, D. (2018). *China, India and Japan in the Pacific: Latest Developments, Motivations and Impact*. Department of Pacific Affairs. Available online: http://dpa.bellschool.anu.edu.au/sites/default/files/publications/attachments/2018-09/dpa_dp2018_6_zhang_final.pdf (Accessed on 11 February 2023)

Williams, M. (2020). *Tropical Cyclone Harold Rapid Gender Analysis*, Care International, 14 April 2020. Available online: https://reliefweb.int/report/vanuatu/tropical-cyclone-harold-rapid-gender-analysis-14-april-2020-version-1 (Accessed on 19 March 2025)

World Risk Report. (2021). Bündnis Entwicklung Hilft Ruhr University Bochum – Institute for International Law of Peace and Armed Conflict (IFHV). Available online: https://weltrisikobericht.de/wp-content/uploads/2021/09/WorldRiskReport_2021_Online.pdf (Accessed on 6 March 2023)

Chinese Mining Projects in Ecuador and Peru

Gender Impacts and Women's Agency

by Diana Castro Salgado

1. Introduction

This paper explores the impacts of the Las Bambas (Peru) and Rio Blanco (Ecuador) mining projects on women in local communities and their agency in the defence of nature and land. The two mining projects have been controlled by Chinese companies since 2014 and 2013 respectively, Las Bambas by MMG, whose main shareholder is China Minmetals Corporation, and Rio Blanco by Ecuagoldmining, owned by the Chinese company Junefield Gold Investments. In both cases, environmental and social conflicts are latent, and women have played an active role in the resistance processes.

This paper is divided into three parts. The first section contextualizes Chinese involvement in the mining sector in Latin America in general terms and reflects on the gender approach in Chinese guidelines for foreign investment in the mining sector. The second section introduces the projects with a brief historical overview and explores the impacts of mining activities on women's lives and how women have responded to these challenges in defense of nature and their land. The third section concludes with a comparative analysis and the main findings.

2. China in the Latin American Mining Sector

Of all extractive activities, mining in particular most exacerbates patriarchal culture and deepens gender inequalities (Ulloa 2016: 124). Latin American women researchers and feminists (Abnal 2015; Aliaga et al. 2021; Guzman 2022; Pérez, De la Puente and Ugarte 2019) have found that in mining exploitation there is a great masculinization of affected areas caused by the increased population of men who are attracted by employment in the industry. These changes reconfigure community spaces around the interests and values of a hegemonic masculinity. Thus women, whose traditional roles are directly related to the care of life – human, animal and natural – perceive the impacts of mining activities more directly in their daily lives. They also face differentiated impacts that deepen material and symbolic violence.

In her recent study 'Building Power in Crises: Women's Responses to Extractivism', Katrina Anderson (2022) argues that gender-based violence is not only structural, rooted in institutional systems and social practices, but also multidimensional; that is, it occurs in diverse spheres such as the economic, environmental, political, and sociocultural. This research analyses the impacts of mining projects on women based on these categories.

2.1 Context and Characteristics of Chinese Mining Operations in the Region

In Latin America, Chinese companies increased their presence in the first decade of the 21st century during the 'commodity boom'. This boom, initially driven by the need to secure raw materials for China's industrial development, is nowadays also motivated by the urgency of sustaining global mineral supply chains such as copper and lithium for the energy transition.

According to the database compiled by Enrique Dussel (2022) on Chinese investments in Latin America, between 2000 and 2021, of the nearly $172 billion (USD) that entered Latin America through foreign direct investment (FDI) from China, almost forty per cent went to the mining and metals sector, of which fifty-six per cent came through mergers and acquisitions of mining projects previously operated by the US, Canadian, and European companies.

Latin America holds a high percentage of the world's mineral reserves: sixty-one per cent of lithium, thirty-nine per cent of copper, thirty-two per cent of silver, twenty-five per cent of tin, eighteen per cent of bauxite and alumina, thirty-two per cent of nickel, twenty-five per cent of molybdenum, and fifteen per cent of iron (Bárcena 2018). Ecuador and Peru have played a strategic role in China's mining expansion in the region. In Peru, projects such as Toromocho, Mina Galeno, Las Bambas, Marcona mine, and Río Blanco stand out. In Ecuador, there are projects such as Mirador, San Carlos Panantza, and Río Blanco. More recently, Bolivia, Argentina, and Chile have gained great relevance as they contain the largest lithium reserves in the world.

Although some researchers have found that in the mining sector, Chinese companies do not act significantly differently compared to transnational companies from other nations (Valderrey and Lemus 2019: 398), others argue that Chinese operations display 'capitalism with Chinese characteristics'. For Rubén González-Vicente (cited in Sacher 2017: 137-40) Chinese mining investments abroad have three characteristics.

First, because of their 'hybrid' nature in terms of ownership (they are state-owned and publicly traded), Chinese companies have relative independence from private shareholders and short-term profitability requirements. This gives them leeway to operate in ways and take risks that their Western counterparts are unwilling to (Sacher 2017: 140).

Second, Chinese companies negotiate, on a par with mining acquisitions, other contracts for infrastructure construction – roads, railways, ports, and electricity generation and transmission systems – which allows them to create alliances and consortia with other actors and control the supply chain (Sacher 2017: 138). Thus, companies such as Zijin Mining Group, Tongling NonFerrous Metals Group, China Minmetals, Jiangxi Copper, Tianqi Lithium, Junefield Mineral Resources, Shougang Corporation, and Aluminium Corporation of China invest in the exploration, exploitation, processing, and refining stages and transportation infrastructure. According to Inclusive Development International (IDI 2021), this investment is further leveraged by a steady source of long-term financing from Chinese policy and commercial banks.

Third, Chinese companies such as the ones analyzed in this paper have shown themselves to be unprepared to address the demands of local communities regarding transparency, accountability, human rights, and other areas.[1] For González-Vicente, this happens because Chinese companies 'face no pressure from "civil society" in China' and can therefore bypass public opinion (Sacher 2017: 139). Therefore, companies lack effective mechanisms for due diligence, comprehensive risk assessment, dialogue, and compensation.

On this last point, it is worth mentioning that between 2013 and 2020, a non-governmental organization (NGO) – Business and Human Rights Information Centre (2021) – recorded 679 complaints globally of human rights abuses linked to Chinese business conduct abroad. Of these, seventy-six per cent were in extractive sectors, thirty-five per cent in metal mining. More than a third of the complaints were related to conflicts between Chinese mining companies and local communities, as well as environmental impacts. Latin America was the region with the highest number of reported cases (forty-three per cent). In addition, the 2022 and 2023 reports led by the Collective on Chinese Finance and Investment, Human Rights and the Environment (CICDHA) have reported twelve and six mining projects respectively, which shows that Chinese operations in Latin America have been accompanied by increasing complaints of human rights abuses and significant environmental impacts.

2.2 Gender and Chinese Guidelines for the Mining Sector

Over the past few years, Chinese government authorities, regulators, and business associations have issued a growing number of plans and guidelines to promote good performance by companies operating abroad. These documents reflect the concerns, priorities, and political will of Chinese lawmakers and often signal the beginning of a process of regulatory strengthening within the country.

As Chinese companies have become more internationalized, these guidelines increasingly refer to compliance with international agreements and standards such as the Universal Declaration of Human Rights, the Guiding Principles on Business and Human Rights, the Organization for Economic Cooperation and Development (OECD) Due Diligence Guidance for Responsible Business Conduct, and the Ten Principles of the Global Compact, which contain important indicators and guidance on gender issues. This signals 'a growing commitment by the Chinese government, business and financial sectors to assume co-responsibility for the results of their intervention in projects' (Garzón 2020).

Over the last five years, while in the most relevant guidelines for international operations gender specifically is largely absent, in the mining sector there has been progress largely due to the guidelines issued by the Chinese mining industry association, the China Chamber of Commerce of Metals, Minerals & Chemicals Importers & Exporters (CCCMC) (Table 1). Both mining sector guidelines make at least one mention of gender or women's issues in areas such as risk assessment, labor discrimination, mitigation of negative impacts, due diligence, gender-based violence, and human rights violations. Unfortunately, by their very nature, the guidelines are not binding and the CCCMC, like other business associations, has no regulatory powers to enforce them, which creates a large implementation gap between narrative and reality. The Latin American case, and in particular the projects analyzed in this chapter, illustrate this.

Interestingly, in May 2023, the CCCMC published a *'Complaints and Consultation Mechanism for the Mining Industry and the Minerals Value Chain'*, which, in its draft version, was put out for consultation to both Chinese and international organizations. LAS, together with the NGOs – BRICS Policy Centre (Brazil), CooperAcción (Peru), FARN (Argentina), and Sustentarse

Table 1 Main applicable guidelines for international Chinese operations in the mining sector (2017–2022)

Name	Year of issuance	Issuing entity	References to international frameworks	Specific references to gender or women
General				
Sustainable Infrastructure Guidelines for Overseas Chinese Companies	2017	International Association of Chinese Contractors and Dagong Global Credit Rating	International Finance Corporation (IFC) Environmental and Social Sustainability Performance Standards	The section on workers' rights and interests mentions they prohibit employment discrimination based on race or gender' (3.1.2-8).
Circular to Regulate Foreign Investment and Cooperation of Chinese Companies	2018	Ministry of Commerce; Ministry of Foreign Affairs; and the Commission for the Administration and Supervision of State-Owned Assets	None	None
Guiding Views on Promoting High-Quality Development of Projects Contracted Abroad	2019	Ministry of Commerce and 19 other Departments	'international norms and standards'	None
Guidelines for the Ecological Environmental Protection of Foreign Investment Cooperation and Construction Projects	2022	General Directorate of the Ministry of Ecology and Environment and the General Office of the Ministry of Commerce	'international commitments' 'international practices' 'international standards'	None

Table 1 (*Continued*)

Name	Year of issuance	Issuing entity	References to international frameworks	Specific references to gender or women
Sectoral: Mining sector				
Guidelines for Social Responsibility in Overseas Mining Investment	2017	CCMC, with the support of the Sino-German Bilateral Corporate Social Responsibility Project	– Agenda 2030 – UN Guiding Principles – Ten Principles of the Global Compact	– 'do not discriminate against workers on the basis of [...] gender...' (3.5.3) – 'Conduct social impact assessments [...] and develop a comprehensive plan to mitigate negative [...] gender-related [...] impacts...' (3.8.1) – 'Develop [...] programmes against gender-based violence...' (3.8.10)
Due diligence guidelines for responsible mineral supply chains. Version 2.	2022	CCCMC	– UN Guiding Principles – OECD Due Diligence Guidance for Responsible Business Conduct	– 'Due diligence is proportional to the risk'. This implies 'taking into account how these risks affect different groups [...] and conducting due diligence from [...] a gender perspective.' (4.3) – '... mining activities entail risks to the health and safety of communities [...] caused by (among several factors ...) gender-based violence' (6.2.2.20) – Recognizes as 'adverse impacts' 'human rights violations caused by involuntary relocation [...] especially on vulnerable groups such as women and children' (6.2.2.19).

Source: Based on the guidelines monitoring and dissemination work of Latinoamérica Sustentable (LAS).

(Chile) – provided a series of comments and noted that the creation of the mechanism shows the CCCMC's interest in providing a space to address the grievances of people affected by Chinese mining operations abroad, which is key, considering that women are a particularly vulnerable and excluded group in participatory spaces. However, this mechanism needs to have a focus that promotes respect for and compliance with human rights with a gender perspective and not just a space for negotiation between actors.

3. Women and Mining Projects in Peru and Ecuador

This section has been prepared in collaboration with researchers Yovana Mamani of CooperAcción (Perú) and Ana Gabriela Castro from the University of Cuenca (Ecuador), who conducted seven in-depth interviews with women from the peasant communities where the mining projects are located – four women at the Las Bambas project and three women at the Río Blanco project. The names of the women interviewed have been changed to maintain their anonymity. All the interviewees have experienced first-hand the effects of mining operations and the socio-environmental conflicts they generate and are active women's advocates and leaders in resistance efforts.

3.1 Las Bambas

The Las Bambas project is an open-pit copper mine located in southern Peru at 4,000 meters altitude in the department of Apurimac. In 2016, it started commercial production and consolidated its position as the largest copper mine in Peru and one of the ten largest in the world. As of 2022, it is estimated to supply two per cent of the world's copper production and contribute one per cent of Peru's GDP (LAS and Schmidt 2022).

Exploration of the mine by transnational companies began in the 1990s. In 2014, the consortium of Chinese companies MMG (majority owned by China Minmetals Corporation), Guoxin International Investment Company Limited, and CITIC Metal Company Limited acquired the mining project for $5.85 billion (CooperAcción 2015).[2] This was, at that time, the largest acquisition of foreign mining assets by a Chinese company (SASAC 2014). The purchase was financed through a $7 billion syndicated loan from the China Development Bank (CDB), the Industrial and Commercial Bank of China (ICBC), the Bank of China, and the Export-Import Bank of China (China Eximbank).

The Las Bambas project has been characterised by latent conflict with the communities, which was exacerbated by the entry of MMG in 2014. This happened largely because the Chinese company approved, without prior, free, and informed consultation, changes in the studies and in the mode and route of transport of the extracted minerals: it discarded the project of a mining pipeline and established a bimodal mining transport consisting of a road and a railroad. The road crosses more than 150 villages and was built on communal land and public roads (Leyva 2018). This change had a great impact on the population, particularly on women.

The area of direct influence of the project is a historically indigenous territory belonging to eighteen peasant communities. The total population of the province of Cotabambas is 50,656 people, of which fifty-three per cent are male and forty-seven per cent female. Seventy per cent of the population lives in rural areas (INEI 2017). Women are mostly engaged in household support, care activities, minor agricultural work, and trade and exchange of their agricultural production at the local level. Men are engaged in major agricultural work and are largely unskilled labour for mining operations.

3.1.1 Main Impacts of the Project on Women

– **Economic Impacts**

Mining projects such as Las Bambas are often promoted for the jobs they generate; however, it is often not noted how this demand for labor, generally male, modifies gender roles in a differentiated way, a situation in which women are the most affected (Pérez, De la Puente and Ugarte 2019). Women have been affected in at least three areas: land tenure, increased cost of living, and access to work.

The historical inequality in land tenure has been further exacerbated by individual and economic interests inherent in mining activity. The continued buying and selling of land necessary for the expansion of mining operations has meant that women have less and less access to the community land on which they depend for their daily activities. Furthermore, in communities such as Cotabambas, land ownership is recognized as the exclusive to men, and women have no decision-making capacity (2019: 50). This in turn has led to division and the breakdown of family and communal ties. Matilde wonders, 'How can it be that in your village, where you were born, because you are a woman, you have no right to land? It is unfair'. She continues, '. . .before, although we were poor, we were happy; it was a union. Now, it is no longer the same; there is a lot of selfishness'. Her testimony reflects the situation of many women in Cotabambas; they have no right to land in their own community, let alone in their husband's community; they have no voice in communal decisions.

The rising cost of living in the area surrounding the mining project is a problem for women who are responsible for the care and feeding of the family. Costs have risen along with the increase in income and consumption generated by mining among local workers, most of whom are men. Verónica, for example, states that mining activities have affected the cost of the family's food: '... being with the mining company is very expensive; it is not like before when you could buy and it cost you less'. She also states that '... not only the family food, but also in clothing [...] in medicines as well'.

In terms of labour access, research such as that of Pérez, De la Puente and Ugarte (2019: 23) has shown that, in mining contexts such as Las Bambas, women obtain far less benefits than men. Although they find that MMG has made efforts to include women in value chains, traditional gender roles have deepened, and women play the role of ensuring care for workers and their families (2019: 25-6). In other words, women are the main caregivers and providers for the mining activity, falling back on an invisible dynamic of a female 'triple burden' – home, family and work – that coincides with the beginning of the construction phase of the Las Bambas megaproject (2019: 42).

In addition, women have found it difficult to engage in work activities at the mine even when they have the education for the required functions. In 2021, only 8.9 per cent of Las Bambas' direct workforce was made up of women (Energiminas 2021). Those women who do manage to get jobs report that wages are not enough to cover the cost of living, as they tend to work in lower paid jobs such as cleaning and cooking (Pérez, De la Puente and Ugarte 2019: 25). Matilde says, 'we do not have work; it is very difficult for the people of the area, even worse if we are women'. For Verónica, it is not only difficult but also discriminatory: 'here in the district of Chalhuahuacho, [women] are not in demand by the mining company [... and when they give us work] the salary here, being next to the mining company, is not enough for us'. Furthermore, access to employment is not linked to the level of education: 'Sometimes it brings tears to my eyes to see what is happening in our district: we have professional young women, but they are not working'.

– **Environmental Impacts**

The mining project has caused environmental and health impacts, due to constant noise, contamination of water sources and pastures, tremors, and dust largely caused by the traffic of 370 heavy trucks that transport minerals daily through 169 population centers (CICDHA, 2022). Although these impacts affect all villagers in general, they have a differentiated impact on women whose care and livelihood activities depend mainly on natural resources such as water, land, and animals.

Matilde expresses her concerns about this: because of 'the dust that comes from the crusher, the sheep, cows and vicuñas die... I wonder how they are going to give us a solution to the pollution issues.' She also states that 'if we sell meat, they ask where it is from; if we say Chicñawi,[3] they don't want to buy it because they say it is contaminated with lead'. She mentions that before the mining activity they did not have these problems. Juana is also concerned: 'the dust and the noise they make [...] in terms of the environment, it strongly affects agriculture and livestock'. Verónica mentions that 'in our streams we have our trout [...] but unfortunately because of this polluted water we have almost no trout anymore'.

– **Political Impacts**

Between 2015 and 2016, the conflicts generated by the change in the mode of transport took the lives of four community members, and three women advocates were deemed to be criminals (Bueno 2019). The conflicts were characterized by the excessive use of force, criminalization, and persecution by the national police in the context of private security contracts with the Chinese company. There are orphaned girls and widowed women who have been completely abandoned by the state and the company. This is the case of Maria, whose husband was murdered: 'I have suffered a lot because I didn't know that they were going to kill my husband [...] I couldn't work because my children were small. I didn't know how to do anything'. The hopelessness is evident in the testimony of another woman: 'My son died, I depended on him [...] I can no longer work, I don't have the strength to work the land [...] I don't know what I will eat, I have no animals, I have no water, it no longer rains in my community. We have lost all the crops.' Another widow claims: 'My husband was killed like an animal. Neither the state nor the MMG have helped us [...] I would like them to be in our shoes and know how we suffer'.[4]

Furthermore, criminalization has been a tool that the state and the company have used to persecute and threaten advocates. Although most of the accusations are brought against men, they have a significant impact on women, who generally desist from resisting in the face of threats (Vargas Díaz 2017). Of the four women interviewed, two have complaints for assuming leadership positions and demanding the fulfilment of rights. For example, Juana commented: 'I have been denounced for claiming our rights on environmental issues, on the issue of prior consultation, which we had to be informed about'. Verónica was denounced by the mine for 'aggravated robbery' for the mere act of expressing herself publicly in a protest. In addition, three of the four interviewees have been threatened or have been victims of these conflicts. For Matilde, the threats go hand in hand with the company's strategies for territorial, population, and information control. She asserts that 'the mine buys everyone and there is nowhere to complain [. . .], the authorities have been bought off by the mine [. . .], those who speak out against the mine are threatened or offered money'.

Even though women are at the forefront of the complaints and protest actions, there are no spaces that encourage their representative and active participation in decision-making or dialogue with the Chinese company. This is aggravated by workloads, deepening of roles, lack of access to information, community structures and norms, limited access to education, discrimination, and other factors. Much information is not in their Quechua language or is disseminated through channels to which they do not have access. Verónica says, 'we hardly participate, because [. . .] we still need a change, we lack more knowledge about our rights, more leadership, to be able to participate in this dialogue'.

– **Socio-Cultural Impacts**

The mining activity at Las Bambas has injected economic resources into the male population, which has led to an alarming rate of alcoholism, domestic and sexual violence, abandonment, and the breakdown of family ties. Juana says, 'when they have money, they dedicate themselves to drinking and other activities, [. . .] they neglect their health, there is a lot of alcoholism, a lot of machismos, and violence'. Another problem perceived by women is discrimination and exclusion both within the family and at the community level where they are limited in their participation. As Matilde mentions, 'your own brother tells you that you have no rights; that big mouth is talking'.

In addition, in order to relate to the communities, MMG has established bilateral dialogue spaces that are carried out in a differentiated manner by districts within its direct sphere of influence. This has generated confrontation regarding negotiations and benefits vs. harm obtained in each one and has weakened grassroots social organizations and communities, breaking the social fabric of the areas. As a result, it also affects relations at family and community levels, as Matilde relates: '. . .We women are not registered, there is a lot of division in the family, my brothers do not want to give me my share of the land [. . .] all because of mining and ambition'.

Mining activity has also aggravated the sexual division of labor. The masculinization of the area generated by the increase in the population of men in mining activities has caused sexual violence against women. According to a woman from the community, 'where there is a mine, there is human trafficking; women are treated as sexual objects.' Verónica also mentions: 'I have been discriminated against by other organizations [...] they have treated us as an object'.

3.1.2 Women's Agency in the Face of the Mining Project

In the Las Bambas project, the main demands of the communities are related not to the suspension of the project but to the fulfilment of the agreements between the company and the government in relation to resettlement, social and economic development, and compensation for environmental damage and land use. Communities have protested through informal mechanisms, such as demonstrations and blockades, and formal ones, such as dialogue roundtables (LAS and Schmith 2022).

Despite the structural limitations that women face, women's organization has been strengthened by the elaboration of a rights agenda. This has, to some extent, allowed them to place their demands in the broader local social organizations and with the municipal authorities. Women are representative at the provincial level and there are women leaders with great popular legitimacy; however, their work is still incipient. Women's participation is very limited, and, according to all interviewees, there is a need to improve women's access to positions of power and decision making.

Women's organizations were formed in Las Bambas as early as 2000 although in the following decade they were weakened, and some even disappeared due to the division of the peasant organization (Cuadros 2010: 40). After the arrival of the MMG company, the organizations returned to action, and today women are organized in different ways based on common interests in organizations, federations, and agricultural committees. However, in many cases, women's participation is still subject to the approval of their husbands. Verónica recounts her concerns as a leader: '... sometimes women, to being able to go to a meeting [...] say, "I'm going to talk to my husband", it's like saying I'm going to ask for permission'. She also sees it as important to organize and strengthen their autonomy as women and as a federation: 'We, as a federation, are thinking of creating a dressmaking project, and another project to raise trout, in the communities to raise guinea pigs and thus be able to work with everything [...] and bring a livelihood to our home'.

3.2 Río Blanco

The Río Blanco mining project is located in southern Ecuador, at 3,900 meters altitude in the vicinity of the Cajas National Park, declared a Ramsar[5] site and world biosphere reserve. It is one of five large-scale mining projects in Ecuador.

Exploration of this mine by transnational companies began in 1998. In 2013, the company Ecuagoldmining South America S.A., a Chinese consortium formed by Junefield Mineral Resources, acquired the project and in 2016 began construction work on the mine (Calle 2019). In 2017, the non-compliance with labor agreements and the dispossession of lands increased the demands of the communities to the Chinese company. In May 2018, the Molleturo community demanded through the courts a protection action and suspension of the project due to the violation of the right to prior, free, and informed consultation, based on their self-identification as Kañari peoples. The local court ruled in favor and ordered the suspension of mining activities (Quizhpe 2020; Quizhpe and Vallejo 2022). In 2020, Junefield filed an 'international arbitration dispute' with the Ecuadorian state for $480 million, and in October 2022 it filed the claim for lack of guarantees under the bilateral China-Ecuador Investment Treaty. Community and women's resistance continues to this day.

The parish of Molleturo has a rural population of 7,166 inhabitants, of which forty-nine per cent are women and fifty-one per cent men (SIN 2023). It contains seventy-two communities, three of which have been in constant contact with the mining project: Río Blanco, Cochapamba, and San Pedro de Yumate (Alcaldía de Cuenca 2022). Land ownership in the community of Río Blanco, the main community affected by the mining activity, is characterized by a greater concentration of land in the hands of men. Men own thirty-eight per cent while women own seventeen per cent of the land. The rest of the owners are communal or legal persons, who own about forty-five per cent of the land (Torres 2022: 107).

3.2.1 Main Impacts on Gender Issues

- **Economic Impacts**

Mining activity in the Río Blanco project has modified the agrarian structure through the commodification of individual and collective land (paramos) for mining (Carpio 2022). Since its arrival, Ecuagoldmining has acquired more than 600 hectares of land, much of it communal lands crossed by muleteers' paths used in everyday life. This has limited women's freedom to move and led to a process of reconcentration of land in the hands of a few (Torres 2022: 106). Eliza states that before the arrival of mining, 'It was a collectively owned commune, and the company bought it and said that now it is private property, and we could not pass'. Miriam also asserts that 'the company did not recognise us as an indigenous community [...] and thus justified the purchase of the land'.

- **Environmental Impacts**

The environmental effects of the exploration and construction phases caused extensive destruction and contamination of water sources and land. In Eliza's words, with 'the loss of quite a few stream flows, water is now quite scarce [...] If it affects nature, it affects us as women because we work the land; of course, there are men who also do, but the majority of those who work are women'.

Women notice the difference between before the mining activity and now. Certain paramo territories have dried up or been contaminated due to drilling, especially since 2016. According to Miriam, 'it makes us wary of drinking [water]; we are really afraid that it is contaminated with so many chemicals. It's scary. [...] Imagine growing crops with that same water, irrigating the crops. Not anymore, it's not good, even for your health'. Eliza also comments on the irreversible drying up of the Cruz Loma lagoon: 'the Canadian company dries it up, the Chinese company fills it with rubble. So, this is the conflict that mining leaves behind; [...] if we were to leave it like this, it would be a desert'.

- **Political Impacts**

Mining activities have caused confrontations between communities that support the project and those that resist it, resulting in polarization and the rupture of internal social ties, as well as confrontations with state forces and private guards aligned with the interests of the Chinese company. According to the testimonies and experiences of the women, the police and military forces attacked the women physically and emotionally. Monica remembers it like this: 'The police, they wanted to attack us; they did all that to us. They wanted to drive over us with the car [...] but I didn't move out of their way'.

Women's participation at the family and community levels has been immersed in a historical patriarchal logic, which has deepened with the presence of mining activities. Men make the decisions within community spaces. The stigmatization of women who speak has caused some women to withdraw from the resistance. This is confirmed by Eliza when she says, '[...] the mining companies say that because you are a woman you cannot lead, that because you are a woman you cannot speak, you cannot raise your voice [...] In the communities, men do not accept that women lead, they do not accept that there is a woman's organization'. Eliza adds, 'If there was a company meeting, only men went; if a woman went, she had to remain silent, bowing her head without being able to express an opinion'.

- **Socio-Cultural Impacts**

The breakdown of family and social ties is part of the reality of the Río Blanco community. The offer of jobs on the construction sites was the source of numerous conflicts between families and communities. Men fought for jobs, which, among other things, increased the insecurity of women, girls, and adolescents (Carpio 2022). Eliza mentions that mining activities have caused 'confrontations or provocations between us, even between us as families. For us it is complicated to be divided between our own family, between siblings, cousins or uncles, neighbors in the same community'.

The mining conflict has also caused women to be away from their homes for long periods of time doing organizational and administrative work due to various criminal lawsuits. In their place, their daughters or grandmothers take on the workload of the household, a job that is rarely recognized economically or socially.

Furthermore, the masculinization of the area has led to situations of insecurity and symbolic and physical violence against women. Ana Castro and Steven Cevallos (2023) investigated these incidents among women of the organization *Mujeres en Resistencia Sinchi Warmi* (Women in Resistance Sinchi Warmi). They found that more than sixty per cent had been affected (discriminated against, stigmatized, humiliated, or beaten, etc.) as women in the mining context. In addition, the mining project increased violence against women by 86.7 per cent: emotional (eighty per cent), physical (66.7 per cent), symbolic (33.3 per cent), sexual (13.3 per cent) and economic (13.3 per cent).

Many women have suffered sexual harassment by mine workers and private guards. Fear and threats prevented them from reporting the cases. Eliza recalls, 'When I started working at the mine, I was also harassed [...] when I told him that I was going to report him, he told me "just report it, but the bosses here do it too"'. She also affirms that the mine workers 'started to want to set up a women's house project for prostitution [which] was stopped'.

Finally, the suspension of mining activities in 2018 led to the entry of irregular groups and illegal mining, which have generated insecurity for women. Women accuse the company's own private guards of giving weapons to the men in the community. Mónica says, 'The company armed the men when they left. It armed the community. They told them, "we are leaving, but you are left here to defend the mining"'. The conflict escalated to such a level that in 2022 a pregnant woman was killed, a case that is still under investigation (Paz Cardona 2022).

3.2.2 Women's Agency in the Face of the Mining Project

The participation and leadership of women in the resistance to the Río Blanco project has attracted the attention of various researchers (Carpio 2022; Zibechi 2019; Quizhpe and Vallejo 2022; Torres 2022; Castro and Cevallos 2023). Not surprisingly, 'without women there would be no resistance to mining and no social movement', argues one local resident, while another adds, 'the greatest value in the organization is the women' (Zibechi 2019).

Women have been at the forefront of the resistance. When the villagers took over the camp in 2018, the women were at the forefront. As Monica points out, 'we were half and half, men and women, but we women were more aggressive in the front line [...] because we as women are more resistant, we do not allow ourselves to be conquered, to be deceived by the companies [...] of course there are others who do, but we are more resistant'. Zibechi (2019) also emphasizes that on that occasion, 'the police [...] soon gave up in the face of women's firmness'.

In this context of conflict and resistance, the 'Organization of Women in Resistance Sinchi Warmi'[6] was born in 2018. The organization is made up of young women, peasants, and indigenous, rural, and urban women who are resisting extractive activities. Sinchi Warmi, which in Quechua means 'Strong Woman or Woman in Resistance', has as its main objective the defense of human rights and nature through community projects, advocating for the recovery and revitalization of the knowledge and wisdom of the territories, and the strengthening of support networks between women from different resistance fronts.

In 2018, in the framework of the protection action filed by the community, the organization participated in the *amicus curiae* where the women detailed in their own words what they experienced in the process of defending the territory. They also promote work alternatives within the framework of strengthening the capacities of women and young people through mutual learning. Their women's community art project 'Warmi Muyu' ('seed woman' in Quechua) is an attempt to generate a dignified economic alternative with the creation of handicrafts.

4. Main Findings and Final Reflections

China's presence in Latin America is closely linked to extractive activities in order to ensure global supply chains of natural resources to sustain its industrial development and energy transition. Mining activities, in particular, change societies in many ways, and these transformations have differentiated and disproportionate impacts on women due to their direct relationship with nature and the care of life. The masculinization of the territory and the conflict generated by mining irreversibly alter community-family dynamics and women's daily lives. Raúl Zibechi (2019) sums it up as follows: 'Men dream of work. Women dream of preserving life.'

Despite the Chinese government's efforts to guide better performance of its companies, the cases of Las Bambas and Rio Blanco show that these efforts are not being implemented in practice. The weak response of Chinese companies to the demands of women reflects the deepening of the patriarchal model of extractivism. Company operations have also shown themselves to be risk-tolerant (projects with social conflict) with weak due diligence mechanisms (projects without processes of free, prior, and informed consultation or comprehensive environmental studies).

The interviews conducted in the communities surrounding Las Bambas and Río Blanco, as well as the various research studies referenced in this paper, are just a small sample that reveal the impacts suffered by women at the economic, environmental, political, and socio-cultural levels in the mining environment. Although these impacts affect the entire population, women perceive and experience them in a differentiated and more direct way, as they deepen traditional gender roles and patriarchal dynamics.

In the economic sphere, mining projects alter the agrarian structure through the commodification of land in favor of the mining project and to the detriment of collective property, which leads to more land tenure in the hands of men. This hinders women's access to sources of survival and care (crops, water, and food) and services (housing, security, and health). As guardians of life and community, women also have the additional burden of repairing or rebuilding what has been lost. For Pérez, De la Puente and Ugarte (2019) this link between care activities and mining is related to the creation of value in the mining chain; that is, women's care, generally invisible in the local economy, sustains mining activities.

In the environmental sphere, women are affected by the destruction and contamination of water and land sources, the main resources for family and community sustenance. This has an impact on their daily life of care, as well as on their health and that of the community.

In the political sphere, women, particularly leaders and advocates, are persecuted, threatened, and criminalized in situations of conflict and resistance. They suffer discrimination and humiliation for raising their voices and participating. In addition, there is evidence of the disproportionate use of force by public forces and private guards in alliance with companies and the government.

Finally, in the socio-cultural sphere, the main impact is the rupture of the social, community, and family fabric. Chinese companies tend to take advantage of the weak presence of the state to control the population and the land through economic compensation mechanisms, negotiations, and social services that break social cohesion and polarize communities. In turn, the masculinization of territories exacerbates discrimination, insecurity, and violence against women.

Beyond the impacts on women in the communities surrounding the project, mining activities have been fertile ground for the emergence and consolidation of women leaders and women's social movements. Women have exercised their

Table 2 Comparison of mining projects: impacts and resistance

	LAS BAMBAS	RÍO BLANCO
Chinese operating companies	MMG, Guoxin International and CITIC.	Ecuagoldmining (Junefield Mineral Resources and Hunan Gold Corporation)
Status	Operational	Suspended
Exploitation phase	2016–present	2016–2018
IMPACTS		
Economic	Changes in land tenure, increased cost of living, and access to work.	Changing agrarian structure, disputes over jobs. Girls and elderly women take on workload.
Environmental	Contamination of water sources and land, constant noise, tremors, and dust from truck traffic.	Destruction and contamination of water sources and land. Desiccation of the Cruz Loma Lagoon.
Political	Criminalization and threats to women advocates, excessive use of force. Obstacles to participation. Murder of husbands and fathers.	Criminalization and persecution of women advocates, polarization between communities, use of force and aggression. Obstacles to participation.
Sociocultural	Masculinization and deepening of gender roles, discrimination and exclusion, rupture of the social fabric, threats and violence, sexual division of labour.	Masculinization and deepening of gender roles, discrimination against women defenders, breakdown of social and family fabric, insecurity, violence.

AGENCY AND RESISTANCE		
Demands	Fulfilment of agreements and commitments regarding access to water and land, reparation, political participation, family diet, increase in the cost of living.	Recognition as Kañari peoples, lack of free, prior, and informed consultation. Definitive suspension of the project.
Achievements	– Strengthened women's organization. – Women leaders with great popular legitimacy. – Rights agenda with a gender focus in local and municipal organizations. – Personal and economic empowerment projects for women.	– Creation of the 'Organization of Women in Resistance Sinchi Warmi'. – Women on the front line in uprisings and denunciations. – They achieve protection action and suspension of the project. – Alternative work initiatives and mutual learning.

Source: Elaborated by Latinoamérica Sustentable (LAS) based on interviews and other field work.

capacity for agency, enabling the reconfiguration and occupation of new spaces in the social environment and thus taking actions that transform the order or practices in which they are immersed and from which they have been historically excluded.

Thus, as Valderry and Lemus (2021: 404) rightly point out, women '... articulate for the defence of communal property, community rights, better working conditions or respect for the environment. They propose a different model of understanding the relationships between human beings, work, and nature'. Consequently, they constitute a paradigmatic challenge to the extractive patriarchal model that historically underpins the transnational mining dynamic, of which China is part.

Acknowledgments

This research would not have been possible without the contribution of Yovana Mamani from CooperAcción (Peru) and Ana Gabriela Castro, researcher at the University of Cuenca (Ecuador), who conducted the field research and interviews. Their experiences and closeness to the territory and the women provide a unique perspective to this work. Thank you!

Notes

1. For more information on similar cases in other regions, see the case of Myanmar and the Letpaduang Copper Mining project. Available online: https://media.business-humanrights.org/media/documents/files/documents/SRI_The_Social_Responsibility_of_Chinas_OFDI_and_NGOs_Engagement.pdf. Also, see Jingjing Zhang's paper. Available online: https://www.business-humanrights.org/en/latest-news/interview-with-environmental-lawyer-zhang-jingjing-on-the-need-for-legal-requirements-for-chinese-overseas-investments/
2. Despite the changes in ownership, it is worth noting that many of the company's officers and directors have remained the same since 2004. This explains the continuity of bad practices regardless of the nationality of the company.
3. Chicñawi is the peasant community where Matilde is from. It belongs to the district of Challhuahuacho, province of Cotabambas. It is a community in the direct sphere of influence of the mine and is close to the processing plant.
4. These two testimonies were taken at the workshop held by CooperAcción and Latinoamérica Sustentable in November 2022 in Cusco, Peru with residents of the affected localities.
5. It is a wetland of global importance under the Convention on Wetlands, or Ramsar Convention, which promotes the conservation and wise use of wetlands.
6. 'Sinchi Warmi' means 'Strong Woman or Woman in Resistance' in Quechua. Instagram: @sinchiwarmirb_ / Facebook: Sinchi Warmi Río Blanco.

References

Aliaga, C., N. Fuentes, A. Rojas, S. Vega and Eva Vázquez. (2021), *Mujeres contra el extractivismo minero en el Abya Yala defensoras,* Red Latinoamericana de mujeres defensoras de derechos sociales y ambientales. Available online: https://www.redlatinoamericanademujeres.org/mapa/wp-content/uploads/2021/11/Mujeres_contra_el_extrativismo_minero_en_el_abya_yala_defensoras_compressed.pdf (Accessed 17 February 2025).

Anderson, K. (2022), *Building Power in Crisis. Women's Responses to Extractivism,* SAGE Fund. Available online: https://static1.squarespace.com/static/56e04646f699bb070acdb6f3/t/648b194c9a89cd6d3f6d0398/1686837583849/Extract+Report_Long_Eng_LoRes_Final_6.6.23.pdf (Accessed 17 February 2025).

Bueno, K. (2019), 'La situación de las mujeres campesinas en Las Bambas', *Observatorio de Conflictos Mineros de América Latina* (OCMAL). Available online: https://www.ocmal.org/la-situacion-de-las-mujeres-campesinas-en-las-bambas/ (Accessed 17 February 2025).

Business and Human Rights Resource Centre. (2021), 'Going out' responsibly. The Human Rights Impact of China´s Global Investments. Available online: https://media.business-humanrights.org/media/documents/2021_BHRRC_China_Briefing.pdf (Accessed 17 February 2025).

Calle, D. (2019), 'El proyecto minero Río Blanco y la aplicación del derecho a la consulta previa, libre e informada', Lawyer diss., University of Azuay, Cuenca. Available online: http://dspace.uazuay.edu.ec/handle/datos/9516 (Accessed 17 February 2025).

Carpio, P., ed (2022), *Resistencia: minería, impactos y luchas*. [*Resistance: mining, impacts and struggles*], Cuenca: Universidad de Cuenca Press. Available online: https://editorial.ucuenca.edu.ec/omp/index.php/ucp/catalog/book/19 (Accessed 17 February 2025).

Castro, A. and Cevallos, S. (not yet published). '*Análisis de la experiencia organizativa de mujeres "Sinchi Warmi" en el contexto del conflicto ecoterritorial minero, periodo 2018-2023*', diss., University of Cuenca, Ecuador.

Colectivo sobre Financiamiento e Inversiones Chinas, Derechos Humanos y Ambiente (CICDHA). (2022), *Derechos Humanos y Actividades Empresariales Chinas en Latinoamérica. Casos de Argentina, Bolivia, Brasil, Chile, Colombia, Ecuador, México, Perú y Venezuela*, Mid-term report of the Universal Periodic Review of the People's Republic of China. Available online: https://cicdha.org/wp-content/uploads/2023/08/HUMAN_RIGHTS_AND_CHINESE_BUSINESS_ACTIVITIES_IN_LATIN_AMERICA-EN-full_.pdf (Accessed 17 February 2025).

Colectivo sobre Financiamiento e Inversiones Chinas, Derechos Humanos y Ambiente (CICDHA). (2023), *Informe: Las Obligaciones Extraterritoriales en Derechos Humanos de la República Popular de China con Relación a Actividades Empresariales en América Latina*, Report for the review of the People's Republic of China by the Committee on Economic, Social and Cultural Rights of the United Nations (UN). Available online: https://cicdha.org/wp-content/uploads/2023/09/Informe-ENG-.pdf (Accessed 17 February 2025).

Comisión Económica para América Latina y el Caribe (CEPAL). (2016), *La Inversión Extranjera Directa en América Latina y el Caribe*, Santiago: CEPAL. Available online: https://repositorio.cepal.org/bitstream/handle/11362/40213/S1600664_es.pdf?sequence=7&isAllowed=y (Accessed 17 February 2025).

CooperAcción (2015), *Caso 'Las Bambas': Informe Especial 2015* [*The 'Las Bambas' Case: Special Report 2015*], Lima: CooperAcción. Available online: https://cooperaccion.org.pe/publicaciones/2114/ (Accessed 17 February 2025).

Cuadros, J. (2010), *Impactos de la minería en la vida de hombres y mujeres en el sur andino. Una mirada desde el género y la interculturalidad. Los casos Las Bambas y Tintaya*, CooperAcción. Available online: https://cooperaccion.org.pe/publicaciones/impactos-de-la-mineria-en-la-vida-de-hombres-y-mujeres-en-el-sur-andino-una-mirada-desde-el-genero-y-la-interculturalidad-los-casos-las-bambas-y-tintaya/ (Accessed 17 February 2025).

Dussel Peters, E. (2022), *Monitor de la OFDI china en América Latina y el Caribe 2022*. Mexico: Red ALC-China. Available online: https://www.redalc-china.org/monitor/index.php?option=com_content&view=article&id=437 (Accessed 17 February 2025).

Energiminas. (2021), 'El 8.9 porciento de la planilla directa de Las Bambas está constituida por mujeres', *Revista Energiminas*. Available online: https://energiminas.com/el-8-9-de-la-planilla-directa-de-las-bambas-esta-constituida-por-mujeres/ (Accessed 17 February 2025).

Garzón, P. (2020), *Compilación de Directrices Ambientales y Sociales Chinas para las Operaciones en el Extranjero*, Quito, Ecuador: Iniciativa para las Inversiones Sustentables China-América Latina (IISCAL). Available online: https://latsustentable.org/wp-content/uploads/2022/07/Compilacion-de-Directrices-Ambientales-y-Sociales-Chinas-para-las-Operaciones-en-el-Extranjero.pdf (Accessed 17 February 2025).

Inclusive Development International, (IDI). (2022), *Development of Chinese Overseas Investment Standards*. Available online: https://www.followingthemoney.org/development-of-chinese-overseas-investment-standards/ (Accessed 17 February 2025).

Leyva, A. (2018), *Una carretera que nadie aprobó* [A Road That Nobody Approved], Lima: CooperAcción. Available online: https://cooperaccion.org.pe/wp-content/uploads/2018/08/Libro-Carretera-Las-Bambas.pdf (Accessed 17 February 2025).

National Information System (SIN). (2023), *Population statistics*. Available online: https://menucloud.sni.gob.ec/web/menu/#(Accessed 17 February 2025).

National Institute of Statistics and Informatics (INEI). *Population and Housing Census 2017*. Peru.

Paz Cardona, A. (2022), '¿Minería ilegal de oro cobra la vida de una defensora ambiental en Ecuador y desata violencia', *Mongabay*. Available online: https://es.mongabay.com/2022/11/mineria-ilegal-de-oro-cobra-la-vida-de-una-defensora-ambiental-en-ecuador/ (Accessed 17 February 2025).

Alcaldía de Cuenca (2022), '*Plan de Desarrollo y Ordenamiento Territorial del Cantón Cuenca y Plan de Uso y Gestión del Suelo (PDOT-PUGS)*' [Development and Territorial Planning Plan of the Cuenca Canton and Land Use and Management Plan]. Available online: https://www.cuenca.gob.ec/content/pdot-pugs-2022 (Accessed 17 February 2025).

Pérez, L., L. De la Puente and D. Ugarte (2019), '*Las cuidadoras de los mineros: género y gran minería en Cotabambas*', Research Paper No. 12. Lima: University of the Pacific. Available online: https://repositorio.up.edu.pe/handle/11354/2491 (Accessed 17 February 2025).

Quizhpe, C. (2020), '*La commoditización de las subjetividades: la minería en la provincia del Azuay, Ecuador y los casos de los proyectos Río Blanco y Loma Larga*', MA diss., Department of Socio-Environmental Studies, FLACSO-Ecuador. Available online: http://hdl.handle.net/10469/16552 (Accessed 17 February 2025).

Quizhpe, C. and I. Vallejo (2022), 'Procesos de juridificación y defensa del agua en el sur andino del Ecuador' [Processes of juridification and defense of water in the southern Andean region of Ecuador], *Íconos, Revista de Ciencias Sociales*, 72/26(1): 33-56. Available online: http://hdl.handle.net/10469/17783 (Accessed 17 February 2025).

Sacher, W. (2017), *Ofensiva Megaminera China en los Andes. Acumulación por desposesión en el Ecuador de la 'Revolución Ciudadana'*, Quito: Editorial Abya Yala. Available online: https://www.rosalux.org.ec/pdfs/Ofensiva-megaminera-china-en-los-Andes.pdf (Accessed 17 February 2025).

State-owned Assets Supervision and Administration Commission of the State Council (SASAC). (2014), '*China Minmetals Consortium Acquires Peru Copper Mine Project for US$5.85 Billion*'. Available online: http://www.sasac.gov.cn/n2588025/n2588124/c3858517/content.html (Accessed 17 February 2025).

Torres, N. (2022), *Mujeres en Resistencia: configuraciones de género y extractivismo minero en la provincia del Azuay* en *Resistencia: minería, impactos y luchas*. Cuenca: University of Cuenca Press.

Ulloa, A. (2016), 'Feminismos territoriales en América Latina: defensas de la vida frente a los extractivismos', *Nómadas*, 45: 123-39, Colombia: Central University. Available online: https://www.redalyc.org/pdf/1051/105149483020.pdf (Accessed 17 February 2025).

Vargas Díaz, W. (2017), 'Violencia, poder y minería en Perú: ¿cómo Las Bambas ha agravado la represión?', *Open Democracy*. 8 December 2017. Available online: https://www.opendemocracy.net/es/violencia-poder-y-miner-en-per-c-mo-las-bambas-ha-agravado-la-r/ (Accessed 17 February 2025).

Yang, H., B. Simmons, R. Ray, C. Nolte, S. Gopal, Y. Ma, X. Ma and K. Gallagher (2021), 'Risks to global biodiversity and Indigenous lands from China's overseas development finance', *Nature Ecology & Evolution*, 5: 1520-9. Available online: https://doi.org/10.1038/s41559-021-01541-w (Accessed 17 February 2025).

Zibiechi, R. (2019), 'Defensoras de la Pachamama. La lucha de las comunidades contra la minería' ['Women: Pachamama's Defenders. The communities' fight against mining'], *Rebelión*. Available online: https://rebelion.org/defensoras-de-la-pachamama/ (Accessed 17 February 2025).

4

Organised Abandonment and Gendered Impacts of Extractivism in Bikita, Zimbabwe

By Hibist Wendemu Kassa and Zinzile Siphiwo Fengu

1. Introduction

Zimbabwe's indigenisation policies have aimed to reconfigure ownership and control over land and natural resources in order to redress historical injustices in pursuit of autonomous development (Moyo and Yeros, 2011). This policy shift emerged against a broader context of discontent with liberalization of the economy (Seddon and Zeilig, 2005; Saul and Saunders, 2005) and a failure to redress land dispossession tied to colonialism and apartheid. In response to the policy shift, sanctions were imposed by the governments of the United States, the United Kingdom, Australia, and the European Union because of human rights violations and political repression (Gov.UK, 2022; Global Affairs Canada, 2023), which has had an impact on constraining the country's access to development finance and investments (Dendere, 2022).

Zimbabwe's woes bring into focus the challenges facing Global South countries, which after independence remain locked in systems of accumulation that undermine their capabilities to reconfigure their economies, political institutions, and societies. The conditions that gave rise to the fast-track land reforms are not solely external (Moyo, 2018) but rather also reflect a growing gap between the black bourgeoisie and smallholder producers within a system of white supremacy (Moyo and Yeros, 2018).

This sets the scene for lithium mining in the Bikita district, where political, socio-economic, and environmental problems center on land conflicts. Bikita had been earmarked for resettlement after land redistribution. Women are particularly adversely affected since their rights to land are restricted. Women in Bikita face multiple challenges that emanate from mining activities that have a disproportionate impact on mine host communities. The prevalence of artisanal lithium mining in Bikita has also reproduced elements of the challenges arising from large-scale mining in a fragile environment. A combination of limits of access to and control of land, scarcity of water, boundary disputes, and social problems are further amplified by the Bikita mine. Altogether, this has had an impact on health, social reproduction, and food and water security.

Extractivism, which broadly refers to the uneven integration in the global system of production, reproduction, and trade, leaves countries where primary production occurs with a lower share of value generated and a higher burden of environmental, health, and labor costs (including social reproductive labor). Zimbabwe has introduced mining reforms to encourage minerals beneficiation (Chimwamurombe and Gona, 2023) and as a means for communities to be more directly involved in minerals extraction (Mathibela, 2022). This raises the possibility of women's integration in the minerals value chain (AMV, 2009). This has had a bearing on lithium mining since, unlike gold mining, which feeds into a state-owned refinery, such processing capabilities did not exist. The absence of such capabilities in lithium extraction and processing had ensured Zimbabwe was unable to capture a greater share of the mineral value.

Corporate accountability frameworks are dominated by voluntary processes in which corporations are largely expected to 'do no harm' and 'respect' but not 'protect' human rights (UNHR, 2011; Bernaz, 2021: 50-53). Human rights here are understood as inclusive of rights to public goods. The latter, which is the purview of the state, under neoliberal structural adjustment has in practice become a form of 'organized abandonment' (Gilmore, 2022). In practice, investors rely on local laws which operate within a policy vacuum within which violations occur. Without effective monitoring and remedy mechanisms the violations can be ignored and, in extreme cases, supported by the state. The securitization of mineral extraction areas is an outcome of this.

What does this mean about the nature of investments from China, when the government of China has offered consistent support for Zimbabwe through its crisis (Guo, 2022)? Do they create new patterns that reverse uneven capitalist development? This case study, in focusing on how racial, gendered, and class inequalities are reproduced in sites of resource extraction, acutely highlights these contradictions. It assesses the nature of the state and existing corporate accountability frameworks that also create enabling conditions for the erosion of women's rights.

While these are the conditions in which Western investors have operated at great cost to mine host communities and countries, new sources of investment offer an opportunity to strengthen regulatory capacity and explore relations of mutual benefit. Traditional Western investors have been focused on environmental, social, and governance in response to protests and campaigns from civil society groups, especially indigenous-led movements, and international human rights law. Corporations are considered 'duty bearers,' whilst domestic courts in their countries of origin are relied upon to intervene in violations and prosecute them (Bernaz, 2021). Therefore, where the country in question is not amenable to this, the opportunity is unavailable.

We do not aim to hold up Western traditional investors as models for corporate accountability. These actors have relied on corporate social responsibility (Blowfield, 2005) and, more recently, local procurement to legitimize their operations (Kassa, 2020). On their own terms, these have not been effective to secure the social license to operate in the long run. Instead, this case study analyses how gendered inequalities are reproduced in areas of resource extraction and the importance of a balance between community engagement platforms framed in free, prior, and informed consent to anticipate and prevent known harmful impacts and strengthening the capabilities of state agencies to prevent violations, and where they do occur, to prosecute them. The state must be reclaimed and repurposed to secure human rights and equitable, just development outcomes.

The first section outlines the theoretical framework guiding the paper. We draw on 'Organized Abandonment,' by Ruth Wilson Gilmore, to analyze how the state has been hollowing out its human rights obligations to regulate the mining sector. This section examines how Zimbabwe has attempted to break out of extractivism and China's role as a strategic partner. This section also outlines the methodology and feminist movement building strategy deployed. The next section examines the case of Bikita and the experiences of women affected by the lithium mine. Based on the main findings of the case study, in the final section, we offer some reflections and recommendations to improve the governance and accountability mechanisms that go beyond corporate social responsibilities to strengthen the obligation of state and corporations and the participation of the affected communities for gender equality and sustainability.

2. Research Framework and Methodology

2.1 The State, Gender Inequality, and Uneven Development

In reference to lithium mining, the Chinese ambassador to Zimbabwe highlights how its investments are 'revitalizing the resources that were long idled by western companies' (Guo, 2022). This draws attention to how China's investments are regarded as stimulating growth and accumulation in an economy that remains in the periphery under the dominance of white supremacy. The possibility of stimulating new areas of production and accumulation, and its wider importance for self-reliance and autonomy, is of prime importance. This is a political question that is amplified in Southern Africa due to extreme land dispossession.

Archie Mafeje (2003), in analyzing the obstacles facing European style agrarian transition, highlights that accumulation within the economy was constrained by tensions between those who produced value and the ruling elites and the petty bourgeoisie. Gendered hierarchies in relation to land tenure systems and labor distribution among small producers also reproduce gender inequality. In the case of Zimbabwe, this is reinforced by calls for women's land rights to be focused on collective action as opposed to land titles (Manji, 2006), while others highlight a strategy involving what secures women's ability to secure and assert their land rights (Goldman, Davis, and Little, 2016). As a result of structural adjustment in Zimbabwe, there are growing class inequalities between the black bourgeoisie and smallholder producers (Moyo and Yeros, 2005), which in turn increase racial and gender inequality. These class relations also have a bearing on governance systems and the nature of the state.

The growing contradiction between these classes creates a governance vacuum that enables corporations and what Ruth Wilson Gilmore (2022: 23) refers to as the 'anti-state state' to 'disorganize' production systems and property relations (Gilmore, 2007: 28), including land. In a wider perspective, this forms uneven development shaped by factors such as environmental damage, labor super-exploitation, structural adjustment, and privatization (Gilmore, 2022: 64). Organized abandonment theorizes not only the absence of the state but also how the state intervenes to shape market-based approaches and contain its outcomes. Securitization is required to contain the consequences of structural adjustment. Gilmore lumps together technocrats, corporations, and political parties as holding similar interests in wielding the state for this purpose.

The nature of resource extraction leads to contestations over control of land and natural resources in the context of historical extreme dispossession in Southern Africa. The UN Guiding Principles for Human Rights has set the framework for accountability globally, including for the China Chamber of Commerce of Metals, Minerals and Chemicals Importers and Exporters (CCCMC). China's Due Diligence Guidelines for Responsible Mineral Supply, which identify conflict mineral supply chains and environmental and social governance, is itself a voluntary framework which drew upon OECD due diligence guidelines (Castillo and Purdy, 2022).

The underlying assumption of self-regulation is that corporations can achieve a balance between securing a social license to operate and the profit maximization interests of shareholders. A state that neglects its responsibility to protect human rights and regulate corporate entities creates a vacuum in which violations occur. When the state itself violates rights on behalf of or alongside corporate interests, this is a form of 'organized violence' (Gilmore, 2022). On the other hand, progressive human rights approaches draw on international law and seek domestic and international courts to intervene. In practice, community organizations, civil society organizations, and journalists are those who document abuses and seek redress in specific cases (Bernaz 2021, Kassa and Nyirongo 2020).

The governance vacuum creates conditions in which policies developed from above do not reflect the interests of smallholder producers, especially women. It is in these conditions that organized abandonment prevails with varying degrees of coercion by the state and private actors. This intersects with racial and gendered inequalities in violations of bodily integrity and autonomy, of environmental, health, labor, and property rights, and of the rights to association and movement, which are the issues this case study scrutinizes.

2.2 Methodology and Data Collection

The study is guided by the mapping of rare earth minerals investments made across the continent. While the dominant investments have come from China, the emergence of export bans of raw critical minerals in Namibia, Ghana, and Zimbabwe shows a rise in resource nationalism on the continent.

A focus on Zimbabwe was informed by consistent policy interventions that emphasize economic indigenization and the significant growth of artisanal mining. While attempts to break from the extractivist orientation of the policy exist on paper, the relations that govern land tenure arrangements, vulnerabilities arising from climate change, and declining living standards result in challenges that have gendered impacts. The context of political instability, imposition of sanctions, dramatic hyperinflation, and food insecurity make this an important case in order to understand what has been different about China's investments in Zimbabwe's geo-strategically important lithium mining operations. This makes it particularly useful to examine the nature of China's investments and their gendered impacts to inform policy recommendations.

The fieldwork draws on data collected between 2019 to 2022 in Bikita in Zimbabwe's Masvingo Province. Focus group discussions were held with twenty women and snowball techniques were used to identify ten women for individual interviews. The women interviewed were between twenty-five and forty-six years old and were those who offered the most impactful narratives and experiences and those who were leading interventions to improve women's social, economic, and political position in Bikita.

The women were affected by resource extraction differently, so there was a lot of trauma rooted in the patriarchal nature of extractivism. As we document those experiences, we are trying to give the women a voice because they have been silenced through violence. With the aim of avoiding an extractivist research approach, mutual benefit is ensured through trauma healing as a prerequisite of sharing experiences in a community. This sets the stage for outlining what development goals should look like and what we need investment to do for us. We also felt that from this platform the women were then able to take power back according to their own terms, experiences, world views, and perspectives.

The focus group discussions were meant to understand the experiences of the women living in Bikita and how they have been impacted by resource extraction. The women in the focus group discussions have been directly and indirectly affected by the mining activities by loss of land, sexual assault, or turning to sex work or transactional sexual relations, while others have had spouses that were injured in the Bikita mine. The focus groups included storytelling in therapy circles to give a voice and a face to women's suffering due to resource extraction.

3. Main Findings and Analyses

3.1 Persistent Crisis, Mining Reform, and Chinese Investment in Zimbabwe

This section examines the context of persistent crisis and mining reforms, especially in the lithium sector in Zimbabwe and Chinese investment. Zimbabwe is a landlocked country in southeast Africa with a population of almost 16 million and a size of 390,745 square kilometers. It has a literacy rate of 86.5 percent. Zimbabwe's National Statistics Authority estimates that 3 to 4 million Zimbabweans are living abroad (The Chronicle, 2023). Formerly a major exporter of food, it is becoming import dependent due to disruption caused by land redistribution policies.

Economic sanctions imposed by the UK and US worsened an economic decline, causing hyperinflation, political instability, and eventually a turn to the US dollar. In 2019, Zimbabwe entered its worst economic depression, with shortages in food, medicine, and energy (The Economist, 2020). These conditions have resulted in political isolation and low levels of foreign direct investment (FDI), making China with its continued support a strategic ally that provides aid and investments.

About two decades after the Fast Track Land Reform (FTLR), which led to expropriation of land initiated by veterans of the liberation struggle, a prolonged economic crisis and political upheaval and protest against the governing party led to a change in leadership in the ruling Zimbabwe African National Union-Patriotic Front (ZANU-PF). ZANU-PF, which has been ruling Zimbabwe since independence in 1980, has been weakened by internal factional struggles for power that culminated in a 2017 coup against Robert Mugabe.

The new government under Emmerson Mnangagwa have not made significant changes to ZANU-PF rule (Vambe, 2023), but there have been significant concessions. In 2020, the government agreed to compensate white farmers and resettle black farmers who occupied farms under FTLR (Chingono, 2023). The African Development Bank has offered to raise funds in the capital markets to fund the compensation (Gbane, 2023).

While there has been debate and contestation over agrarian reforms that have impacted Zimbabwe's political stability and economic development (Moyo and Yeros, 2007; Bond, 2007, Moyo, 2011), these reforms have also had an impact on mining. Indigenization in the mining sector took the form of the requirement that fifty-one per cent of controlling shares in foreign companies and mines be allocated to designated entities that in the mining sector tended to be community share ownership trusts (Russel, 2011; Nechena and Kurebwa, 2018; Makoni, 2014). Initially seeking controlling shares of platinum and diamond mines, it had been amended to enable extension to other minerals (Veritas, 2021).

However, after much uncertainty and pushback (Motsoeneng, 2019), the government decided to delete the amendment to assuage investors' fears about their investments and assets (Kuyedzwa, 2021). Nonetheless, community share ownership trusts have been the key vehicles in the mining sector to ensure inclusion of mine host communities and to secure social license. In practice, since the ten per cent shares that the government asks companies to give to community share ownership trusts is not paid for by the government (or the community groups are not able to secure capital to purchase these), and there is a lack of clarity on their role in governance over mining operations, it is merely symbolic. Companies are not even obliged to pay dividends into community shared ownership trusts, and mine host communities have no legal standing to question mining companies (Nechena and Kurebwa, 2018).

Bolivia, Chile, and Argentina, known as the lithium triangle countries, as well as Canada, Australia, United States, and China, also have significant lithium resources (Kaunda, 2020). China Mineral Resources has invested $380 million in Bikita mine in Zimbabwe, which has 11 million tonnes reserves of lithium ore, the largest single deposit in the world. China Mineral Resources has expanded the initial extraction of minerals, which was for ceramics and glass production, to battery inputs. China Minerals Resources is one of eighty Chinese state-owned enterprises operating in Zimbabwe since 2005, which have a value of $10.45 billion. Another major lithium mining operation in Zimbabwe is Arcadia, which is also owned by a Chinese company (Sydney Boyo et al., 2023).

The government of Zimbabwe has increasingly sought to process its lithium in the country to retain a greater share of the value. In 2020, Zimbabwe was the largest producer of lithium. Artisanal mining also contributes to the lithium value chain. A base mineral control act from 2022 prohibits the export of raw lithium except in cases where mines are being developed and processing plants set up in Zimbabwe (Philip de Wet, 2022). It is presumed that this law intends to control smuggling attributed to artisanal small-scale mining. The ban affected livelihoods dependent on artisanal mining (Sydney Boyo et al., 2023), including of lithium (Boyo, 2023). The environmental impacts of lithium mining and its social consequences on women and communities are also grave, which is elaborated on in the following section.

The leading FDI sources to Zimbabwe from 2000 to 2018 were South Africa, China, and Mauritius (Chinyanganya and Sunge, 2021: 150), with China as a leading source since 2021 (Sharara, 2023). According to the Zimbabwe Development Agency, out of 427 investments from China, 228 are in the mining sector. Key mining companies are Sinomine Resource Group, Zhejiang Huayou Cobalt, and Chengxin Lithium Group, which have invested in lithium mines and processing plants (Sharara, 2023). Zhejiang Huayou bought out the Arcadia mine for $422 million in 2022. Huayou announced it was building a $300 million plant to process 4.5 million tons of lithium ore as part of a strategy to 'secure and build a chain of lithium assets' (Banya, 2023).

ZELA and AIEL (2023) highlight that China's capacity to process exceeds its lithium reserves, requiring it to diversify and control its supply. Therefore, it is strategically advantageous for China to control lithium mineral extraction. It must be considered how China, despite its existing mineral processing capacity, has been responsive to Zimbabwe's measures to build domestic processing capacity. Zimbabwe, on the other hand, has conferred Special Economic Zone status to lithium investments to date, meaning companies are exempt from taxes until January 2025 (ZELA & AIEL, 2023). Concerns about weak regulatory systems that investors have been exploiting tended to be amplified by the range of Chinese investments and businesses that are active in Zimbabwe. Chinese investments range from large scale investments to buyers of artisanal mining (ZELA & AIEL, 2023). Recently, operations in Bikita mine had to be briefly stopped to enable government inspection of labor management and subcontractors (Reuters, 2023).

3.2 Mining Reform and Indigenization in Zimbabwe

The current cycle of critical minerals rush has given new impetus to reviving an agenda for formulating a coherent regional strategy (Chikwanka, 2023). In July 2022, Zambia, Mali, and Guinea ratified a statute for the establishment of the African Mineral Development Centre (AMDC) along with eight other member states. The AMDC will coordinate and oversee the implementation of the AMV, ensuring a mechanism to pursue its implementation (African Minerals Development Centre, n.d.). The AMV is also undergoing review and will be complemented by a new strategy for green minerals in Africa (ANRC, 2022; Zimbabwe Environmental Lawyers Association, 2023). Zambia and Zimbabwe have both adopted a new National Mineral Development Policy to pursue this at a national level.

Women are considered only in terms of owning mineral rights and being included in the value chain (AMV, 2009). Supporting women in the mining sector requires addressing obstacles to property rights and also recognizing social norms in the form of taboos and demands for women to undertake care work that can discourage, preclude, or constrain women from running mining operations. This is not to say women do not overcome these obstacles or actively challenge social norms and policies.

However, this is still an individualistic strategy that only includes women who can raise capital to license operations and purchase and manage mining equipment and labor. It excludes women who do not have an asset base to raise resources. Nevertheless, both categories of women would still be constrained by customary laws that undermine women's land rights. This is a limited approach that does not cater for women whose social position and livelihoods have been eroded such that their ability to shape governance processes in remote and rural areas is extremely limited and risky. There needs to be attention given to explicit governance mechanisms that support women in shaping developmental outcomes (Kengne, n.d.). The lack of attention to explicit mechanisms is consistent with UN Guiding Principles for Business and Human Rights (UNHR, 2011; Bernaz, 2021).

While emphasis has tended to be on egregious labor rights violations in mining, the interconnected environmental and gendered impacts of mining also need to be understood. The environmental cost and gendered nature of extractivism amplified by the ongoing climate crisis which threatens the viability of agrarian livelihoods need to be considered. Masvingo Province, where the Bikita lithium mine is located, highlights these interlinked issues.

3.3 Environmental and Gender Impacts of Mining Activities in Bikita

Masvingo, a province in southeastern Zimbabwe, is composed of seven districts, one of which is Bikita, which has the highest poverty levels (Viceisza, Aflagah, Abner and Hippolyte, 2020). According to the Food and Nutrition Council report (2022a), maternal mortality increased in 2021 to 269 per 100, 000 deaths, from 230 per 100,000 in 2016. It had previously fallen to 212 in 2018 and 145 in 2019. Livelihoods in Masvingo are largely dependent on rainfed agriculture, further impacted by degradation linked to resettlement programs. Chronically poor households' characteristics include dependence on less than a hectare of land for food production and lack of access to irrigation for food planting.

Bikita is also particularly vulnerable to climate change, with droughts, heatwaves, and floods directly impacting agricultural activities, which are the key economic activities. Deteriorating health facilities and road networks also undermine the quality of life and resilience to these harsh conditions (Chikoko and Chihiya, 2023). Largely dependent on growing cereal crops, a marked fall in production has worsened food insecurity in Bikita. The prevalence of food insecurity has risen from 12% in 2011, reaching a peak of 54% in 2018, and 44% in 2022 (Food and Nutrition Council, 2022b).

The larger part of the district is communal, with some wards sharing both communal and resettled communities, leading to land conflicts, a trend that also prevails in the Masvingo district (Mafukidze, 2018). With the economic decline that Zimbabwe has faced since the 2000s, many people have resorted to relocating from urban to rural areas, which has resulted in the creation of resettlement areas. The economic crisis has also led to a surge of emigration from Zimbabwe by male household heads, leaving women as de facto household heads.

Mavis (2024), a thirty-two-year-old woman in Bikita, explains:

> There are too many people and too little land to settle on. The increase in population has also led to a serious water crisis in the area, and the massive use of water by the mine has further fueled the water crisis.

Resettlement areas in Zimbabwe arise out of the redistributive land reform programs where small holdings were supposed to be prioritized and encouraged in communal grazing or arable lands. In practice, the state's role was predominant and tended to control decision-making at the farm level (Marongwe, 2011). Women whose land ownership depended more on indigenous cosmology, culture, and politics, as opposed to title deeds or permits, did not benefit from land reforms. These multiple exclusions place women in a vulnerable situation. FTLR was skewed by a chaotic process of resettlement marked by violence that did not have a place for women, especially those who were single or widowed (Zvokuomba and Batisai, 2020).

One of the two wards in the district has a resettlement area, and the other has a lithium mine concession, which makes them extremely volatile. The competing claims and interests to access and control land and resources is further amplified by the presence of artisanal mining operations, which have offered a livelihood to impoverished households. The major means of livelihood in the district are crop production, livestock production, horticulture, and artisanal lithium mining.

Artisanal mining activities have grown significantly in the Zimbabwean economy, especially in the gold sector, where 23.3 tons out of a total of thirty-five tons were produced by artisanal miners (Moyo, 2023). In Bikita, artisanal miners also extract petalite and co-exist with the Bikita mine. The export ban on lithium was ostensibly aimed at stopping smuggling by artisanal miners, therefore ensuring local processing and value addition.

Artisanal miners in Bikita also encroach on and dig up people's fields, which has resulted in the landscape becoming a death trap, destroying arable lands. Mavis (2024) explains that 'the shafts have not been well set up and supported, and we have had incidents where shafts have collapsed, and there have been deaths and injuries from the accidents.' This land degradation has dire implications for the women in Bikita because they rely on subsistence farming for their sustenance. The open shafts where artisanal miners operate also increase the burden of unpaid care work for injured children and spouses.

Given lithium bearing petalite reserves can be processed into lithium carbonates, and there has been a rise in the global demand for lithium batteries, it has become more valuable as a mineral deposit (Sitando and Crouse, 2011).

Land and environmental degradation in Bikita was observed after the massive clearing of land and opening of deep pits at the lithium mine sites. Sharon, a forty-five-year-old woman in Bikita, highlights that 'the location of some of the mines is on some of the pieces of land we used for our farming, and that has rendered us food insecure. Our school-going girls have also become vulnerable because of food insecurity.'

Large scale and artisanal mining activities in Bikita have resulted in water, air, and land pollution. Mercy (2024), a twenty-five-year-old woman, explains that 'water shortages have really hit us hard, and we are at risk of getting diseases that emanate from the lack of water.' Large scale extractivist processes cause an imbalance in these geological systems and can have disastrous consequences on water resources and soil health (Adeel et al., 2019).

In 2017, the Business & Human Rights Resource Centre (2019) documented allegations of negative environmental impacts arising from waste dumps in Bikita operations. This legacy of labour and environmental violations and discontent existed before Sinomine Resource Group started operations in Bikita (Bikita Minerals, 2017) in 2022 after operations had closed for two years. However, in the focus group discussions and interviews, there was a consensus that their operations have further deteriorated the situation due to a rapid expansion of operations since 2022. The timeline below illustrates the historical dominance of Anglo-American entities.

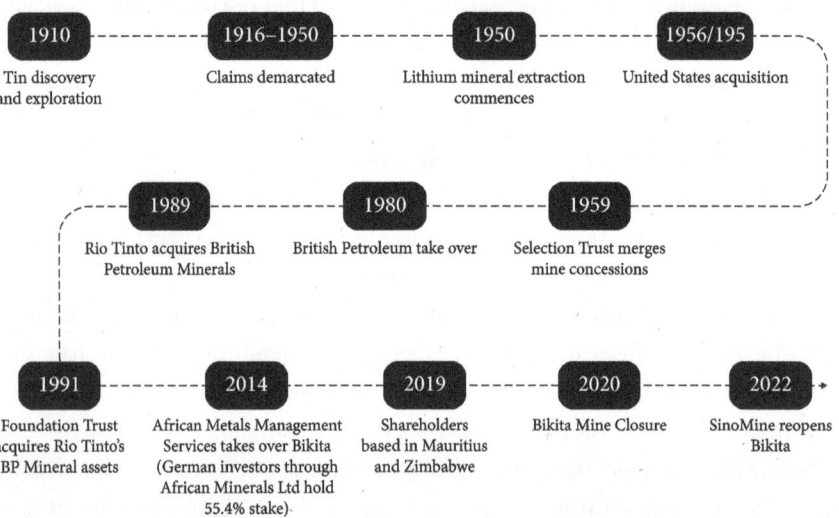

Figure 1 Bikita Mine History timeline

Source: Bikita Minerals (2017) and Southern Africa Resource Watch (2024).

Sinomine Resource Group has been accused of violating labor rights (Reuters a, 2023) and not taking cognizance of the impact of their activities on the environment. The general secretary of the Zimbabwe Diamond and Allied Workers Union described an 'existential threat of a new colonizer in the form of Chinese miners' (Mangirazi and Sithole, 2021). A 2017 report of workers being shot at and threatened with guns by Chinese owned mines invokes the trauma of recent massacres (as in South Africa) (Sinwell and Mbatha, 2016), as well as historical colonial strategies of labor control (Laning and Mueller, 1979).

Joy (2024) and Mercy (2024) describe a practice of employment gender discrimination: 'The first preference when it comes to employment is light skinned, slender women, and they even earn better wages than their bigger and darker colleagues' (Joy, 2024). 'Us, the fat and ugly ones are not recruited because we are not attractive, and that means we cannot even try to get jobs at the mine. These Chinese have not benefited us in any way; they have ruined our good relations as a community and left us vulnerable and worse off than we were before' (Mercy, 2024).

There have been clashes between the company and Bikita community members over the pollution caused by Sinomine. Industrial plastic has been used to demarcate some of their operational areas. This material tears easily and mixes with chemicals used in mineral extraction. In May 2023, Sinomine Resource Group was forced to suspend its operations for government inspections (Reuters b, 2023).

Joy (2024) further explains:

> The coming of the Chinese has been disastrous to us; the amount of air, land, and noise pollution has been alarming. There is plastic everywhere, dust everywhere, and they blast at all hours of the day, and there are sirens going off at all times of the day. In general, there is no peace here.

To understand how Sinomine Resource Group operations have had such an impact, it is necessary to consider ongoing tensions in Bikita. The incidence of land conflicts from competing land claims are concerning. Land rights in Zimbabwe is a thorny and problematic issue; the constitution states that all communal land in Zimbabwe is vested with the president, who shall permit it to be occupied and used in accordance with the Land Act. Communal chiefs are the custodians of said land (Section 71 of the Zimbabwean constitution). This means that the president and chiefs can arbitrarily decide what happens to the land.

Sinomine Resource Group manages the biggest lithium mine in Bikita and are by law the only entity legally permitted to mine lithium in Bikita. Over the years, the mine has expanded to take up more land than had initially been gazetted. It has been observed that as more lithium deposits are discovered in Bikita, the mine expands. This expansion is problematic since the Zimbabwean constitution states that mining takes precedence over all other land uses.

As a result, where lithium deposits are discovered, agriculture retreats, and mining takes precedence, which has created more conflict and chaos. In Zimbabwe, men are ascribed social and cultural rights as landowners and women as land users. Thus, women are at the bottom of the hierarchy when it comes to decisions on how land is used and allocated. Due to the clauses highlighted above, land repurposing is rampant, and female headed households are disproportionately affected by the land repurposing.

Meanwhile, Sinomine Resource Group have not had meaningful engagements with the mine host community with regards to their operations, which have had an immediate impact on mine host communities. Since Sinomine took over Bikita mine, Mavis (2024) says that 'we have had more problems than solutions in our area. They create new rules and laws every day, and that has been hard for us to keep up with.'

Mavis (2024) explains how the Sinomine Resource Group arbitrarily demarcated areas without consulting the community: 'Our transport from the markets would leave us at our homesteads, but now because of the cordoning of the concession area, we struggle to bring in our goods'. Mercy (2024) further describes the gender-based violence risks arising from this: 'They have killed our transport network, and now we are dropped off very far from our homesteads, putting us at risk of being robbed and sexually assaulted in the bushy areas'. The arbitrary nature of the company's decision-making and disproportionate impact reflect how in practice mining companies and states are equally complicit in creating and sustaining organized abandonment.

In terms of environmental impacts, leaching into the soils and water sources in the mineral extraction process leads to dangerous concentrations of chemical-based acid that is absorbed into plant and aquatic life, thereby entering the food system, causing serious health problems. While there are developments in bioleaching using micro-organisms, this is not yet possible at an industrial scale (Moazzam et al., 2021). Over time, pollutants will accumulate in underground water systems as acid mine drainage.

Women who carry the burden of social reproduction in these communities are directly impacted by the increase in unpaid care work. Their livelihood activities rely on the soil and water resources that are poisoned by ecologically destructive methods of leaching in lithium mining. Water pollution greatly affects women and girls as this means that they must walk long distances to get clean water for their households, which also puts them at risk of sexual assault and has implications for the time they spend on their daily chores.

Some of the mining sites are close to schools, resulting in the closure of Gaururo and Guruva high schools, in addition to Maringambizi secondary school (Makado and Makado, 2015). Meanwhile, Sinomine has set up science laboratories for Bikita-Fashu high school alongside electricity transformers also supplied to Mangondo secondary school. Electrification was also provided to Marinda primary school. In Chiwara, other schools and health facilities were also provided access to water (Maponga, 2023).

The economic situation in Zimbabwe, coupled with the low levels of education amongst women in Bikita, has made it a hub for commercial sex work and increased gender-based violence. The incidence of sex workers being killed is alarming. A 2022 study found that ninety-three per cent of respondents perceived gender-based violence as prevalent, while sixty-three per cent thought the drought was linked to increased cases (Muto, 2022).

This proximity of mining operations (both artisanal and large-scale) to schools poses a grave danger to young girls as they are then exposed to sexual abuse, femicide, the risk of contracting HIV/AIDS, and unwanted teenage pregnancies. Girls in school face vulnerabilities when men offer them lifts to school when they struggle with time scarcity since they also have domestic responsibilities (Gwarisa, 2021). Since there is a high incidence of food insecurity and need to pay for basic needs for themselves and their siblings, girls are very susceptible to transactional sexual relations (Dziro, 2020).

Artisanal miners, who earn an income selling their ore, and mineworkers, who earn salaries from the mine, create demand for commercial sex work, which creates risks for women and girls, usually from older men and criminals, and creates turmoil in families (Dziro, 2020).

Traditional leaders play critical roles in dealing with the closure of schools, boundary disputes, and securing jobs for locals in the mining sector (Chanakira, Mujere and Spiegel, 2019). The Traditional Leaders Act 1998 enabled them to extend their roles into resettlement areas and was further strengthened by their inclusion in the boards of community share ownership trusts. Earlier, this had been described as a superficial initiative, which in real terms is used to placate communities without transformative possibilities. Although chiefs may mobilize for securing local jobs (Chanakira, Mujere and Spiegel, 2019), they remain largely unreliable allies for women, whose interests require concessions that support their livelihoods and land rights.

In some instances, chiefs infringe on women's rights by parceling out land belonging to female-headed households as there is no pushback from women. This has implications for who is eligible to access, control, and manage land. There is, therefore, a gap between national governments and local administrations. The political areas that chiefs occupy are also contested. This makes the context within which mining investments are made complex, conflictual, and tending to marginalize women.

Corporations such as Anglo American have developed a broad and complex strategy for engagement with a range of actors to identify partnerships for mutually beneficial development strategies. The corporation says it employs spatial analysis to identify ways of building local economies (Anglo American, 2023). Nonetheless, Anglo American is being held to account for human rights and environmental violations in South America and Africa (AIDA, 2021; BHRC, 2020, Amnesty International, 2023) and cannot be a model to be replicated. Meanwhile, Sinomine does not have an engagement strategy in Bikita, and there are no mechanisms to hold them accountable apart from one instance of an investigation of labor violations. There is also no evidence of the outcome of this process, or changes made as a result.

It is important to factor in the scale at which mining operations can damage natural resources such as arable land and water, including in lithium mining. This includes the historical legacy of previous cycles of production, which in Bikita traces back to 1911. The process of extracting the mineral ores and producing the lithium concentrate will impact ecosystems, which will in turn impact livestock and arable lands beyond the immediate mining concession (Sierra Club, 2021).

To emphasize this point, Joy (2024) considers how her loss of land has put girls 'at risk of being manipulated and abused'. Young girls are abused by male workers at Sinomine, both internal migrants and Chinese, who 'take advantage of our girls, leading to teenage pregnancy, school dropout, and sexually transmitted illnesses. There is an endless cycle of sexually transmitted diseases within the community, and it is scary.'

Sharon (2024) explains that the root cause of this vulnerability is the scarcity of arable land, which causes competing mining operations to make communities food insecure. The vulnerability extends to women and girls becoming targets for transactional sex with older men: 'Our livelihoods have been affected deeply by the coming of the Chinese corporation'. Mavis (2024) and Mercy (2024) also describe a cycle of infections transmitted between mineworkers, sex workers, underaged girls, and women in Bikita. This has further triggered gender-based violence. Underaged girls face risks from Chinese workers who 'want relationships with the young girls, and also due to poverty levels here the girls become vulnerable to abuse from mine workers and artisanal miners as well. The Chinese workers call the fresh young girls "Small Marias". We even have a young girl who was impregnated by a Chinese national' who abandoned the girl (Mercy, 2024).

Given how violence is amplified by mining, as highlighted earlier in Bikita, there is urgency for the creation of spaces for women to share their experiences, center their healing, and rebuild their lives and communities. In practice, these activities go beyond counselling and include livelihood activities (WoMin, 2021). An example is the Rape Survivors Network in Zimbabwe. Women come together to be trained in counselling, so they can provide support to rape survivors in their communities. These spaces should be supported to guide interventions to stop gender-based violence, protect the rights of sex workers, and give other women and girls social support to avoid being pressured by working men into transactional sexual relations.

4. Concluding Reflections

Zimbabwe's indigenization policies have sought redress by retaining a greater share of value through beneficiation. This aims to avoid a central aspect of extractivism, the unevenness of capitalist development that results in economies in the periphery. China appears to be an effective partner in working towards this, with processing capacity being built in Zimbabwe, which supports the government's ban on raw lithium exports.

Nonetheless, there is an inevitable tension between global demand and the possibilities of gaining a fairer share of value generated by minerals extraction, on the one hand, and long-term economic, social, and ecological impacts, on the other. The extent to which land conflicts, transactional sexual relations, child abuse, and gender-based violence are amplified in mining areas also raises further concerns about how racial, class, and gendered forms of inequalities are reproduced. Sinomine Resource Group in Bikita mine has a direct and profound negative impact, but this company is not unique. Rather, with voluntary due diligence frameworks and an absence of punitive measures, a state of impunity prevails. While due diligence laws are being introduced in Europe, these are also being watered down due to fears of being unable to compete with China. This implies that China is in a strategic position to set the terms of global corporate governance by ensuring that environmental and social governance standards are mandatory and punitive measures are introduced.

Mathibela (2022) asserts that without reforming mineral resources governance and enabling bottom-up processes, ongoing conflicts and tensions will not be resolved. Mathibela proposes a shift to devolution of power to local communities. They will need to ensure there are transparent processes, including prosecutions for grievous harm, in place to hold corporations accountable for environmental, human rights, and labor rights violations while also creating opportunities to build local economies. There also should be a flow of communication that is transparent and inclusive of women's leadership as a means of trust building, to facilitate understanding of the context in areas like Bikita where corporations operate.

Community share ownership schemes can play a part if they are made effective, representative, and meaningful partnerships instead of operating as a form of corporate social responsibility fund. It is fair to conclude that any accountability mechanism or community engagement platform that takes on board traditional leaders, local government, and the mine host community must be explicitly inclusive of women and girls.

Another critical governance issue is the securitization and militarization that characterizes mining in Zimbabwe. While attention has been on diamond and gold mining in Zimbabwe, concerns around securitization also apply to lithium mining where illicit financial flows, smuggling, and organized crime concerns are coming to the fore (Glass, 2021). In practice, securitization has been an important tool for conformity to extractivism. This is not peculiar to Zimbabwe or Sinomine Resource Group but is an outcome of the organized abandonment of mineral governance by states. A core issue remains the need for 'secure land tenure rights' (Mathibela, 2022) and support for platforms such as the Rape Survivors Network as a model for intervention.

Nevertheless, without weighing the environmental and social costs, including social reproduction, which is integral to the value creation process, this can reproduce patterns of the feminization of poverty. Traditional investors have developed instruments such as corporate social responsibility and voluntary mechanisms of corporate accountability, but in practice this has not been effective in responding to local demands for equitable, fair, and environmentally sustainable forms of economic activities. Narrow interventions as utilized in corporate social responsibility projects hardly offer a solution to these broader resource governance issues. To create these spaces, states must develop capabilities of monitoring and regulation of mining companies, complemented by accountable local governance systems that prevent violations, and when they do occur, ensure meaningful remedy.

References

Adeel, M., Lee, J. Y., Zain, M., Rizwan, M., Nawab, A., Ahmad, M., Shafiq, M., Yi, H., Jilani, G., & Javed, R. (2019). Cryptic footprints of rare earth elements on natural resources and living organisms. *Environment International*, 127, 785–800.

African Minerals Development Centre. n.d., African Union. Available online: https://au.int/en/amdc (Accessed on 19 March 2025)

Africa Natural Resources Management and Investment Centre (ANRC). (2022), *Approach Paper to Guide Preparation of an African Green Minerals Strategy*. African Development Bank. Abidjan, Côte d'Ivoire. Available online: https://www.afdb.org/sites/default/files/documents/publications/approach_paper_towards_preparation_of_an_african_green_minerals_strategy.pdf (Accessed on 19 March 2025)

Amnesty International, *South Africa hears historic class action for lead poisoning launched by Zambian children*, January 23, 2023. Available online: https://www.amnesty.org/en/latest/news/2023/01/south-africa-hears-historic-class-action-for-lead-poisoning/ (Accessed on 19 March 2025)

Anglo American (2023) *Collaborative Regional Development*, Available online: https://www.angloamerican.com/sustainable-mining-plan/collaborative-regional-development (Accessed on 19 March 2025)

AIDA (Inter American Association for Environmental Defense) *Parallel complaints also filed in Ireland against state owned-company for purchasing coal and Dublin-based sales wing of mining enterprise*, 19 January 2021. Available online: https://aida-americas.org/en/press/oecd-to-investigate-human-rights-abuses-filed-against-the-owners-of-cerrejon-coal-mine (Accessed on 19 March 2025)

Banya, N. (2023) *Sinomine's Zimbabwe unit resumes operations*, Reuters. Available online: https://www.reuters.com/markets/commodities/sinomines-zimbabwe-unit-resumes-operations-2023-05-24/ (Accessed on 19 March 2025)

Bernaz, N. (2021), Conceptualizing Corporate Accountability in International Law: Models for a Business and Human Rights Treaty, *Human Rights Review*. 22:45 64. Available online: https://doi.org/10.1007/s12142-020-00606-w (Accessed on 19 March 2025)

Blowfield, M. (2005), Corporate Social Responsibility – The Failing Discipline and Why it Matters for International Relations. *International Relations*, Vol 19 (2): 173–191. Available online: http://ire.sagepub.com/cgi/content/abstract/19/2/173 (Accessed on 19 March 2025)

BHRRC (Business & and Human Rights Resource Centre) *Anglo American faces question at AGM human rights and mining activities in South America*, 14 May 2020.

Available online: https://www.business-humanrights.org/en/latest-news/anglo-american-faces-questions-on-human-rights-and-mining-activities-at-from-ngos-at-agm/ (Accessed on 19 March 2025)

Bikita Minerals. Response to Investigating Illicit Financial Flows in Zimbabwe's Lithium Mining Sector, *Trust Africa*, July 2017. Available online: https://media.businesshumanrights.org/media/documents/files/documents/Bikita_Minerals_Response_PDF.pdf (Accessed on 19 March 2025)

Bond P. (2007), Competing Explanations of Zimbabwe's Long Economic Crisis, *Safundi*, 8:2, 149-181. DOI: https://doi.org/10.1080/17533170701370976

Boyo, S., Pettitt, J. & Baldwin, S. *Why all eyes are on Zimbabwe's lithium industry*, 29 March 2023. Available online: https://www.cnbc.com/video/2023/03/09/why-all-eyes-are-on-zimbabwes-lithium-industry.html (Accessed 19 March 2025)

Castillo R. and Purdy C. (2022), *China's Role in Supplying Critical Minerals for the Global Energy Transition: What could the Future Hold. Leveraging Transparency to Reduce Corruption.* July 2022.

Chanakira, DL, Mujere, J & Spiegel S. (2019), Traditional leaders and the politics of labour recruitment in Zimbabwe's platinum mining industry, *The Extractives Industries and Society*, Volume 6, Issue 4, November 2019, Pages 1274–1281.

Chikoko W. and Chihiya P. (2023), Climate change and vulnerabilities of children in rural Zimbabwe: The case of ward 14 of Bikita District, Zimbabwe. *African Journal of Social Work,* 13(2), 78–86. https://dx.doi.org/10.4314/ajsw.v13i2.4 (Accessed on 19 March 2025)

Chikwanka N. *Wanted-a common vision for mining clean-energy transition minerals in Africa. Daily Maverick.* January 31, 2023. Available online: https://www.dailymaverick.co.za/opinionista/2023-01-31-wanted-common-vision-for-mining-transition-minerals-in-africa/ (Accessed on 19 March 2025)

Chimwamurombe, F. and Gona., L. (2023), *Review of the base Minerals Export Control (Unbeneficiated Base Mineral Ores) Order 2023*. 28 April 2023. Available online: https://www.mondaq.com/export-controls--trade--investment-sanctions/1309576/review-of-the-base-minerals-export-control-unbeneficiated-base-mineral-ores-0rder-2023 (Accessed on 19 March 2025)

Chingono, N. (2023), *African Development Bank proposes 'fast track' compensation for Zimbabwe white ex farmers*, May 15, 2023. Available online: https://www.reuters.com/world/africa/african-devt-bank-proposes-fast-track-compensation-zimbabwe-white-ex-farmers-2023-05-15/ (Accessed on 19 March 2025)

Chinyanganya, K. and Sunge, R. (2021), 'Growth Effects of Foreign Direct Investments in Zimbabwe: Do Sources Matter?', *African Journal of Economic Review*, vol. 9(4), September.

Dendere, C. (2022), *Zimbabwe: The Long Shadow of Sanctions.* June 29. https://carnegieeurope.eu/2022/06/29/zimbabwe-long-shadow-of-sanctions-pub-87313

Dziro, C. (2020), Challenges and Opportunities Experienced by Young Adults Transitioning Out of Informal Kinship-Based Foster Care in Bikita District, Zimbabwe. *Emerging Adulthood*, 8(1), 82–91. https://doi.org/10.1177/2167696819870019

Fliess, B., Idsardi, E. and Rossouw, R. (2017), "*Export controls and competitiveness in African mining and minerals processing industries*", OECD Trade Policy Papers, No. 204, OECD Publishing, Paris. Available online: http://dx.doi.org/10.1787/1fddd828-en (Accessed 19 March 2025)

Food and Nutrition Council. (2022a), *Masvingo District Food and Nutrition Security Profile*. Available online: http://www.fnc.org.zw/wp-content/uploads/2023/04/Masvingo-District-Profile.pdf (Accessed on 19 March 2025)

Food and Nutrition Council (2022b) *Bikita District Food and Nutrition Security Profile*, Available online: https://www.fnc.org.zw/wp-content/uploads/2023/04/Bikita-District-Profile.pdf (Accessed on 19 March 2025)

Gbane, NC. (2023), *Zimbabwe: New African Agricultural Power House*. Available online: https://www.africanews.com/2023/01/08/zimbabwe-new-african-agricultural-power-house// (Accessed on 19 March 2025)

Gilmore, R.W. (2007), *Golden gulag: Prisons, surplus, crisis, and opposition in globalizing California*. Berkeley: University of California Press.

Gilmore, R.W. (2022), *Abolition geography: Essays towards liberation*. Brooklyn: Verso Books.

Glass, F.C. (2022), Preventing Environmental Crime and Human Vulnerability through the MGPOC Framework: The Case of Zimbabwe's Lithium Industry. *Journal of Illicit Economies and Development*, 4(1), p.34–43.

Global Affairs Canada, *Canadian Sanctions Related to Zimbabwe*, March 2023. Available online: https://www.international.gc.ca/world-monde/international_relations-relations_internationales/sanctions/zimbabwe.aspx?lang=eng (Accessed on 19 March 2025)

Gov.UK, *Financial Sanctions Zimbabwe*, 18 March 2022. Available online: https://www.gov.uk/government/publications/financial-sanctions-zimbabwe (Accessed on 19 March 2025)

Goldman, M. J., Davis, A. & Little, J. (2016), Controlling land they call their own: access and women's empowerment in Northern Tanzania, *The Journal of Peasant Studies*, 43:4, 777–797, DOI: 10.1080/03066150.2015.1130701

Graham, Y. (2022), Reflections on the African Mining Vision: The Fragmented Terrain of Mineral Governance in Africa. *New Agenda: South African Journal of Social and Economic Policy*, 2022 (83), 15–18.

Guo, S. (2022), *China remains the true friend of Zimbabwe on its development path forever*. Available online: http://zw.china-embassy.gov.cn/eng/xwdt/202208/t20220823_10749341.htm#:~:text=In%20the%20fight%20for%20national,increasing%20the%20scope%20of%20cooperation (Accessed on 19 March 2025)

Gwarisa, M. (2022), *Long Distance Exposes Bikita School Girls to Sugar Daddies and Unintended Pregnancies*. Available online: https://healthtimes.co.zw/2021/03/01/long-distance-exposes-bikita-school-girls-to-sugar-daddies-and-unintended-pregnancies/ (Accessed on 19 March 2025)

Hughes, C. *Zimbabwe's developing lithium industry is shifting the market balance*. CRU, July 2023. Available online: https://www.crugroup.com/knowledge-and-insights/insights/2023/zimbabwe-s-developing-lithium-industry-is-shifting-the-market-balance/ (Accessed on 19 March 2025)

Joy. Interview with the author in Bikita. February 2024.

Kaunda, R. B. (2020), Potential environmental impacts of lithium mining. *Journal of Energy & Natural Resources Law*, 38(3), 237–244.

Kengne G. (n.d.), *Understanding the Right to Say No*. Available online: https://womin.africa/understanding-the-right-to-say-no/ (Accessed on 19 March 2025)

Kuyedzwa, C. (2021), Foreign entities can now fully own mines in Zimbabwe following outcry, *News24*. Available online: https://www.news24.com/fin24/economy/foreign-entities-can-now-fully-own-mines-in-zimbabwe-following-outcry-20210203-2 (Accessed on 19 March 2025)

Laning, G. and Mueller, M. (1979), *Africa undermined: a history of the mining companies and the underdevelopment of Africa*. By Greg Lanning and Marti Mueller. Harmondsworth: Penguin.

Sinwell, L. and Mbatha, S. (2016), *The Spirit of Marikana: the rise of insurgent trade unionism in South Africa*. London: Pluto Press.

Mafukidze, J. (2018), "Let them starve so that they 'hear' us": Differing perspectives on unresolved land occupations and livelihoods at Mushandike small-holder irrigation scheme, Masvingo District. *The Political Economy of Livelihoods in Contemporary Zimbabwe* (pp. 170–183). Routledge.

Makadoc, R.K. and Makado, E. (2015), An Assessment of Intercessory Skills and Abilities of Traditional Leaders Viewed as Important in Handling Conflict between Schools and Communities and Their Impact on Education: A Case of Zaka and Bikita Districts. Masvingo: Zimbabwe, *The International Journal Of Humanities & Social Studies*, 3:12, December 2015, Available online: https://www.internationaljournalcorner.com/index.php/theijhss/article/view/138375/97127 (Accessed on 19 March 2025)

Mavis. Interview with the author in Bikita. February 2024.

Makoni, P. L., (2014) The Impact of the Nationalization Threat on Zimbabwe's Economy, *Corporate Ownership & Control* / Volume 12, Issue 1.

Manduna, K., & Muchadenyika, D. (2021), Indigenization policy in the extractive sector in Zimbabwe: A critical reflection. *Routledge Handbook of Public Policy in Africa* (pp. 373–383). Routledge.

Maponga, G. (2023), *Bikita Minerals expansion to create 3000 jobs*, 13 June 2023. Available online: https://www.herald.co.zw/bikita-minerals-expansion-to-create-3-000-jobs/ (Accessed on 19 March 2025)

Marongwe, N. 2011. *Redistributive land reform and poverty reduction in Zimbabwe*. Available online: https://assets.publishing.service.gov.uk/media/57a08ae4ed915d622c000985/60332_Zimbabwe_Land_Reform.pdf (Accessed on 19 March 2025)

Maurice Taonezvi Vambe. (2023), Zimbabwe: the Fall from a Jewel Status, *Third World Thematics: A TWQ Journal*, 8:4-6, 181-188. DOI: 10.1080/23802014.2023.2287495

Mercy. Interview with the author in Bikita. February 2024

Moazzam, P., Boroumand, Y., Rabiei, P., Baghbaderani, S. S., Mokarian, P., Mohagheghian, F., Mohammed, L. J., & Razmjou, A. (2021), Lithium bioleaching: An emerging approach for the recovery of Li from spent lithium ion batteries. *Chemosphere*, 277, 130196. https://doi.org/10.1016/j.chemosphere.2021.130196

Motsoeneng, T. (2019), *Zimbabwe Mulls Use it or Lose it Approach to Mining Rights*, 10 April 2019. Available online: https://www.reuters.com/article/zimbabwe-mining-idINKCN1RM1TR (Accessed on 19 March 2025)

Moyo, S. (2011), Three decades of agrarian reform in Zimbabwe, *The Journal of Peasant Studies*, 38:3, 493–531.

Moyo, S. and Yeros, P. (2007), Intervention the Zimbabwe question and the two lefts. *Historical Materialism*, 15(3), 171–204.

Moyo, S. (2018), Debating the African Land Question with Archie Mafeje, *The Agrarian South Journal of Political Economy*, 7(2), 211–233. https://doi.org/10.1177/2277976018775361

Moyo, S. (2023), Increase bankability of projects, artisanal miners urged, *The Chronicle*, April 2023. Available online: https://www.chronicle.co.zw/increase-bankability-of-projects-artisanal-miners-urged/ (Accessed on 19 March 2025)

Munyati, S., Chandiwana, B., Mahati, S., Mupambireyi, P., Buzuzi, S., Mashange, W., Moyana, T., Gwini, S., and Rusakaniko, S. (2008), *Situation analysis of orphaned and vulnerable children in eight districts in Zimbabwe*, Pretoria: HSRC.

Muto, Y. (2020), *Gender-Based Violence in Emergencies Response in Bikita District in Masvingo*, Institute of Development Studies, National University of Science and Technology, August. Available online: https://www.academia.edu/47763202/GENDER_BASED_VIOLENCE_IN_EMERGENCIES_RESPONSE_IN_BIKITA_DISTRICT_IN_MASVINGO (Accessed on 19 March 2025)

Nechena, H. and Kurebwa, J. (2018), Community Participation in Community Share Ownership Trusts in Bikita Rural District of Zimbabwe, *International Journal of Research in Humanities and Social Studies*, Volume 5, Issue 9, 2018, pp:30-40.

News24. *Zimbabwe bans lithium unprocessed lithium exports demands beneficiation*, December 2022. Available online: https://www.news24.com/news24/bi-archive/zimbabwe-bans-unprocessed-lithium-exports-demands-benefaction-2022-12 (Accessed on 19 March 2025)

Nex, P., Goodenough, K., Shaw R., and Kinnaird J. (n.d.), *A review of lithium occurrences in Africa*, University of Witwatersrand, British Geological Survey, Centre for Excellence and Meteorological Analysis. Available online: https://www.geolsoc.org.uk/~/media/shared/documents/events/Past%20Meeting%20Resources/Lithium/Paul%20Nex.pdf (Accessed on 19 March 2025)

Nkala, S. (2022), Predatory Politics and the Indigenization and Economic Empowerment Policy in Zimbabwe's Mining Sector. *Africa Review*, 14(3), 277–304. https://doi.org/10.1163/09744061-tat00004

Owusu-Koranteng, H. (2018), *Operationalising Free Prior and Informed Consent: The case of Mining Communities*, Keynote Address at ACCA General Assembly, Nairobi. Available online: https://accahumanrights.org/images/resources/reports/Operationalising_FPIC.pdf (Accessed on 19 March 2025)

Peng-Fei, S. & Huang, J. (2023), Rural transformation, income growth, and poverty reduction by region in China in the past four decades, *Journal of Integrative Agriculture*, 22(22), 3582–3595. Available online: https://doi.org/10.1016/j.jia.2023.10.037 (Accessed on 19 March 2025)

Philip de Wet. *Zimbabwe has banned the export of raw lithium from its globally-important reserves*. News24. December 2022. Available online: https://www.news24.com/news24/bi-archive/zimbabwe-bans-unprocessed-lithium-exports-demands-benefaction-2022-12 (Accessed on 19 March 2025)

Randriamaro, Z. (2018), Beyond Extractivism: Feminist Alternatives for a Socially and Gender Just Development in Africa, *Feminist Reflections*. Available online: https://library.fes.de/pdf-files/bueros/mosambik/15208-20190325.pdf (Accessed on 19 March 2025)

Reuters a. *Sinomine suspends Zimbabwe lithium ops over authorities' concerns*, May 2023. Available online https://www.reuters.com/markets/commodities/sinomine-suspends-zimbabwe-lithium-ops-over-authorities-concerns-2023-05-15/ (Accessed on 19 March 2025)

Reuters b. *Sinomine's Zimbabwe unit resumes operations*, May 2023. Available online: https://www.reuters.com/markets/commodities/sinomines-zimbabwe-unit-resumes-operations-2023-05-24/ (Accessed on 19 March 2025)

Russel, A. (2011), Zimbabwe's tough line on nationalisation, *Financial Times*, published April 15. Available online: https://www.ft.com/content/9ca62a74-6775-11e0-9138-00144feab49a (Assessed on 19 March 2025)

Saul J.S. and Saunders R. (2005) Mugabe, Gramsci and Zimbabwe at 25, *International Journal*, Autumn, 2005, Vol. 60, No. 4, Africa: Towards Durable Peace (Autumn 2005), pp. 953–975. Available online: https://www.jstor.org/stable/40204093 (Accessed on 19 March 2025)

Seddon, D. and Zeilig L. (2005), Review of African Political Economy, Vol. 32, No. 103, *Imperialism & African Social Formations* (March 2005), pp. 9–27. Available online: https://www.jstor.org/stable/4006907 (Accessed on 19 March 2025)

Sharara, K. (2023), *China now Zim's largest FDI source*, June 2023. Available online: https://www.herald.co.zw/china-now-zims-largest-fdi-source/ (Accessed on 19 March 2025)

Sharon. Interview with the author in Bikita. February 2024

Sierra Club. (2021), *Guidance on lithium mining and extraction*, November 2021. Available online: https://www.sierraclub.org/sites/www.sierraclub.org/files/Lithium-Mining-Guidelines.pdf (Accessed on 19 March 2025)

Sitando, O. and Crouse, P. (2011), Processing of a Zimbabwean petalite to obtain lithium carbonate. *International Journal of Mineral Processing*, October. No 102. https://doi.org/10.1016/j.minpro.2011.09.014

Smits, J., and Steendijk, R. (2015), The International Wealth Index (IWI). *Soc Indic Res* 122: 65–85 (2015). https://doi.org/10.1007/s11205-014-0683-x

The Chronicle. (2023), *Zimbabweans in South Africa sent bulk of remittances in 2022*, February 2023. Available online: https://bulawayo24.com/index-id-news-sc-national-byo-227532.html (Accessed on 19 March 2025)

The Economist. (2023), Zimbabwe's worst economic crisis in more than a decade. *The Economist*. July 2020. Available online: https://www.economist.com/middle-east-and-africa/2020/07/09/zimbabwes-worst-economic-crisis-in-more-than-a-decade (Accessed on 19 March 2025)

United Nations Office of the High Commissioner on Human Rights (UNOHCHR). (2011), *Guiding Principles on Business and Human Rights: Implementing the United Nations "Protect, Respect and Remedy" Framework*, New York and Geneva: United Nations Office of the High Commissioner. Available online: https://www.ohchr.org/sites/default/files/documents/publications/guidingprinciplesbusinesshr_en.pdf (Accessed on 19 March 2025)

Viceisza A., Aflagah K., Abner J., Hippolyte K. (2020), *Poverty and Malnutrition in Zimbabwe: Findings from Masvingo Province*. Research Technical Assistance Centre: Washington, DC. Available online: https://www.rtachesn.org/wp-content/uploads/2020/01/RTAC_Food-Security-Analysis_Masvingo-1.pdf (Accessed on 19 March 1025)

WoMin. (2021), *Guns, Power and Politics: Research Paper*. Available online: https://womin.africa/wp-content/uploads/2020/09/Zimbabwe_Report-_FINAL.pdf (Accessed on 19 March 2025)

ZELA (Zimbabwe Environmental Law Association) and AIEL (Africa Institute of Environmental Law). (2023), *Implications of the Lithium Mining Rush in Zimbabwe: Analysis of Legal Developments*, February 2023.

Zimbabwe Environmental Lawyers Association. (2023), *Leveraging the Africa Mining Vision to Unlock the Sustainable Development Dividend*. February 2023. Available online: https://zela.org/leveraging-the-africa-mining-vision-to-unlock-the-sustainable-development-dividend/ (Accessed on 19 March 2025)

Zimbabwe National Statistics Authority. (2022), 2022 *Population and Housing Census: Preliminary Report on Population Figures*. Available online: https://zimbabwe.unfpa.org/sites/default/files/pub-pdf/2022_population_and_housing_census_preliminary_report_on_population_figures.pdf (Accessed on 19 March 2025)

Empowering Women in Nigerian Agriculture

Assessing the Effects of China-Nigeria Agricultural Cooperation on Female Smallholders' Livelihood, Capacity-Building, and Shifting Social Norms

by Ishola Itunu Grace

1. Introduction

China's experience in combating food shortage in the last few decades positions it as a suitable and exemplary partner of Africa for agricultural development (Brautigam and Tang 2009). Drawing on its successes and approaches to investment and development assistance flows for fast-tracking economic growth across several sectors, including agriculture, China supports many African countries that aim to replicate the 'China development model.' Previous studies argue that China adopts different modalities for its agricultural cooperation with African countries. These include establishing agriculture technology demonstration centers (ATDC), offering technical training and scholarships that facilitate technology and knowledge transfer, land investments, joint business ventures and equity between the host countries by Chinese state-owned and privately-owned companies (Brautigam and Tang 2009; Harding et al. 2021; Gu et al. 2016; FOCAC 2009). The modalities' effectiveness has relied on implementing agricultural cooperation via bilateral agreements, trilateral cooperation, and public-private partnerships (PPP) (Olasehinde et al. 2023; Ebula and Qi 2011; Food Agriculture Organization n.d.).

These modalities are evident in cooperation mechanisms such as the Forum for China-Africa Cooperation (FOCAC) and the United Nations Food Agriculture Organization (UNFAO). The Addis Ababa Action Plan (2004–2006) catalyzed China-Africa agricultural cooperation. China pledged to send 100 agriculture experts to different African countries to provide training and expertise in the agricultural sector for food security and development. Several government institutions and ministries from China, including the Ministry of Commerce (MOFCOM), the Ministry of Agriculture and Rural Affairs, and the Ministry of Science and Technology, were assigned to work with their African counterparts to provide their expertise while maintaining good diplomatic relations with the host countries. To facilitate sustainable agricultural cooperation with various African countries, China introduced the 'One Province, One Country' cooperation model – a Chinese province serves as the development partner to one African country, ingeniously executing its political and business tasks in one bid. A vital feature of this model is establishing ATDCs in twenty-four African countries, including Nigeria, since 2006 (Harding et al. 2021; Liu and Peter 2023; Buckley et al. 2017; Jiang et al. 2016; Amanor and Chichava 2016).

Before launching ATDCs across Africa, between 2003 and 2014, under the United Nations Food Agriculture Organization South-South Cooperation Programme (UNFAO-SSC), Nigeria received about 650 Chinese agriculture experts and technicians and over 200 agricultural technologies. Many of these rural-based experts and technicians introduced non-traditional agriculture technologies, provided training and technical support to smallholders and enhanced local farm practices, significantly improving the income and livelihood of many Nigerian smallholders (FAO 2019). According to Sun (2011), China's increased engagement in Africa's agriculture investment in the last few decades is not coincidental. As the impacts of climate change worsen worldwide, China aims to diversify its energy structure, downscale fossil fuels and increase biofuel production to meet its energy demands while ensuring food security domestically. Notably, Africa produces many staple crops for biofuel production, creating more channels for China-Africa agricultural cooperation. For instance, Nigeria is one of the world's largest cassava exporters, and China is the world's largest cassava importer. The rising demand for biofuel feedstock creates an avenue for trade and investment between both partners, helping to offset part of the China-Africa trade imbalance.

Like the triple helix model, the state, industries and universities are active actors in China-Nigeria agriculture cooperation. The implementers of Chinese agricultural aid projects in Nigeria include the Chinese embassy, China's Ministry of Commerce, Chinese state-owned, private businesses and several research institutions. These actors collaborate with ministries, including Nigeria's Federal Ministry of Agriculture and Rural Development, the Ministry of Budget and National Planning, and the Federal Ministry of Women Affairs, to implement projects in Nigeria. In 2022, the Chinese ambassador to Nigeria launched the Juncao technology workshop in partnership with the University of Agriculture, Nigeria, aiming to establish a twenty-hectare ATDC dedicated to planning and training Nigerians in agro-technologies (Oyoyo 2022). While Chinese agriculture experts and agribusiness firms' introduction of hybrid rice, maize, millet, and cassava variants in Nigeria aims to help Nigerian farmers boost agricultural productivity and food security, many local farmers have both praised and criticized the effort (Ibrahim 2020; Otung 2014). However, little is known about how smallholders, specifically females, will benefit from this programme due to existing cultural and institutional barriers to assessing education, training, agriculture inputs, extension services and credit facilities (World Bank 2022; Ogunlela and Mukhtar 2009; Olaosebikan et al. 2019).

Despite the growing body of research on the modalities, prospects and challenges of China-Nigeria agriculture cooperation, there is a dearth of studies considering women's roles and the impacts of China's agricultural engagements on gender equality and women's rights in Nigeria's agricultural sector. Thus, this paper aims to examine China-Nigeria agricultural cooperation from a gender perspective, focusing on the impacts on female smallholders. It seeks to answer the research questions: How does China-Nigeria agricultural cooperation influence smallholder women's rights and gender equality in Nigeria? How do China-led training programmes impact the income and livelihood of female smallholders in Nigeria? What strategies do women adopt to overcome gender norms while pursuing economic and social empowerment in Nigeria's agriculture sector?

This study contributes to the knowledge about China's agricultural engagement in the Global South, drawing on a feminist perspective and a micro-level analysis. It provides a lens that shows the impacts of Chinese agricultural aid projects on female smallholders beyond food production in Nigeria. The study examines the effectiveness of existing institutional provisions within Chinese agricultural aid projects in promoting women's rights and gender equality in Nigeria's agricultural sector. This research adopts a case study approach and qualitative method, evaluating a Chinese public-private-owned agribusiness firm in Nigeria – Green Agriculture West Africa Limited (GAWAL). GAWAL is a facilitator of Chinese-led agriculture training in Nigeria and the sole implementer of the Chinese-donated ATDC in Abuja. As a Chinese public-private agriculture enterprise operating in Nigeria, it displays a hybrid model of China-Africa agriculture cooperation. China strives to make its aid project sustainable in host countries by introducing a mixture of business strategies and aid initiatives, asserting the win-win cooperation narrative (Jiao, 2014). This study sheds light on GAWAL's business operations in Nigeria through a gender lens. Insights from respondents on GAWAL-led training programmes suggest that they influence the livelihood and welfare of hundreds of participating Nigerian smallholders. However, information is scant regarding the programmes' effects on improving gender equality and women's rights, calling for attention and challenging the rhetoric of gender mainstreaming in the training designs.

The paper is structured as follows: This opening section offers a background to China-Africa agricultural cooperation and the objectives and contributions of the case study; the second section reviews existing literature on women's participation in China-Nigeria agricultural cooperation and the conceptual framework guiding the research, as well as its methodology and data analysis; the third section contains its findings and discussions; and the last section concludes and proposes recommendations.

2. Examining the Role of Women in China-Africa Agricultural Cooperation

This section reviews existing literature on China-Africa agricultural cooperation, women's participation in China-Nigeria agriculture cooperation, the conceptual framework guiding the study and its methodology.

2.1 China-Africa Agricultural Cooperation

Recent reports on the impacts of China-Africa agricultural cooperation, drawing upon data from multiple field studies, show that Chinese aid to the agriculture sector positively influences various socioeconomic outcomes across African countries. Several studies in the China-Africa agricultural aid effectiveness literature have focused on the impacts of this cooperation on rural development and poverty reduction (Gubak and Samuel 2015; Paulin 2017), youth empowerment and job creation (Akinnifesi and Setshawelo 2014), farmers' productivity and income levels (Olasehinde et al. 2013). Other scholars, including Ebula and Qi (2011), Jiao (2015) and Bakare (2019), have explored the nature, impacts and challenges of China's approach to partnering with African countries through a PPP perspective that stresses the relationships between the public and private sectors. However, Gu et al. (2016) take a different view, describing China's agricultural engagements in Africa as a hybrid model that blurs the relationship between the donor (state) and investors (state-owned and privately-owned firms) and creates a symbiotic relationship – 'development cooperation' – between the recipient and the donor. Nonetheless, while these studies offer numerous details about the nature and effects of Chinese-led agriculture interventions in recipient African countries, they do not address several core issues, including the role of female smallholders.

Female farmers are on the front line in the agriculture sector and are critical rural development actors (Ogunlela and Muktar 2009). Nonetheless, impediments, including customs, beliefs and unpaid domestic labor, affect women's access to credit facilities, education, and healthcare, limiting their productivity and socioeconomic development prospects (Ogunlela and Muktar 2009). Veliu et al. (2009) conclude that religious beliefs impede land ownership and depress earnings for Muslim and non-Muslim women in Nigeria's northern region, prompting many female smallholders to seek alternative income sources. Moreover, Das et al. (2023) find that restrictive gender norms, occupational segregation and regional variations in Nigeria influenced women's choice of agribusiness value chain training programs, deepening the income gap and socioeconomic inequalities between male and female agribusiness entrepreneurs.

Despite the importance of women in agriculture, several studies on China-Nigeria agriculture cooperation failed to include the participation of female farmers in their analysis and findings (Gubak and Samuel 2015; FAO 2019; Olasehinde 2023). The preceding literature reveals little about the impact of Chinese agricultural aid on women and how development assistance influences gender equality and reduces the income gap in Africa's agricultural sector. Moreover, the literature exploring the hybrid model of China's agricultural cooperation with Africa has only recently begun to emerge, offering limited insights into its application to specific cases of Chinese enterprises and their real-world effects on productivity, income and gender equality. This study, therefore, attempts to fill these research gaps by exploring female smallholders' participation in China-Nigeria agricultural cooperation. Recognizing the hybrid model as a critical element of China's agricultural engagements in South-South cooperation (SSC), the paper undertakes a case study of GAWAL, a Chinese agribusiness operating in Nigeria, investigating how its activities, including training and technology transfer, affect women participants. This approach reveals the specific mechanisms of Chinese interventions in Nigeria, contributing to the literature on women in agriculture and the localized impacts of China-Africa cooperation.

2.2 Conceptual Framework

This study integrates the gender, economic and ecological justice (GEEJ) framework proposed by Development Alternatives with Women for a New Era (DAWN) on the gender impact of China's global engagement in the Global South and the sustainable livelihood approach. The GEEJ framework addresses the interlinkage between gender, economic and ecological justice from a feminist perspective. It connects these areas to explore the interactions between gender and social trends such as globalization, development and climate change. Moreover, it creates a lens for gender awareness in the discourse of China's global engagement in the Global South and how it influences and is influenced by human rights, gender equality and women's rights in the host countries (Cai and Yu 2022).

Although the GEEJ framework helps illuminate connections between gender and the factors listed above, using the framework to analyze diverse social, political and economic contexts requires in-depth theoretical underpinnings that address the multifaceted dynamics behind outcomes of gender-related issues in a micro-level analysis. Thus, this study also adopts the sustainable livelihood framework proposed by Robert Chambers and Gordon Conway.

Chambers and Conway (1992) proposed the concept of livelihood from a people-centered discourse, highlighting the complexities behind humans' actions and behavior in the confines of the opportunities available to them at any given time. This study aligns its definition of livelihood with Chamber and Conway's as the 'adequate stocks and flows of food and cash to meet basic needs.' Livelihood is sustainable when one can manage and cope with various challenges to enhance consistent provision for future needs (Chambers and Conway 1992: 5). Scoones (1998) transformed the concept of sustainable livelihood into a conceptual framework for analysis, which describes different resources needed to achieve sustainable livelihood, individuals' strategies and the influence of formal and informal institutional structures on sustainable livelihood outcomes. The resources the author regards as capital include human, natural, financial, physical and social or political capital and the structures are the public and private sectors, laws, culture and institutions.

In the wake of globalization, digitalization, and technological development, several scholars have expanded the scope of capital to analyze various case studies and research in other fields and disciplines (Odero 2006; Horsley et al. 2015; De Haan 2011). Odero (2006) adds information capital to the framework, arguing that information is critical in individuals' strategies to attain a sustainable livelihood. For a holistic understanding of the studied phenomena, this study adopts the framework with six types of capital (human, social, economic, financial, physical and information) to assess the impact of China-Nigeria agricultural cooperation on female smallholders' income and livelihood. Here, **human capital** includes educational levels and competence in various agricultural practices; **natural capital** is access to land and water; **physical capital** comprises agricultural machinery and various assets used to enhance productivity and income (a truck to transport crops to market or good storage for harvested crops); **financial capital** comprises cash and access to credits, loans and grants; **social capital** refers to social and political connections, membership in farmers' organizations and networks of friends and partners; and **information capital** is an individual's access to information relevant to their agriculture practices, such as training, extension services, and market access (value-chain).

2.3 Methodology and Data Collection

This paper adopts a case study approach to assess the impacts of China-Nigeria agriculture cooperation on female smallholders' income and livelihood and the promotion of women's rights and gender equality among smallholders in Nigeria. This approach transcends the state of food production and the operations of Chinese agribusinesses in Nigeria. The study adopts qualitative methods, drawing primary and secondary data from semi-structured interviews, policy documents, academic journals, books, and news articles. Interviews were conducted via WhatsApp, WeChat, and audio phone calls between October and December 2023. The interview questions were drawn from the study's research questions, and respondents engaged in open discussions, sharing their experiences of Chinese-led training initiatives in Nigeria and their impacts on their income and livelihood.

The study includes fourteen respondents, five males and nine females. They include a company representative from GAWAL, a representative from Nigeria's Ministry of Agriculture, a regional director of the International Fund for Agricultural Development (IFAD) trilateral cooperation, and two male and nine female farmers who participated in GAWAL-led agricultural training exercises in Abuja between September 2019 and December 2023. This range of participants provides a holistic viewpoint of the impacts of the training in different stages and periods. While respondents from the 2023 training are still implementing the knowledge acquired at the training, those from the 2019 training have adopted the acquired skills in their farming practices and could discuss the effects on their yields, income levels, and livelihood. The researcher adopts the snowball technique, which requires the respondents to introduce other participants willing to join the study. The researcher selected participants using an approach aimed at achieving a sample with maximum variability (Creswell 2007). The purpose of such a selection is not for representation but rather an understanding of the studied phenomenon through the real-life experiences of the respondents. Due to constraints on onsite visits, the researcher conducted virtual meetings with the respondents. All data collected and disclosed by interviewees is kept confidential, and the interview data do not contain the interviewee's personally identifiable information, such as name, address, or telephone number.

3. Gender Disparity vs. Women's Empowerment: China-Nigeria Agricultural Cooperation through a Gender Lens

This section presents and discusses the research findings. The results are divided into sections: the effects of Chinese-led agricultural training programmes on women's rights and gender equality in Nigeria; agricultural training programmes' impacts on the income and livelihood of female smallholders in Nigeria; and women's bargaining power and strategies to shift gender norms in Nigeria's agriculture sector.

3.1 GAWAL – A PPP Model of China-Nigeria Agricultural Cooperation

Examining Nigeria's agricultural development through a gender lens is vital for several reasons. First, Nigeria is one of China's most prominent African trade partners, with a trading volume of over $13 billion in 2021. Agriculture accounted for about twenty-two per cent of Nigeria's total gross domestic product (GDP) in the first quarter of 2023 (National Bureau of Statistics 2023). The sector employs thirty-five per cent of Nigeria's labor force, about half of which are female smallholders (International Labour Organization 2021). Nigeria has welcomed around 650 Chinese agriculture experts and technicians since 2003 under the FAO South-South cooperation. These experts spent two years each training Nigerian smallholders, extension agents, and other local agriculture experts on some of China's cost-efficient and new agricultural technologies (FAO 2019). Hence, China-Nigeria agriculture cooperation continues to evolve, involving many stakeholders, including the Chinese embassy, state- and privately-owned companies operating in Nigeria, and township and friendship associations. These new actors execute China's hybrid model of development assistance and serve as contact points for China-Nigeria agricultural cooperation. This study focuses on Green Agriculture West Africa Limited (GAWAL), a public-private agribusiness established by CGCOC Group Co., Ltd., formerly named CGC Overseas Construction Group Co., Limited (中地海外建设集团: *zhongdi haiwai jianshe jituan*) and Yuan Longping High-Tech Agriculture Co. in 2006 in Nigeria.

CGCOC Agriculture Group entered Nigeria owing to its agriculture technology expertise and the country's market prospects, favorable agricultural conditions, and vast human resources. Chief Executive Officer Wang highlighted the company's dedication to aligning its business interests with corporate social responsibility (CSR) goals, emphasizing CSR as crucial for their reputation and sustainable growth and food security in Nigeria (Li 2021). GAWAL's activities include large-scale seed production, agricultural machinery and equipment sales, agro-processing, training and consultancy, and constructing and operating agriculture industrial parks in Nigeria (Kebbi and Abuja). GAWAL also partners with several Chinese agriculture and research institutions to conduct seed manufacturing-related research, training, and knowledge exchanges[1].

GAWAL is a strategic partner and supplier of hybrid rice seed under the Growth Enhancement Support (GES) scheme and Anchor Borrowers' Programme (ABP) launched by the Nigerian Federal Ministry of Agriculture and Rural Development. The company runs a 2,025-hectare mechanized demonstration farm in Kebbi state, Nigeria, and has its operational office in Abuja, Nigeria. GAWAL implements Chinese aid projects in Nigeria through agricultural training for Nigerian government officials and farmers and operates Nigeria's sole ATDC in Bwari, Abuja[2]. This study investigates GAWAL because it epitomizes China's hybrid aid model – a mixture of business and aid conducted by the state and independent business actors in its agricultural cooperation with Nigeria (Harding et al. 2021; Brautigam and Tang 2009). Also, it conducted the first agricultural training under the Chinese aid project in Nigeria in 2016 and has trained over 400 farmers and government parastatals since then (Zhang 2016; GAWAL 2023).

3.2 Who Attends What? GAWAL Agricultural Training for Nigerian Smallholders

A central feature of China-Nigeria agricultural cooperation is technology transfer and provision of technical assistance in agriculture-related issues. This study found that capacity building, food security, sustainable agribusiness, and farming mechanisms are firmly embedded in China's agriculture cooperation in Nigeria (Gubak and Samuel 2015). China organizes training and technical assistance through various mechanisms, including bilateral and trilateral agreements and state-owned and privately owned Chinese businesses in Nigeria. The Chinese government funds several agricultural and technical training programmes to introduce Chinese agricultural technologies and facilitate agricultural technology transfer between China and Nigeria. Over the years, GAWAL has organized eight Chinese government-backed training programmes to equip Nigerian smallholders with cutting-edge skills in adopting hybrid seeds, using agriculture machinery, applying pesticides and chemicals, processing, and agribusiness value chain knowledge.

Unlike the FAO-Nigeria-China agriculture cooperation that provides agricultural training mainly to farming households and extension agents (FAO 2019; Olasehinde 2023), GAWAL trains these groups and government officials regarding Chinese agro-technologies. Between 2016 and 2019, GAWAL trained over 400 government officials, smallholders, and technicians and launched seven seed production cooperatives boasting about 5,000 members across different states in Nigeria to disseminate Chinese agricultural technology and contribute to Nigeria's agricultural development and food security[3]. Besides implementing Chinese agricultural aid projects in Nigeria, GAWAL partners with different ministries and government bodies, including the Nigerian Ministry of Agriculture and Rural Development, the Ministry of Budget and National Planning, and the Federal Ministry for Women Affairs, to recruit participants for its agricultural training programmes. Nonetheless, gender segregation for specific crops and value chains, poor dissemination of programme information, and reliance on local ministries to recruit participants have led to a higher male than female participation rate in training, as indicated in the company's records. The average ratio of male to female participants in each training was 30:9, with females comprising less than one-third of the total participants (see Appendix 1 Figure 1).

The agricultural training programme does not mandate a ratio for male and female participants, resulting in gender imbalances. While the interviewed company representative expressed GAWAL's intention to recruit more female smallholders, they noted that this decision and process lacked formal policies or guidelines since the recruiting ministries had the discretion to choose participants. Moreover, no public announcements specified the recruitment process, eligibility criteria, or gender distribution for training programme participants. While some respondents reported that being a member of a registered farmers' association or cooperative group is a prerequisite to participating in the training, the study found some exceptions. This suggests that the recruiting ministries use other requirements and metrics to determine the eligibility of training participants. Hence, the recruitment method needs to be reassessed to increase female smallholders' involvement in training programmes.

Furthermore, GAWAL effectively implements agriculture aid projects and sustains its business by outsourcing some of its seed production to local farmers. Male smallholders in this study stated that they were invited to work as rice outgrowers to help produce hybrid rice seeds and sell them to the company at a reasonable rate. Respondent Six explained that:

> 'During the (last) rainy season, GAWAL gave us seeds to produce for them. They give the seeds to the farmers for free, and then after production, no matter the amount the farmers produce, they buy back everything even if it amounts to a billion (naira).'

While this implies that the company can localize its production, helping smallholders diversify their income and improve the adoption of modern Chinese-made agro-technologies, it raises questions about women's lack of involvement.

Also, as in other Chinese-led agricultural training programmes in Nigeria, a large part of the training concentrates on hybrid rice and cassava stem cultivation and processing, agrochemical usage, and farm machinery and equipment operation (Osheinde 2023; Guhbak and Samuel 2015). In Nigeria, male smallholders dominate rice and sales of cassava stem for cultivation (Umeh and Atarboh 2006 as cited in Omiunu 2014; Aboaba et al. 2019; Olaosebikan et al. 2019), discouraging many female smallholders from participating in these kinds of agricultural training programmes. Hence, implementers of Chinese agricultural aid projects, including GAWAL, should consider gender roles, norms, culture, and occupational segregation in Nigerian agriculture when designing and implementing training programmes. This approach would promote inclusivity by offering courses on crops traditionally cultivated by women, such as tubers and vegetables.

Furthermore, the training programmes adopt an 80/20 principle: eighty per cent theoretical knowledge and twenty per cent practical, leaving the participants with limited opportunities to have practical experiences of the skill taught for most of the training. The company representative acknowledged that their training programmes before 2022 lacked adequate demonstrations due to space constraints and the participants' demographics. Different training formats were used: government officials had more theoretical information, while smallholders and local agricultural experts had more demonstrations. The representative explained that since starting the ATDC facilities in December 2022, the company has increased the practical sessions in its training programme.

Moreover, despite initial theoretical and practical knowledge imbalances during the training, this study found that participants adopted Chinese agro-technologies, including hybrid rice seeds and pest control techniques, suggesting GAWAL's successful transfer of Chinese agriculture knowledge and technologies for improved crop production. Respondent Five reported that:

> 'For rice with improved rice seeds (GAWAL R1 and Faro 44)[4] and better extension services, farmers have recorded three to five tons per hectare or even six tons around lowland areas with dry season farming. Millet farmers find it difficult to adopt the foxtail millet[5] against the local millet varieties – sosat and super sosat millet[6] varieties are very good. Instead, they use the information on millet cultivation techniques that allowed them to increase the quality and yield of the product.'

This finding lends credence to the study by Olasehinde et al. (2023), which argued that while farmers benefit from training, an imbalance in the appropriation of training resources and information persists among farmers. Most training participants have relatively high financial and social capital compared to others without similar backgrounds and economic incentives (Olasehinde et al., 2023). The data found no evidence of female participation in the six-month activity organized by Chinese agricultural experts in Ogun state, Nigeria. This study analyses the variations between male and female smallholders following the training to fill this gap.

3.3 Impacts of Chinese-led Agricultural Training on the Income and Livelihood of Female Smallholders in Nigeria

This study examined smallholders' livelihood and income post-training, focusing on four indicators: agricultural products and outputs, income diversification, access to credit and production units (labour, seeds, fertilizer and agricultural machinery). The findings indicate increased satisfaction with the training programmes vis-à-vis production. A respondent practicing subsistence farming initially with little yields to feed her family described improved outputs, providing enough for her family and surplus for sale or exchange for other goods and services. The respondent, however, did not specify the kinds of goods and services acquired with the extra income. These could be education, health products, livestock, and tangible and intangible assets that might boost farmers' income and livelihood, living standards and overall rural development (DFID, 1999).

This study also found that trainees decided to diversify their income streams post-training, drawing on their newly acquired skills. Respondent Two noted that while she learned to make oil from sesame seeds for private consumption, she could not afford the hybrid rice seedlings for mass production on her farm. This acquired sesame oil manufacturing skill can be harnessed in Nigeria's agro-processing industry if enough credit and capital are allocated to these farmers post-training. GAWAL's representative expressed that this is a challenge because some participants cannot execute most of the knowledge acquired during the training in their usual farm operations owing to a lack of funding to purchase agro-materials and technologies. Also, Respondent Five stated that the improved rice seeds and better extension services have helped increase rice yields to about six tonnes per hectare in Sokoto, even in dry seasons.

Nonetheless, the study discovered gender disparities in the impacts of the training on farmers' income. Compared to female smallholders, male farmers experienced a significant rise in income levels and opportunities to improve their livelihood post-training. Male smallholders reported about a thirty per cent higher agricultural yield, participation in GAWAL's outgrower scheme, and access to credit facilities to scale up farm production, helping to increase their income post-training. Respondent Six explained that GAWAL offered him the opportunity to join its outgrower scheme, where he produces rice seeds for the company and earns extra income. Also, he obtained a loan from the government to expand his agribusiness after the training, planning to purchase a harvester[7] and rent it to other farmers to generate more income. In contrast, female smallholders face financial constraints when upscaling their agriculture businesses. They operate small businesses, including selling cows, sheep, and goats for meat, processing farm products, tailoring, and buying and selling beverages and small house items, thereby diversifying their income and reinvesting their profit in their agriculture business.

The gender imbalance in budget allocations and access to credits, training, and extension support for crops and value chains puts female smallholders at a disadvantage compared to males. Besides institutional barriers that hinder female smallholders from accessing opportunities that could improve their agricultural income and livelihood, enshrined cultural beliefs, gender norms, and occupational segregation keep some female smallholders from farming valuable crops such as cereals, coffee, cocoa and different kinds of tubers. Female farmers classify these as 'male crops' (World Bank 2022 p. 33) and are unwilling to plant them.

Furthermore, the power dynamics between men and women in Nigeria's agricultural sector significantly affect the productivity of female-managed farms and agricultural outputs. Gender roles impact women's decisions on crop selection, land access, agricultural inputs, machinery, and physical labor, shaping the power structure between male and female smallholders. Respondent Nine stated that male smallholders dominate rice farming in her community, and the minority of females who plant rice have smaller farms than their male counterparts. Respondent Seven explained women's challenges, including the limited affordability of leasing large farmlands, as they often dedicate productive hours to physical labor on their husbands' farms. Also, male smallholders typically control land assets through inheritance, leaving many women without access. Respondent One, who plants mainly fruits and vegetables rather than maize, rice, millet or other grains, reported that women need their male counterparts to help them bargain for machinery rentals, wages for manual labor, and inputs such as fertilizers and other agrochemicals. She explained that:

> 'Even if you're interested in growing rice, you can't do it alone; it requires a lot of capital. Besides, women can work in the agriculture sector, but no matter what we say, it is still male dominated. So, even as a woman, you are expected to be at the back, not the forefront of the farm operations. You need a man to manage the farm. As someone with some staff under my jurisdiction, I know how it is being a woman and wanting to give orders. Yes, you can give the orders, but it's more challenging than when a man does it.'

The preceding aligns with existing knowledge that married female farmers need more incentives or motivation before investing their time and resources into their farms because of the long hours spent working on their husbands' farms or doing chores (Pierotti, Friedson-Ridenour, and Olayiwola 2022). Although women constitute a significant portion of Nigeria's agriculture workforce, male farmers predominantly control the resources and higher agriculture value chain (Ogunlela and Mukhtar 2009; World Bank 2022). This phenomenon influencing the socioeconomic inequality between male and female smallholders illustrates the transforming structures and processes highlighted in Scoone's (1998) sustainable livelihood framework. It explains how institutions (private and public), policies, laws, and culture directly and indirectly impact an individual's livelihood.

Overall, training and skills formation alone may not bring about desired structural and transformative changes in the short term. This may be due to the training programmes' limitations in fast-tracking broader shifts in socioeconomic dynamics that are culturally and religiously embedded in specific settings. Simultaneously, prevalent power disparities can obstruct access to technical training, creating a cyclical challenge. These findings have a complementary nature. On the one hand, acquiring technical knowledge and skills without addressing power disparities sustains the barriers hindering female smallholders from accessing agro-related opportunities. On the other hand, restructuring power dynamics without offering training might result in missed opportunities for meaningful socioeconomic progress. Nonetheless, long-term changes are possible, which is seen in the behavioral changes among female smallholders in the study who engaged in rice farming and are willing to grow more cash crops, including ginger and groundnuts, in larger quantities. Also, higher farm yields among female farmers result in increased disposable income. Financial independence, in turn, improves female smallholders' autonomy, giving them greater influence on decision-making processes regarding agricultural practices, household expenditures, and community development.

3.4 Shifting Gender Norms through Capital Acquisition

This study finds that female smallholders' participation in Chinese-led agricultural training influences the adoption of modern agriculture practices in their communities, leading to a shift in gender norms in the agriculture sector. Post-training, more female smallholders grow large quantities of rice and other staple foods, increasing their income and their communities' food security. The respondents also discussed sharing the new farming techniques and methods with their communities, friends, and farmers' association members, especially women-led cooperative associations in Nigeria's northern region. Hence, two beneficiary groups are identifiable: direct beneficiaries who attended GAWAL's agricultural training and indirect beneficiaries, including household members of trainees, members of the same farmers' associations, friends and the community at large. Out of the nine female respondents, five of them are farmers' association leaders. They noted that they shared the knowledge they gained from the training with around 300 women in their various cooperatives. Respondent Seven said:

> 'As the chairperson of a farmers' cooperative in my community, I attended the training, jotted down the important points, and went back to train the other farmers. These women also have other farmers whom they train in smaller villages.'

This information-sharing process is crucial for the Federal Ministry of Women's Affairs, requiring beneficiaries to teach fellow smallholders in their farm associations and communities. Respondents recruited through this ministry said that leadership roles in farmer associations, language proficiency, and willingness to train other farmers constituted part of the eligibility criteria for the training. Participants were asked to submit a comprehensive report, including photos, name lists, challenges, and community feedback on their 'step-down' training[8]. While institutional provisions exist to address language and cultural barriers smallholders might face in accessing agricultural training opportunities themselves, the study found a lack of ad-hoc policies and frameworks to monitor the step-down programme across different localities. Ministries rely solely on reports and pictures without systemic measures to measure the impact and sustainability of training programmes on smallholders in their communities.

Nonetheless, this process creates a ripple effect, where one female smallholder's participation in agricultural training enlightens others who could not directly access the training, thereby reducing the gender gap in cash crop and staple food farming in Nigeria. Building on Farnworth et al.'s (2020) perspective, this finding suggests that adopting new technologies can restructure the power dynamics of men and women in agriculture. These technologies help farmers improve their productivity, farm yields, and income and enhance the participation of women in household decision-making processes and their economic contributions to their households (Farnworth et al. 2020).

This finding further validates the use of information capital to create livelihood strategies to achieve the desired outcomes. Interviewees report obtaining the agricultural training information through professional and personal relationships. Respondent Eight mentioned obtaining information about the training from an acquaintance who serves as a special advisor to the governor of her state. Respondent Eight reckoned that language proficiency significantly influenced participants' selection for the training. Those who attended were adept in English and capable of communicating in Hausa or other indigenous languages to effectively conduct training for fellow farmers in their communities. Olasehinde et al. (2023) highlight that some farmers prefer to learn from other farmers due to their familiarity with the individual, language, and culture (Olasehinde et al. 2023). In this informal setting, female smallholders can learn about new farming techniques, apply them to their farms, and increase their yields and income.

Furthermore, the study shows that many female smallholders in Nigeria are aware of the cultural, political, and institutional barriers they encounter in the agriculture sector. In response, they leverage their agency to develop strategies to combat or mitigate these limitations, including income diversification and involvement in community leadership. Land assets connote financial stability for most female smallholders, serving as production means and collateral during emergencies. In regions where women face constraints in land ownership[9], they employ strategies such as acquiring land through their parents, relatives, or male children. For instance, an unmarried female respondent acquired farmland through her parents, acknowledging the difficulties she would have faced in acquiring it independently. Financial constraints further drive female smallholders' dependence on loans, inheritance, and support from parents or spouses to invest in capital-intensive assets, including land and agriculture machinery. In some parts of Nigeria, especially the north, where agriculture is prevalent, most women are not allowed to own or inherit land due to religious or cultural beliefs (Veliu et al. 2009).

Similarly, Umaru Baba and Van der Horst (2018) noted that in the last decade, women in Nigeria's northern region have been negotiating their rights to own livestock and properties through various relationships, including marriage and other social networks. This aligns with the theory that social capital is an asset for sustainable livelihood, enabling individuals to acquire physical capital such as land, livestock, and agriculture equipment, thereby generating financial capital over time. Many women actively challenge gender norms that limit their production capacity and income. They depend on diverse networks, including religious, township, and farmers' associations, for knowledge sharing and financial support. This study reveals that women's empowerment can help address limiting and discriminatory cultural norms. Knowledge and economic empowerment give women in Nigeria's agriculture sector some leverage to exercise their agency and bargaining power to purchase more assets and participate in decision-making in their families and communities.

4. Conclusion and Recommendations

This case study on China-Nigeria agriculture cooperation and its impact on female smallholders assesses the effects of Chinese-led agricultural training programmes on the income and livelihood of recruited female smallholders. The study reveals that Chinese-led agricultural training at GAWAL does less to promote women's rights and gender equality in Nigeria's agriculture than it could do. The challenge lies in the training recruitment mechanism, existing gender segregation for specific crops and value chains in Nigeria, and poor dissemination of programme information, resulting in fewer female trainees than men. Besides, GAWAL and ATDC possess no institutional provisions to provide a quota for more female smallholders to participate in the training. Likewise, the study shows that male smallholders report more crops yield post-training, leading to an increase in income compared to female smallholders. Nevertheless, the training helps female smallholders improve their agricultural practices and yields, adopt new technologies, and foster social cohesion with other smallholders. Furthermore, the study provides evidence that female smallholders' access to more agricultural training boosts the adoption of new agricultural technologies and techniques in rural areas, fostering food security and developing rural Nigeria.

This study is not without its limitations. First, its scope is limited to a small sample of smallholders in Nigeria who participated in two GAWAL training programmes. These factors highlight the challenge of missing the experiences of other respondents in other training programmes and locations where GAWAL has operated, raising questions about the generalizability and representativeness of the findings. Nonetheless, this research serves as a forerunner, bringing scholars, activists, and policymakers' attention to the issues discussed here and establishing the groundwork for subsequent research on agricultural development cooperation through a gendered lens. Future studies may undertake a comparative analysis with similar (China-led or other international actors') training programmes in different regions or countries to draw cross-cultural and cross-regional insights.

Recommendations

(1) Gender consciousness should be included in the design of the training programmes, and the kinds of training held in the ATDC should be diversified. GAWAL's primary business is rice seed production; they could invite other agriculture

training experts to conduct training in horticulture, tubers and other crops that female smallholders traditionally grow in Nigeria. This would provide opportunities for women who cannot switch to growing 'male crops' and equip them with better ways to improve their agricultural practices in the current value chain.

(2) Degenderize the agriculture sector. Historically, though women contribute significantly to the agriculture sector, they are not considered active actors in agricultural development and have less access to vital resources such as land, credit and extension services. Thus, the government should promulgate new inclusive policies to degenderize the sector and boost sustainable agricultural development. By degenderizing the agriculture sector, women can participate in policy-making and access necessary services for the production and transformation of the agriculture sector.

(3) Adopt the 'small but beautiful' (*xiao er mei*小而美) model. This concept under the Belt and Road Initiative describes small-scale projects in China's cooperation with other countries. The model emphasizes the effectiveness and palpable income of the project. Adopting the model in the China-Nigeria agricultural training and projects can help tackle social and gender inequality. In most cases, big projects are government-led and, to some extent, have political aims; these projects might not benefit ordinary people, especially rural farmers. In contrast, well-structured 'small but beautiful' projects can better the lives of smallholders and give them opportunities to develop their agricultural skills.

Notes

1 Information provided by GAWAL's company representative on 3 October 2023.
2 Information elicited from GAWAL's official website. Available at: https://gawal123.com/ (Accessed: 6 November 2023).
3 Information provided by GAWAL'S company representative on 3 October 2023.
4 Names of hybrid rice seed varieties produced and marketed to the Nigerian market by GAWAL.
5 Name of hybrid millet seed varieties produced and marketed to the Nigerian market by GAWAL.
6 Names of locally sourced millet seeds in Nigeria.
7 A machine used for gathering crops during the harvest season.
8 Step-down is the term by which farmers' associations and recruiting ministries call the agricultural training conducted by local farmers and cooperative leaders. During a step-down training, first-hand beneficiaries of GAWAL's agricultural training pass down the knowledge and techniques acquired from the training in informal settings using some of Nigeria's indigenous languages.

9   Women acquire lands through their spouses, male children, and relatives in different parts of the country, especially the north. Studies show that some regions in Nigeria forbid women from inheriting or owning lands due to their religious status. For instance, Muslim and non-Muslim women in the north have different access and rights to own lands (see Veliu et al. 2009).

References

Abdulrahman, H. (2023), Minister will distribute 26,000 tons of hybrid rice to rural women farmers, *The Federal Radio Corporation of Nigeria (FRCN)*. Available online: https://radionigeria.gov.ng/2023/10/12/minister-to-distribute-26000-tons-of-hybrid-rice-to-rural-women-farmers/ (Accessed on 14 October 2023).

Aboaba, K.O., et al. (2019), Determinants of disease burden among rice farming households in Ogun state, Nigeria. *Journal of Agriculture and Rural Development*, 9(2), pp.264–273.

Akinnifesi, F.K. and Setshawelo, L.L. (2014), South-South Cooperation in Agric is empowering Nigerian farmers, *Daily Trust*. Available online: https://dailytrust.com/south-south-cooperation-in-agric-is-empowering-nigerian-farmers/ (Accessed on 10 October 2023).

Amanor, K.S. and Chichava, S. (2016). South-South cooperation, agribusiness, and African agricultural development: Brazil and China in Ghana and Mozambique. *World Development*, 81, pp.13–23.

Bakare, M. (2019), Farmers groan as Chinese firm grabs land in northern Nigeria, *Premium Times*. Available online: https://www.premiumtimesng.com/agriculture/agric-news/343566-farmers-groan-as-chinese-firm-grabs-land-in-northern-nigeria.html?tztc=1 (Accessed on 10 October 2023)

Bräutigam, D.A. and Xiaoyang, T. (2009), China's engagement in African agriculture: 'Down to the countryside'. *The China Quarterly*, 199, pp.686–706.

Cai, Y. and Yu, Y. (2022), *An Analytical Framework on the Gender Impact of China's Global Engagement in the Global South*. DAWN discussion paper #47. Available online: https://www.dawnfeminist.org/wp-content/uploads/2023/01/20230202-China-Analytical-Framework.pdf (Accessed on 19 March 2025)

Chambers, R. and Conway, G. (1992), *Sustainable rural livelihoods: practical concepts for the 21st century*. Institute of Development Studies. UK.

Das, S., et al. (2023), Occupational sex segregation in agriculture: Evidence on gender norms and socio-emotional skills in Nigeria. *Agricultural Economics*, 54(2), pp.179–219.

De Haan, L.J. (2012), The livelihood approach: A critical exploration. *Erdkunde*, pp.345–357.

Department for International Development (DfID), UK. (1999), *Sustainable livelihoods guidance sheets*. DFID, London.

Egbula, M. and Zheng, Q. (2011), China, and Nigeria: A Powerful South-South Alliance. *West African Challenges* No. 5 November 2011. Sahel and West Africa Club Secretariat (SWAC/OECD). Available online: https://www.oecd.org/china/49814032.pdf (Accessed on 10 October 2023).

FAO. (2019), *Inspiration, Inclusion and Innovation: FAO-China South-South Cooperation Programme (2009–2019)*. Available online: https://www.fao.org/policy-support/tools-and-publications/resources-details/en/c/1365055/ (Accessed on 10 October 2023)

FAO. (n.d.), *FAO and China mark 40 years of hunger-fight cooperation*. Available online: https://www.fao.org/newsroom/detail/FAO-and-China-mark-40-years-of-cooperation-in-hunger-fight/ (Accessed on 13 October 2023)

Farnworth, C.R., et al. (2020), Unequal partners: associations between power, agency and benefits among women and men maize farmers in Nigeria. *Gender, Technology and Development*, 24(3), pp.271–296.

FOCAC. (2009), *Implementation of the follow-up actions of the Beijing Summit of the forum on China-Africa cooperation*. Available online: http://www.focac.org.cn/eng/ljhy_1/dscbzjhy/FA32009/200911/t20091117_7976734.htm (Accessed on 20 October 2023)

Gu, J., Zhang, C., Vaz, A. and Mukwereza, L. (2016), Chinese state capitalism? Rethinking the role of the state and business in Chinese development cooperation in Africa. *World Development*, 81, pp.24–34.

Gubak, H.D. and Samuel, M. (2015), Chinese trade and investment in Nigeria's agricultural sector: A critical analysis. *American International Journal of Social Science*, Vol. 4, No. 2, pp.277–287.

Horsley, J., Prout, S., Tonts, M. and Ali, S.H. (2015), Sustainable livelihoods and indicators for regional development in mining economies. *The Extractive Industries and Society*, 2(2), pp.368–380.

Ibrahim, M.A. (2020), Development of Hybrid Rice Technology and Sustainable Food Security in Nigeria. *International Journal of Authentic Agriculture*. Volume 1, Number 1, June 2020, pp. 42–54.

ILO. (2021), *Employment in agriculture (% of total employment) (modeled ILO estimate) – Nigeria, World Bank Open Data*. Available online: https://data.worldbank.org/indicator/SL.AGR.EMPL.ZS?locations=G (Accessed on 6 November 2023)

Jiao, Y. (2014), Chinese Agribusiness Entrepreneurship in Africa: Case Studies in Ghana and Nigeria. *Policy Brief* 05/2015, August 2014.

Li, R. (2021), *How Chinese companies in Africa adapt to the local environment*. Available online: https://news.cgtn.com/news/2021-03-08/Chinese-companies-in-Africa-look-to-shape-positive-image-VOH8zBurdK/index.html (Accessed on 6 November 2023)

National Bureau of Statistics. (2023), *Nigerian Gross Domestic Product Q1 2023*. Available online: https://nigerianstat.gov.ng/elibrary/read/1241325 (Accessed on 6 November 2023)

Odero, K.K. (2006), Information capital: 6th asset of sustainable livelihood framework. *Discovery and Innovation*, 18(2), pp.83–91.

Ogunlela, Y.I. and Mukhtar, A.A. (2009), Gender issues in agriculture and rural development in Nigeria: The role of women. *Humanity & Social Sciences Journal*, 4(1), pp.19–30.

Olaosebikan, O., et al. (2019), Gender-based constraints are affecting biofortified cassava production, processing, and marketing among men and women adopters in Oyo and Benue States, Nigeria. *Physiological and Molecular Plant Pathology*, 105, pp.17–27.

Olasehinde, T.S., Jin, Y., Qiao, F. and Mao, S. (2023), Marginal returns on Chinese agricultural technology transfer in Nigeria: Who benefits more? *China Economic Review*, 78, p.101935.

Omiunu, O.G. (2014), Investigating the challenges faced by women rice farmers in Nigeria. *Open Access Library Journal*, 1(6), pp.1–14.

Otung, I.A. (2014), Evaluation of Six Chinese Maize (ZEA MAYS) Varieties in the Human Tropical Environment of Calabar, Southeast Nigeria. *Global Journal of Agricultural Research*, 2(3), pp.10–16.

Oyoyo, I. (2022), *Food security:* Auda-NEPAD to Domesticate Juncao Technology, *Leadership News*. Available online: https://leadership.ng/food-security-auda-nepad-to-domesticate-juncao-technology/ (Accessed on 20 October 2023)

Parkinson, S. and Ramirez, R. (2006), Using a sustainable livelihoods approach to assessing the impact of ICTs in development. *The Journal of Community Informatics*, 2(3).

Pierotti, R.S., Friedson-Ridenour, S. and Olayiwola, O. (2022), Women farm what they can manage: How time constraints affect the quantity and quality of labor for married women's agricultural production in southwestern Nigeria. *World Development*, 152, 105800.

Scoones, I. (1998), *Sustainable rural livelihoods: a framework for analysis*. IDS working papers 72.

Su, F., Saikia, U. and Hay, I. (2018), Relationships between livelihood risks and livelihood capitals: A case study in Shiyang River Basin, China. *Sustainability*, 10(2), 509.

Sun, H. L. (2011), *Understanding China's agricultural investments in Africa*. China in Africa Project Occasional Paper No. 102. South African Institute of International Affairs (SAIIA).

Umaru Baba, S. and Van der Horst, D. (2018), Intrahousehold relations and environmental entitlements of land and livestock for women in rural Kano, northern Nigeria. *Environments*, 5(2), 26.

Veliu, A., Gessese, N., Ragasa, C. and Okali, C. (2009), *Gender analysis of aquaculture value chain in Northeast Vietnam and Nigeria*. World Bank.

World Bank. (2022), *Closing Gaps, Increasing Opportunities: A Diagnostic on Women's Economic Empowerment in Nigeria*. Washington, DC: World Bank. Available online: http://hdl.handle.net/10986/37225 (Accessed on 10 February 2024)

Zhang, B. (2016), *First Chinese-aid agriculture training held in Nigeria*, Xinhua. Available online: http://www.xinhuanet.com//english/2016-06/16/c_135442229.htm (Accessed on 5 January 2024)

保林. (2017), 探究尼日利亚与中国之间的经济信任：以农业合作为例[D]. 黑龙江：哈尔滨工业大学.

刘海方 & 皮埃尔. (2023), 大变局时代的国际发展援助——以中国援助布隆迪农业示范中心项目为例. 海外投资与出口信贷(1), 14–17.

中国一带一路网. (2022), 港媒："小而美"成为"一带一路"投资新偏好. Available online: https://www.yidaiyilu.gov.cn/p/266404.html (Accessed on 31 October 2023)

Appendices

Appendix 1

Table 1 List of agricultural training organized by GAWAL between 2016 and 2023

S/N	Year	Type of Agricultural Technical Trainining Progamme	Fund Provider
1	2014	Fish Cage Culture	West Africa Agricultural Productivity Programme in Nigeria(WAAPP Nigeria)
2	2014	Biogas Digester Construction	West Africa Agricultural Productivity Programme in Nigeria(WAAPP Nigeria)
3	2016	Comprehensive Agricultural Technical Training	Chinese Embassy in Nigeria
4	2017	Comprehensive Agricultural Technical Training	Chinese Ministry of Commerce
5	2017	Comprehensive Agricultural Technical Training	Chinese Embassy in Nigeria
6	2018	Comprehensive Agricultural Technical Training	Chinese Ministry of Commerce
7	2018	Comprehensive Agricultural Technical Training	Chinese Embassy in Nigeria
	2018	Cassava Processing and Pepper Cultivation Technology	Chinese Academy of Tropical Agricultural Science
8	2019	Comprehensive Agricultural Technical Training	Chinese Embassy in Nigeria
9	2023	Rice Cultivation	Nigerian Federal Ministry of Women Affairs
10	2023	Peanut Quality Evaluation and Processing Utilization Technology	Chinese Ministry of Science and Technology

Source: table graphed by the author from data presented by the company's representative.

Partner	Period	No. of Participants	No. of Female Participants
Niger and Lagos State governments	2 days*2 sites	300	Unkown
12 State Governments	20 days *12 sites	240	Unkown
Federal Ministry of Agriculture and Rual Development	7 days	40	15
Shandong Foreign Trade Vocational College	45 days	21	7
Federal Ministry of Agriculture and Rual Development	7 days	40	6
Shandong Foreign Trade Vocational College	45 days	103	18
Federal Ministry of Agriculture and Rual Development	7 days	40	15
Different agricultural organizations in Nigeria	2 days	74	15
Federal Ministry of Agriculture and Rual Development	7 days	40	5
	2 days	20	20
Institute of Food Science and Technology, Chinese Academy of Agricultural Sciences(IFST-CAAS) and Agricultural Research Council of Nigeria	1 day	70	Unkown

6

Implications of Security Agreements on Women, Peace, and Security in Solomon Islands

A Comparative Case Study on China-Solomon Islands Bilateral Security Cooperation and the Australia-Solomon Islands Bilateral Security Treaty

by Patricia Sango Pollard

1. Introduction

The year 2019 marked a turning point in the history of diplomatic relationships for Solomon Islands when the country forged a diplomatic relationship with China, letting go of a long-term relationship with Taiwan. This change in allegiance occurred against the backdrop of a country struggling to meet the needs of its citizens and a government seemingly eager to change the direction of the country. Suspicions of China's intentions to expand hegemony over the Pacific region through military might were heightened in March 2021 when China and Solomon Islands signed a security agreement.

Amidst the myriad areas that this development may impact, this research focuses on implications for women, peace, and security. The broad question that this research aims to answer is: What does the Solomon Islands-China security agreement mean for the situation of women in Solomon Islands and the role they play in peace building and security efforts, in comparison to a traditional development partner like Australia?

To answer this question, the author employed two methods, the first, a desk review on relevant literature including but not limited to policies, academic papers, news items, and online public forums and, the second, informal interviews with citizens in government, civil society representatives, and local women. Out of the fifteen people approached to be interviewed, only seven women responded, and given the current sensitivity of this development in the country, no further attempts were made to secure interviews with those who failed to respond. All respondents requested to remain anonymous. Interview questions (See Annex 1) were amended to suit the different groups of people.

The background section of this study brings Solomon Islands into focus, covering the country's recent troubles and need for external security assistance, the status of women and their role in peacebuilding and security efforts, and the 'diplomatic switch' from recognising Taiwan to China. The main body of the paper discusses the findings in the following areas: perceptions of the China-Solomon Islands security agreement and its implementation; concerns about the agreement's implications for women, peace, and security; comparisons with Australia's assistance for women, peace, and security considerations; and opportunities for advancing women's peace and security in Solomon Islands in the current geopolitical landscape.

It is important to note that 'gender' and 'gender equality', when used in this study, refer to a binary construct of the experiences of women and men.

2. Background

2.1 Solomon Islands

Solomon Islands is in the South Pacific Ocean, approximately 2,000 kilometres to the northeast of Australia, with a total land area of 28,466 square kilometres (SPC, 2023; DFAT, 2022). It has over 900 islands with nine island provinces. Honiara, the capital city, is on the largest island of Guadalcanal (SPC, 2023). With a tropical climate, the country is located in the coral triangle, one of the world's richest areas of marine biodiversity (Chapman, 2021). Sadly, this biodiversity is continuously being threatened by a legacy of reliance on logging activities. The country is also at the forefront of sea level rise and adverse impacts of climate change (Chapman, 2021).

Solomon Islands has a population of 744,407, with Melanesians being the majority group alongside Polynesians, Micronesians[1], Chinese and other Asians, and Europeans (SPC, 2021). Culturally, most Solomon Islanders live communally, with people identifying strongly with their kin groups and tribes, land, and provinces. Languages spoken by the majority of the population are English and

Pidgin[2] alongside about seventy main languages with numerous other local dialects (DFAT, 2022).

The country's economy relies heavily on the export of raw materials, namely from forestry, agriculture, and fisheries with recent new developments in the gold, bauxite, and nickel in the mining sector. In 2021, gross national product (GDP) per capita was $2,305 (USD) (CBSI, 2021). Eighty per cent of the population live in rural areas and are dependent on subsistence agriculture and fisheries. The country has a relatively small manufacturing sector, importing most goods and services (Gay, 2016: 3). There is heavy reliance on overseas aid from bilateral and multilateral partners for its budget and development projects.

Solomon Islands was a protectorate under the former British colony and gained independence in 1978, adopting the Westminster system of democracy with the British monarch as the head of state, represented by a governor general. The head of the government is the prime minister, who oversees a cabinet of twenty-three members who form the executive arm of the government. The country is politically demarcated into fifty constituencies that are represented by fifty national members of a unicameral parliament elected in a 'first-past-the-post voting system' (Ace Project, 2014).

Solomon Islands is a member of the United Nations and has diplomatic relationships with a significant number of countries. Important to the country are countries with historical significance, such as the United Kingdom, the United States, Australia, New Zealand, and Japan. The latter three are currently important development partners to the country through trade and development aid relationships. Australia, through its Department of Foreign Affairs and Trade (DFAT) is 'Solomon Islands' largest bilateral donor, re-shaping efforts in response to COVID19, and since 2017, [Australia has] provided over $800 million through their development program in the areas of justice, health, education, agriculture, governance, gender, and security' (DFAT, 2023).

2.2 Diplomatic Switch from Taiwan to the People's Republic of China

Solomon Islands benefited from a 36-years long diplomatic partnership with Taiwan starting in 1983, which ended when the country switched allegiance to the People's Republic of China (PRC) in 2019. The PRC views Taiwan as a 'renegade province' of China, and therefore maintains that there cannot be dual diplomatic recognition by any country (Maizland, 2023). Historically, Taiwan forged diplomatic relationships with several countries, including the Solomon

Islands, to garner support for recognition on the global stage, particularly at the United Nations. During their partnership, Taiwan provided multi-sectoral support to Solomon Islands, including discretionary funds to members of parliament through the Rural Constituency Development Fund (RDCF) (Nanau, 2015: 441-450). Meanwhile, China gradually became Solomon Island's largest export market, absorbing 65.2 per cent or $326 million worth of Solomon Islands' total exports in 2017 (Agorau and Zhang, 2019).

Speculations about a diplomatic switch from Taiwan to China culminated on 20 September 2019 when the government signed a joint communique with China. The switch was seen by members of the opposition group in parliament as conducted in haste with limited public consultation and inadequate adherence to parliamentary processes (Solomon Islands Parliamentary Opposition 2019). However, Prime Minister Manasseh Sogavare stated that this switch has put Solomon Islands on the 'right side of history' as China is a member of the United Nations, thereby acknowledging and supporting China's 'One China Policy' (Iroga, 2020). Among the areas of consensus reached by both countries was the advancement of the Belt and Road Initiative (OECD, 2018). This relationship has accelerated in recent years, with China's major support for the construction of the 2023 Pacific Games facility for the main sporting event of Pacific Island countries – to be hosted by Solomon Islands for the first time in late 2023 (SIG-GCU Press, 2021).

2.3 Political Instability, Violence, and Security Agreements

Solomon Islands has a history of political instability and civil unrest that continue to threaten its political stability and the maintenance of law and order. No-confidence votes are common and at times successful, with a swift change of government and disruption to policy implementation. Solomon Islands experienced a major conflict known as 'ethnic tensions' from 1998 to 2003 fuelled by deep-seated grievances due to claims of corruption, unequal distribution of resources, and land disputes among many others. This conflict was fought mainly by warring groups from two of the larger provinces, Guadalcanal and Malaita, and resulted in the loss of over 100 lives, human rights abuses, and the displacement of people. The unrest ended with the intervention by the Regional Assistance Mission to Solomon Islands (RAMSI) led by Australia with the participation of Pacific Forum member countries, impelling the peace process in 2003. Despite RAMSI's presence, a riot broke out in Honiara in 2006 that burned down the China Town. This riot was fuelled by dissatisfaction with the election of Snyder Rini to the prime minister's post due to allegations of his close ties with the Chinese community, a group blamed for taking over most economic activities in the country (Nautilus Institute, 2006).

RAMSI ended its operation in June 2017, and its departure was closely followed in August by the signing of a security treaty between Australia and Solomon Islands. The treaty allows Australian police, defence forces, associated civilian personnel, and a third state to deploy rapidly to Solomon Islands if the need arises (DFAT Canberra, 2017). A written copy of this treaty was made public, allowing citizens to understand its contents (DFAT, 2023).

In November 2021, another riot broke out, again burning down the China Town and other parts of Honiara. Disgruntled Malaitans requesting dialogue with the government in support of their provincial government's seeking greater autonomy for the province following the country's bilateral switch to China from Taiwan were denied, igniting the riot (Sade, 2021). The country then requested assistance from Australia under the 2017 Security Treaty, which was granted. However, in December 2021, a motion of no confidence was moved by the leader of the opposition against Prime Minister Manasseh Sogavare, with allegations of the latter receiving money from foreign loggers and China to maintain his support among members of parliament (N.A, 2022). The motion was defeated, Sogavare remained in power, and subsequently China and Solomon Islands signed the Solomon Islands-China security treaty in 2022.

2.4 Gender Equality, Women, Peace, and Security in Solomon Islands

Solomon Islands has a patriarchal system that continues to hamper women's progress in the 21st century. Although five of the main islands have matrilineal societies, this has not translated into roles of political and community leadership for women (Caso and Pollard, 2023). In the current parliament, there are only four women members in a house of fifty representatives. Women do not have equal say on benefits from resources on their land and property ownership. Despite incremental improvements, women continue to experience high rates of sexual and physical violence from intimate partners and are vulnerable to unemployment and death from childbirth (Caso and Pollard, 2023). During the ethnic tensions of 1998 to 2003, women experienced many atrocities, including rape, forced marriages, and lack of access to health and justice services (SIG-MWYCFA, 2017: 12). Similarly, the 2021 riots in the capital exacerbated risks to women's safety and caused disruption to livelihoods for women who depended on the informal sector.

Despite this, the country has a strong women's network and movement that advocates for gender equality and improvements in issues affecting women under the auspices of the government's Ministry of Women, Youth, Children and Family Affairs (MWYCFA), the National Council of Women (NCW), and other key civil society organizations. MWYCFA oversees the Gender and Equality and Women's Development (GEWD) and the Elimination of Violence Against Women and Girls (EVAWG) policies and the National Women and Girls Economic Empowerment Strategy (NWGEES). Solomon Islands is also party to the Convention on the Elimination of All Forms of Discrimination Against Women (CEDAW) and has adopted the Beijing Platform for Action and various other regional commitments that support improving the situation of women and girls. With significant assistance from development partners such as Australia, UN Women, and others, the government has been implementing policy actions under these frameworks throughout the country and gradually fostering change.

During the various crises, women have been instrumental in meditating the peace process by interacting with warring parties and law enforcement as well as campaigning through media. 'During the ethnic tension years, women drew on both kastom and Christian doctrines in performing peacemaking roles, which included invoking traditional restrictions (*tambu*) to mediate and exert pressure on militants to disarm' (SIG-MWYCFA, 2017: 12). Similarly, during the 2006 riots, the women's network banded together and used public media to demand change. However, the importance of women's contributions to peacebuilding was never completely recognised. Negotiations to settle the ethnic tensions relegated women who have been dedicated to peace efforts to observers. Similarly, RAMSI did not provide women with adequate room to contribute to the process during their time. An illustration of this occurred when RAMSI personnel advised notable woman Hilda Kari not to dialogue with rioters during the 2006 unrest (George, 2018: 1340). In 2015, through the then Ministry of National Unity, Reconciliation and Peace (MNURP) the government launched the Solomon Islands National Peace Building Policy. This too failed to give significance to women's protection and their contributions to peacebuilding (SIG-MTGPEA, 2020).

These experiences gave rise to the government MWYCFA's endorsement of the Solomon Islands Women Peace and Security (WPS) National Action Plan (NAP) 2017-2021 in 2017, with major support from DFAT, UN Women, and other partners. This strategy drew on both CEDAW General Recommendation number thirty and UN Security Council Resolution 1325 (UNSCR 1325), which calls for recognition of women's full and equal participation in peace building processes (SIG-MWYCFA, 2017). The strategy paved the way for engagement with women and consideration of their rights in issues concerning their own security and in matters of national security.

The next section of the paper will scrutinise perceptions of the China-Solomon Islands security agreement and how it relates to women, peace, and security. It also makes comparisons with similar engagements with Australia, a traditional partner, and highlights opportunities from the China-Solomon Islands security agreement and the Australian-Solomon Islands bilateral security treaty.

3. China-Solomon Islands Bilateral Security Cooperation and the Australia-Solomon Islands Bilateral Security Treaty

3.1 Perceptions of the China -Solomon Islands Security Agreement and Its Implementation

The specific date for the adoption of the China-Solomon Islands security agreement has never been fully disclosed. A leaked copy of the agreement published on Twitter indicated that the agreement allows Solomon Islands to request the 'deployment of Chinese police, armed police, military personnel, and other law enforcement forces to assist in maintaining social order and humanitarian assistance when consented, also allowing for Chinese ships to visit and transition in the country, and allowing relevant Chinese forces to protect Chinese personnel and projects in the country as needed' (ABC, 2022).

In May 2022, China's Ministry of Foreign Affairs released a statement stating the agreement expounds on three principles, to respect the national sovereignty of Solomon Islands, to maintain social stability, and to operate in parallel with regional security agreements and other security arrangements that the country has already entered into with other countries. Moreover, the permanent secretary of the Solomon Islands Ministry of Foreign Affairs and External Trade (MFAET) stated that the agreement aims to address internal security threats, and the impacts of climate change as opposed to external threats and that it will be triggered only as a last resort (Kekea, 2022). Nevertheless, the final text of the agreement is yet to be made public.

The regional and international community commented on the non-transparent manner in which the agreement transpired, its potential to accommodate a Chinese military naval base in the country, and the expansion of Chinese communist ideology into a region with predominantly democratic systems. The possibility of a naval base was vehemently denied by both China and Solomon Islands on multiple platforms. Australia reacted by increasing its security and defence assistance to Solomon Islands, where it has already maintained a military presence since the 2021 riots (DFAT-Minister for Foreign Affairs, 2022). The United States also returned focus to the country, re-establishing its embassy after having closed it thirty years ago. The United States and Australia also made official visits to brief the Solomon Islands government on their latest security pact, the tripartite submarine deal between the United States, United Kingdom, and Australia (AUKUS) (Doherty and Hurst, 2023). In response, both Solomon Islands and China raised concerns about the risk of nuclear proliferation and threats to peace and stability in the region.

Locally, however, the China-Solomon Islands security agreement remains a mystery that only the governments of both China and Solomon Islands are privy to. According to informal interviews carried out in February 2023, Solomon Islanders are not aware of what the security agreement fully entails as the final provisions were never disclosed, unlike the 2017 Solomon Islands-Australia security treaty. The secrecy around the contents of the agreement has raised fears of the threat of Solomon Islands succumbing to China's communist ideologies and therefore undermining democratic processes, principles, and institutions (Solomon Islands National Council of Women (NCW), CEDAW Report, 2023). An example of the threat to freedom of expression was seen when the media was barred from covering the Chinese delegation's meeting with the Solomon Islands government in the wake of the security agreement in May 2022 (International Federation of Journalists, 2022).

Among other sentiments expressed was that there was no significant need for the security agreement as the country has no external security threats but rather socio-economic problems such as high unemployment, poor delivery of goods and services, poor governance and law enforcement, and an increase in corruption, which could be better addressed through sound policy and legislative approaches (Interviewee, 2023). Similarly, there is the view that the provision of guns and other tactical training to police to quell unrest may also provide an effective means of suppressing citizens who demand accountability from their government in a country where public protests and demonstrations have already been heavily policed and routinely suppressed in recent times (Aqorau, 2022).

Another interviewee (2023) voiced that the security agreement may be a means of legitimising elite capture, as well as providing protection for politicians and their Chinese cronies from burgeoning resistance among Solomon Islanders as there was no effective consultation with the public. However, other interviewees (2023) have argued that the security agreement and subsequent capacity building of police and defence in the country is timely to deal with ongoing unrest that has resulted in the loss of lives and economic activity. Altogether, the security agreement and subsequent developments have triggered much speculation among citizens as seen by reactions to a post by Afuga on 18 April 2022 on the Yumi Tok Tok Forum, a Facebook platform that discusses national issues in Solomon Islands.

3.2 Concerns about the China-Solomon Islands Security Agreement's Implications for Women, Peace, and Security

The Solomon Islands Women Peace and Security NAP 2017-2021 (WPS NAP) clearly outlines key pillars to support the inclusion of women in peace building and security. These are:

> (1) Participation – Women's participation, representation, and decision making in peace and security are expanded at all levels.
> (2) Protection – Women's human rights are protected, and women are secure from sexual and gender-based violence.
> (3) Prevention – Solomon Islands actively prevents conflict and violence against women and girls.
> (4) Recovery, Rehabilitation, and Reconciliation – Women's and girls' priorities and rights are reflected in all development and peace building.
> SIG-MWYCFA, 2017:7

In 2020, the Solomon Islands government launched the National Security Strategy (NSS), which mainstreams gender equality and respects all the pillars of the Solomon Islands WPS NAP (SIG, 2020:22).

Like Solomon Islands, China is a state party to CEDAW and has been providing periodic reports on the 'achievements and progress that China has made in promoting gender equality and protecting women's rights' (Cai and Yu, 2022:23). China has also established frameworks to combat gender-based violence and it reports on its observance of its human rights obligations at UN human rights mechanisms including the universal periodic review (UPR) (Cai and Yu, 2022:20). Recently, China's State Council unveiled the outline of development plans for women and children over the next decade (2021-2030), which cover women's issues in health, education, and the economy (The State

Council, PRC, 2023). Since 2015, China has been committed to advancing the *UN Security Council Resolution (UNSCR) 1325,* making progress in the gradual reduction of military expenditure, disarmament, increase in the number of women peacekeepers deployed under UN command, and engagement in combating the international trafficking of women and girls (Guo and Han 2022: 284-292).

Despite the above commitments, there was no consultation with key organizations representing women in the framing and development of the China-Solomon Islands security agreement. The key ministries responsible for the agreement such as the Ministry of Foreign Affairs and External Trade (MFAET) and the Ministry of Ministry of Police, National Security and Correctional Services (MPNSCS) did not consult with the Ministry of Women, Youth, Children and Family Affairs (MWYCFA) to obtain their input, indicating a lack of consideration to consult women despite the adoption of national frameworks that prescribe this. Neither is China's commitment to the WPS translated into this undertaking with Solomon Islands. In the wake of the signing of the deal, the National Council of Women (NCW), the umbrella body for women's NGOs in the country, together with Transparency Solomon Islands (TSI), raised concerns about the ambiguous way the agreement was negotiated with no inputs from women, youth, children, or people with disabilities (Podokolo, 2022). These concerns correspond to issues raised by Cai and Yu (2022: 23) of Chinese foreign policies sometimes trading off women's rights for other priority issues in the name of their 'non-interference principle'.

Similarly, the lack of consultation with women also undermines the important historical legacy that Solomon Islands women have in peace building and security efforts both during the conflicts and in the post-conflict period. The act repeats past practices and solidifies the view that women in the Solomon Islands are always excluded from decision-making. For example, NCW was summoned by government representatives and discouraged from engaging with the media regarding the security agreement (Interviewee, 2022). This also displays nuances of the suppression of the freedom of expression, a practice that is strongly associated with China (Amnesty International, 2022).

Another cause for concern is the effective militarisation of the police by supplying them with guns and ammunition. Australia responded to China's assistance to the Royal Solomon Islands Police Force (RSIPF) by delivering sixty MK18 rifles and thirteen vehicles, some of which will be used in a new mobile protection unit for VIPs (Maka'a and Wright, 2022). Solomon Island's recent history has shown that guns in the hands of both police and civilians resulted in atrocities committed against citizens that severely impacted women and children. During the ethnic tensions in the late 1990s, 'police officers of various units [were] accused of human rights violations' (Amnesty International, 2000: 9-16). Women and girls were raped at gunpoint by militias in various places during the breakdown of law and order (Fangalasuu et al, 2011: 19-28).

The firearms amnesty in Solomon Islands during the early years of RAMSI's operation had seen the surrender and destruction of nearly 4000 weapons. Recently, the RSIPF accelerated its community policing programmes based on building relationships with communities to help maintain peace and security and prevent unlawful activities (Denoon, 2014; RSIPF, 2016). The re-introduction of guns is concerning, raising fears both within the country and abroad that state-sanctioned use of guns may be aimed at suppressing citizens, and atrocities could again be committed. The current leader of the opposition raised concerns that Solomon Islands may be on a path to becoming a militarised state while the country's real problem is lack of sound economic policies, which the acquisition of guns cannot solve (Kusu, 2022). However, Prime Minister Sogavare applauded the assistance, claiming that it is a responsibility to 'protect the lives and welfare, liberty and property of all people in this country' (Maka'a and Wright, 2021).

The China-Solomon Islands security agreement has diverted attention from pressing problems affecting the country, including women's peace and security. Political wrangling between the national government, the opposition group, and some provincial governments and the geopolitical competition that has ensued have dominated public discourse, overshadowing poor health care and education services, deteriorating and deficient infrastructure in rural areas to support the movement of people and markets, mass urban migration, and unemployment, all of which exacerbate problems for women and marginalized groups. A common theme that has emerged from this research is that women associate the country's engagement with China with Pacific Games infrastructure development and police operations, with limited awareness of wider implications. On 7 July 2023, the social media platform Yumi Tok Tok Forum raised concerns that 500 million Solomon Islands dollars (SBD) from China towards building of the Pacific Games complex could be a concessional loan as opposed to a grant, which had been the general understanding. Its status was never fully disclosed by the government media, raising fears that future generations may bear the impacts of the repayments. Moreover, comments were made about the publicity surrounding kung fu trainings carried out by Chinese police with women and children in surrounding communities, asking if this is part of the implementation of the security agreement (Interviewee, 2023). In a country where the rate of domestic violence is sixty-four per cent for women between fifteen and forty-nine years of age (SurfAid, 2021), such training seemingly empowers women, but it also diverts attention from entrenched prejudices against women by perpetrators of violence against women. Furthermore, women's reproductive health remains unprioritised; there are high maternal mortality rates, with cervical and breast cancers the current leading causes of death for women. Maternal mortality in the Solomon Islands is seventeen times higher than in Australia and deaths from cervical cancer are eleven times the rate of Australia (SurfAid, 2021). There has been very slow traction in government responses to these problems.

While Solomon Islands has become a focus of geopolitical rivalries in the region because of its new relationship with China, it is useful to look at how a traditional partner like Australia, which is aligned with the US in its rivalry with China, has engaged with women in its security assistance to Solomon Islands. The next section discusses this.

3.3 Comparison with Australia in Women's, Peace, and Security Considerations

Until 2021, Australia had committed $34.8 million towards progress in gender equality in Solomon Islands, which was channelled through regional and UN agencies, the government, and civil society organizations (DFAT, 2016). In the years that followed, Australia's assistance to women largely targeted initiatives focused on the elimination of violence and promotion of women in leadership and decision-making spaces under the Pacific Women Shaping Pacific Development (now replaced by Pacific Women Lead) (Caso and Pollard, 2023: 3).

Currently, Australia's commitment to gender equality in the Indo-Pacific region[3] covers 'ending sexual and gender-based violence, advancing women's economic empowerment, enhancing women's leadership, strengthening women's and girls' access to and influence on essential services, including in health and education, and implementing the Women, Peace and Security agenda' (DAFT 2023). Australia's National Action Plan on Women, Peace and Security 2022-2031 includes four important targets, namely:

(1) Supporting women's and girls' meaningful participation and needs in conflict prevention and peace processes;
(2) Reducing sexual and gender-based violence;

(3) Supporting resilience, crisis response and security, law, and justice sector efforts to meet the needs and rights of all women and girls; and
(4) Demonstrating leadership and accountability for the women, peace, and security agenda.

DFAT, 2021

This NAP will be implemented through departments' and agencies' programmes in partner countries.

Australia has prided itself as Solomon Islands' leading partner in implementing commitments to gender equality and advancing WPS efforts. However, Australia's women's peace and security commitments on paper did not translate into the 2017 security treaty with Solomon Islands, which made no reference to UNSCR 1325 or to the Solomon Islands National Action Plan on WPS (Caso and Pollard, 2023: 3). In these respects, Australia's approach showed exact similarities to China's. According to an interviewee, the Australia-led intervention in the 2021 riots did not include a gender focus, either. While Australia's commitment to WPS can be seen to support policy formulation addressing domestic violence, promoting women to key leadership positions within the police force, and empowering women's agency to contribute to peace and security working through agencies, Australia still falls short when it comes to bringing women to the table to discuss matters of military security. With the controversial weapons assistance to the police that was introduced without consultations, Australia has also relegated women to the sidelines. Australia's approach is congruent with China's in securing its bilateral security agreement with Solomon Islands.

The final section of this paper will discuss some possible opportunities that might be pursued under the China-Solomon Islands security agreement.

4. Opportunities for Advancing Women, Peace, and Security

The preceding discussions explained at length some underlying issues experienced by Solomon Islands that may have led to the country forging diplomatic ties with China and subsequently signing a security agreement. As reactions to this agreement escalated into a geopolitical tussle between China and Western countries including Australia, New Zealand, the United States, and the United Kingdom, its impacts on pre-existing women's peace and security commitments were seen in how little consideration was given to including women's voices in this development. However, there may be opportunities that

Solomon Islands could utilise to amplify women's voices in WPS and offer an alternative foreign policy guideline – one that works to advance social imperatives and contributes to equitable, gender-sensitive, ethical, and sustainable development.

This session will discuss this in four areas: (1) inclusion of women in discussions on state security and security agreements; (2) forging and strengthening a positive relationship with China to advance women's development; (3) benefiting from increased geopolitical interest in the region by securing support to address root causes of dissent in the country; and (4) strengthening national security policies to ensure optimal outcomes for the country in the face of increasing instability in the region.

4.1 Inclusion of Women in Security Agreement Discussions

Firstly, women in Solomon Islands should continue to demand meaningful participation in discussions regarding the implementation of the country's security agreements. The Solomon Islands NSS and the WPS NAP provide opportunities for women to hold the government accountable for implementing its provisions, allowing women's voices to be heard at the state security level. Similarly, China's and Australia's own frameworks to advance gender equality and their WPS NAPs also provide an opportunity for Solomon Islands women to seek and gain support for refining and implementing their own WPS NAP. In addition, China and Australia could be pressed to adopt the feminist foreign policy approach of 'an instrument of peacebuilding in the hands of states that promotes gender justice and the empowerment of women as prerequisites of peace' (Caso and Pollard, 2023: 4-5). This approach allows for decisions to be made taking into consideration their impacts on women and other marginalised groups, thus placing less emphasis on a militaristic approach. For their legacy in peace building efforts in Solomon Islands, women should be regarded as knowledge holders and their contributions to key decisions around security should not be overlooked.

4.2 Strengthening the Relationship with China to Enhance Women's Development

Despite the concerning discourses surrounding the signing of the security agreements with China and Australia, both these undertakings may provide opportunities to pursue additional assistance to enhance economic benefits and improve infrastructure for women. In complementing Australia's current commitments to women's development in Solomon Islands and learning from their rise to being a major player in the global economy, China could provide targeted advice and assistance for policy implementation that generates opportunities in employment, business creation, and access to credit and financial services for women. The Chinese embassy in Honiara has held meetings with women representatives from government and CSOs to introduce the mandate of the All-China Women's Federation with the possibility of creating partnerships (Interviewee, 2023). Similarly, large scale investment in infrastructure and transport systems will make it easier for people, especially women, to access important services such as health, education, justice, markets, and other key services. In addition, women can also benefit from China's digital technological advancement to gain protection from new threats such as cyber-bullying and trafficking and from China's advancement in medicine to support women's health facilities and similar areas.

4.3 Benefiting from the Geopolitical Situation

Since the diplomatic switch to China and the subsequent security agreement, the Solomon Islands as well as the Pacific region has become the focus of interest from other world powers. Both Australia and New Zealand have strengthened their multisectoral support, including committing multimillion dollar support for the Pacific Games (SIG, 2022). The United States and the United Kingdom have revitalised decades of partnership with the Solomon Islands, which was seen in the United States' new investments and the reopening of their embassy; similarly, the United Kingdom also expanded areas of bilateral cooperation, including new prospects in trade (SIG-MFAET, 2023). With these developments come commitments that offer opportunities for the country to change for the better. The government maintains a 'friends to all, enemy to none policy' that takes maximal advantage of the current landscape (SIG-MFAET, 2022). The country could use this opportunity to leverage support to address significant development needs in health, infrastructure, education, investments and job creation, and general support for social development that may help address the root causes of unrest in the country. In terms of security, the government could potentially broaden its focus to cover the range of security risks facing the country, as outlined in the NSS. These include climate change, health security, security from foreign interference, border security, ethnic conflicts, transnational crimes, cyber threats, terrorism, land disputes, political and social instability, pest infestation, corruption, unemployment, the influx of foreigners, environmental security, and economic security (SIG, 2020). Nevertheless, this needs to be conducted with serious caution whilst including all community groups, including women, and showing respect for Solomon Islands' democratic values, principles, and institutions.

4.4 Strengthening the Implementation of Security Policies

Since the enactment of key security policies such as the WPS NAP and the NSS, the country has faced new issues in security that emerged from new security agreements and the supplying of arms to the RSIPF. The country should now revise these policies to guide this new undertaking to ensure benefits to and the protection of citizens. The WPS NAP (2017-2021) will be undergoing review, and it is imperative that provisions to ensure women's proactive participation in and consideration by state security are included. Similarly, with the current supply of firearms to police, growing geopolitical tensions, and concerns about arms proliferation in the region, Solomon Islands should restrict the use of force and firearms by law enforcement officials to prevent misuse, including the targeting of citizens lawfully exercising their right to protest. The country should also be steadfast in meeting its obligations under international and regional treaties and agreements that recognise non-proliferation, such as the Rarotonga Treaty on the South Pacific Nuclear Free Zone and the Comprehensive Nuclear Test Ban Treaty (CTBT) (SIG-MFAET, 2016). Furthermore, the country's conduct in this area should reflect the interests of its citizens and not undermine the sovereignty of the state.

5. Conclusion

Scrutinizing the China-Solomon Islands security agreement through the lens of WPS reveals that Solomon Islands women have not reconciled this undertaking with how it may impact their daily lives but rather have raised concerns about the way it was conducted. That is, there was no inclusion of women in state security discussions despite policies that allow for such, there was no acknowledgement of women's leadership in peacebuilding and security efforts, and the supply of military weapons is raising fears of guns being used against citizens, as was experienced in the past. While Australia remains the most significant bilateral partner of Solomon Islands, its recent militaristic approach as seen in both its militarisation of Solomon Islands police and its engagement in the AUKUS security pact remains a concern. Solomon Islands women and the country could explore ways to potentially benefit from this situation by holding the government and diplomatic partners accountable in implementing their gender equality and WPS frameworks, bringing women to the discussion table, and pursuing cooperation with China to advance women's development in consultation with women's organizations. With the current interest from world powers and risks of the militaristic approach being taken, Solomon Islands must tread carefully to ensure that its most vulnerable, including women and children, are not further marginalised. Whether the Solomon Islands will be able to carve its own path in the context of likely-to-intensify geopolitical competition and tensions within the Pacific region remains to be seen.

Acknowledgement

My sincere appreciation to certain individuals who have provided their invaluable insights to this study. Your contribution is highly appreciated.

Notes

1 A mixture of English and local dialects. Solomon Islands Pijin is one of the three Melanesian pidgins (along with Tok Pisin spoken in Papua New Guinea, and Bislama spoken in Vanuatu) that are, more or less directly, the offshoots of the Pacific trade jargon of the early 19th century.
2 Micronesians in the Solomon Islands are descendants of I-Kiribati people who were resettled in the Solomon Islands under the British Colonial Administration in the 1950s. The main settlements are in Wagina and Titiana Islands in the western Solomons (Tabe, 2011:20).
3 The Indo-Pacific region – a new geo-strategic designation by the US in its strategy of countering China. US has a relationship with Australia, India, and Japan under the Quadrilateral Security Dialogue (QUAD) that focuses on maritime cooperation, and tackling security, economic, and health issues in the Indo-Pacific region. This relationship has recently intensified to counter China's interests in the region (Smith, 2021).

References

ABC. (2022), 'China and Solomon Islands sign security pact'. [online] *Radio New Zealand*. Available online: https://www.rnz.co.nz/news/world/465534/china-and-solomon-islands-sign-security-pact (Accessed on 3 March 2023)

ACE Project. (2014), *ESD Toolkit: Introduction to Education for Sustainable Development*. [online] Available onlinr: https://aceproject.org/main/english/es/esd01.htm (Accessed on 20 April 2023)

Afuga. B. (18 April 2023), *Sogavare's military deal with China-Secrecy*. [Facebook Post] Yumi Tok Tok Forum. 2nd April 2023.

Amnesty International. (2000), *Solomon Islands: A forgotten conflict*. AI Index: ASA 43/05/00. [online], pp. 9-16. Available online: https://www.amnesty.org/en/documents/asa43/005/2000/en/ (Accessed on 5 May 2023)

Amnesty International. (2022), *China*. Available online: https://www.amnesty.org/en/location/asia-and-the-pacific/east-asia/china/report-china/ (Accessed on 21 April 2021)

Aqorau, T. (2022), 'Rethinking Solomon Islands Security'. *Devpolicy Blog*. Available online: https://devpolicy.org/rethinking-solomon-islands-security-20220404/ (Accessed on 4 May 2023)

Aqorau, T. and Zhang, D. (2019), 'Diplomatic switch in Solomon Islands: Relations with Taiwan or China'. [online]. *Lowy Institute – The Interpreter*. Available online: https://www.lowyinstitute.org/the-interpreter/diplomatic-switch-solomon-islands-relations-taiwan-or-china (Accessed on 4 May 2023)

Australian Department of Foreign Affairs and Trade (DFAT). (n.d.), *Australia-Solomon Islands Bilateral Security Treaty*. Available online: https://www.dfat.gov.au/geo/solomon-islands/bilateral-security-treaty (Accessed on 20 April 2023)

Australian Government Department of Foreign Affairs and Trade (DFAT). (2022), *Solomon Islands Country Brief*. Available online: https://www.dfat.gov.au/geo/solomon-islands/solomon-islands (Accessed on 28 November 2022)

Australian Department of Foreign Affairs and Trade (DFAT). (2021), *Australia's National Action Plan on Women, Peace and Security 2021-2031*. Available online: https://www.dfat.gov.au/sites/default/files/australias-national-action-plan-on-women-peace-and-security-2021-2031.pdf. (Accessed on 5 May 2023)

Cai, Y. and Li, Y. (2021), 'Global China from a Gender Lens'. *IDEES*. No. 52. *China before a World in crisis*. Available online: https://revistaidees.cat/en/global-china-from-a-gender-lens/ (Accessed on 2 May 2023)

Cai, Y. and Yu, Y. (2022), *An Analytical Framework on the Gender Impact of China's Global Engagement in the global South*. DAWN Discussion Paper #47. Suva: DAWN. pp.20-23. Available online: https://dawnnet.org/wp-content/uploads/2023/02/20230202-China-Analytical-Framework.pdf. (Accessed on 4 June 2023)

Caso, F and Pollard, P. (2023), 'Peacebuilding and feminist foreign policy: Can Australia rebuild relations with Solomon Islands?' [online] *Australian feminist foreign policy coalition:* issue number 11. pp. 1-4. Available online: https://iwda.org.au/resource/peacebuilding-and-feminist-foreign-policy/ (Accessed on 9 April 2023)

Central Bank of Solomon Islands (CBSI). (2021), *Annual Reports*. p. 2. Available online: https://www.cbsi.com.sb/publications/annual-report/ (Accessed on 20 April 2023)

Chapman, A. et al. (2021), 'Climate Risk, Country Profile: Solomon Islands'. Washington: World Bank Group, DC. pp. 1-2. Available online: https://climateknowledgeportal.

worldbank.org/sites/default/files/country-profiles/15822-WB_Solomon%20Islands%20Country%20Profile-WEB.pdf(Accessed on 4 February 2023)

DFAT Canberra. (2017), *Agreement between the Government of Australia and the Government of Solomon Islands Concerning the Basis for Deployment of Police, Armed Forces, and other Personnel to Solomon Islands.* Available online: http://www.austlii.edu.au/au/other/dfat/treaties/ATS/2018/14.html (Accessed in December 2022)

DFAT. (2021), *Making Australia Stronger and More Influential in a Contested World.* Available online: https://www.foreignminister.gov.au/minister/penny-wong/media-release/making-australia-stronger-and-more-influential-contested-world (Accessed on 17 April 2023)

Denoon, D. (2014), Solomon's guns amnesty a stunning achievement. *Lowy Institute-The Interpreter.* Available online: https://www.lowyinstitute.org/the-interpreter/solomons-gun-amnesty-stunning-achievement (Accessed on 21 April 2023)

Doherty, B. and Hurst, D. (2023), What is the AUKUS submarine deal and what does it mean? *The Guardian.* Available online: https://www.theguardian.com/world/2023/mar/14/what-is-the-aukus-submarine-deal-and-what-does-it-mean-the-key-facts (Accessed on 2 May 2023)

Fangalasuu et al. (2011), *Herem kam: story blong mifala olketa mere. Women's Submission to the Solomon Islands Truth and Reconciliation Commi*ssion. Available online: https://www.ictj.org/sites/default/files/Solomon-Islands-TRC-Submission-Sept-2011.pdf (Accessed on 21 April 2023)

Gay, D. (2016), *Productive Capacity and Trade in the Solomon Islands.* United Nations Department of Economic and Social Affairs. CDP Background Paper No. 31. pp.5-7. Available online :https://www.un.org/development/desa/dpad/wp-content/uploads/sites/45/publication/CDP-bp-2016-31.pdf (Accessed on 4 February 2023)

George, N. (2018), Gender, Security and Australia's Pacific Pivot: Stalled Impetus and Shallow Roots, *Australian Journal of International Affairs*, 73 (3) pp. 213-18.

George, N. (2021). Solomon Islands deployment: Australia must meet obligations to women. [online]. *Lowy Institute – The Interpreter.* Available online: https://www.lowyinstitute.org/the-interpreter/solomon-islands-deployment-australia-must-meet-obligations-women (Accessed on 2 April 2023)

Guo, Y. and Han, Z. (2022), Achieving sustaining peace through preventive diplomacy. *Asian Regional Cooperation Studies.* Vol. 6. pp. 284-292 Available online https://www.worldscientific.com/doi/epdf/10.1142/11868 (Accessed on 12 May 2023)

International Federation of Journalists. (2019), *Solomon Islands media restricted from attending China ministerial visit.* Available online: https://www.ifj.org/media-centre/news/detail/category/press-releases/article/solomon-islands-media-restricted-from-attending-china-ministerial-visit.html (Accessed on 18 April 2023)

Iroga. R. (2020), China switch puts Solomon Islands on the right side of history. *Solomon Islands Business Magazine Online.* Available online: https://sbm.sb/china-switch-puts-si-on-the-right-side-of-history/# (Accessed on 20 August 2023)

Kabutaulaka, T. (2022), China-Solomon Islands Security Agreement and Competition for Influence in Oceania. *Georgetown Journal of International Affairs.* Available online: https://gjia.georgetown.edu/2022/12/02/china-solomon-islands-security-agreement-and-competition-for-influence-in-oceania/ (Accessed on 6 May 2023)

Kekea, G. (2022), We needed China deal to protect 'domestic security', says key Solomon Islands official. *The Guardian.* Available online: https://www.theguardian.com/world/2022/jun/14/we-needed-china-deal-to-protect-domestic-security-says-key-solomon-islands-official (Accessed on 3 June 2023)

Kusu, F. (2022), Wale slams Australia's guns supply to Solomon Islands. *Solomon Islands Broadcasting Cooperation (SIBC) Online.* Available online: https://www.sibconline.com.sb/wale-slams-australias-guns-supply-to-solomon-islands/ (Accessed on 2 June 2023)

Ligaiula, P. (2022), We needed China deal to protect domestic security, says key Solomon Islands official. *Pacific Islands News Association.* Available online: https://pina.com.fj/2022/06/14/we-needed-china-deal-to-protect-domestic-security-says-key-solomon-islands-official/ (Accessed on 23 April 2023)

Maka'a, G. and Wright, S. (2021), China, Australia give equipment to Solomon Islands police as rivalry escalates. *Radio Free Asia.* Available online: https://www.rfa.org/english/news/pacific/solomons-11042022133221.html#:~:text=China%20and%20U.S.%20ally%20Australia,chaos%20only%20two%20decades%20ago (Accessed on 21 April 2023)

Maizland, L. (2023), *Why China-Taiwan relations are so tense.* Council on foreign relations. Available online: https://www.cfr.org/backgrounder/china-taiwan-relations-tension-us-policy-biden (Accessed on 19 August 2023)

Ministry of Foreign Affairs of the People's Republic of China. (2022), '*China urges Japan to adopt a responsible attitude on nuclear waste disposal in the Pacific*'. Available online: https://www.fmprc.gov.cn/eng/zxxx_662805/202205/t20220526_10693195.html (Accessed on 26 May 2023)

Nanau, G. (2015), *Moving Beyond the Musical Chairs of Solomon Islands Politics. The Round Table,* 104(4), pp. 441-450. Available online: http://repository.usp.ac.fj/8581/1/moving-beyond-the-musical-chairs-of-solomon-islands-politics-20151110.pdf (Accessed on 20 April 2023)

N. A. (2022), Solomon Islands: Sogavare defeats no-confidence motion. *Radio New Zealand.* Available online: https://www.rnz.co.nz/international/pacific-news/457372/solomon-islands-sogavare-defeats-no-confidence-motion (Accessed on 3 April 2023)

Organization for Economic Cooperation and Development (OECD). (2018), *China's Belt and Road Initiative in the global trade, investment and finance landscape.* Available online: https://www.oecd.org/finance/Chinas-B https://sbm.sb/china-switch-puts-si-on-the-right-side-of-history/≤t-and-Road-Initiative-in-the-global-trade-investment-and-finance-landscape.pdf (Accessed on 24 April 2023)

Podokolo, M. (2022), 'Women leaders want security treaty cancelled'. *Island Sun Online.* Available online: https://theislandsun.com.sb/women-leaders-want-security-treaty-cancelled/ (Accessed on 23 August 2023)

Royal Solomon Islands Police Force (RSIPF). (2016), 'RSIPF Working with the Community to Prevent Unlawful Activities'. *Royal Solomon Islands Police Force-Polis blo iu*. Available online: https://www.rsipf.gov.sb/?q=node/2345#:~:text=Police%20work%20together%20with%20the,in%20maintaining%20law%20and%20order (Accessed on 21 April 2023)

Sade. S, (2021), 'Premier Suidani Calls for Self-Autonomy for Malaita'. *Solomon Times Online*. Available online: https://www.solomontimes.com/news/premier-suidani-calls-for-self-autonomy-for-malaita/11345 (Accessed on 2 December 2022)

SIG. (2020), *Solomon Islands National Peacebuilding Policy*. Available online: https://solomons.gov.sb/wp-content/uploads/2020/02/SI-National-Peacebuilding-Policy.pdf (Accessed on 16 February 2023)

SIG. (2021), *Solomon Islands and People's Republic of China Deepened Relations with the Signing of More Development Cooperation*. Available online: https://solomons.gov.sb/solomon-islands-and-peoples-republic-of-china-deepened-relations-with-the-signing-of-more-development-cooperation/ (Accessed on 5 February 2023)

SIG-Ministry of Women, Youth, Children, and family Affairs (MWYCFA). (n.d.), *Solomon Islands Women Peace and Security, National Action Plan 2017-2021*. Honiara: *SIG*. p. 12. Available online: https://solomons.gov.sb/wp-content/uploads/2020/02/Women-Peace-and-Security-National-Action-Plan-2017-2020.pdf (Accessed on 5 November 2022)

SIG-Government Communication Press. (2022), *Sogavare Welcomes Australian SPG2023 Assistance. Solomon Islands Government*. Available online: https://solomons.gov.sb/sogavare-welcomes-australian-spg2023-assistance/ (Accessed on 4 June 2023)

Smith, S. (2021), 'The Quad in the Indo-Pacific: What to Know'. *Council on Foreign Relations*. Available online: https://www.cfr.org/in-brief/quad-indo-pacific-what-know (Accessed on 28 August 2023)

Solomon Islands Government Ministry of Foreign Affairs and External Trade (SIG-MFAET). (2016), *Solomon Islands Ratifies Comprehensive Nuclear-Test-Ban Treaty*. Available online: http://www.mfaet.gov.sb/media-center/press-releases/foreign-affairs-news/383-solomon-islands-ratifies-comprehensive-nuclear-test-ban-treaty.html (Accessed on 24 April 2023)

Solomon Islands Parliamentary Opposition. (15 September 2019), '*Kenilorea disappointed with PM saying there's no need to rush switch decision*'. [Facebook Post] Solomon Islands Parliamentary Opposition Group Page. (Accessed on 5 June 2023)

Solomon Islands Government (SIG). (2021), *High-Level Visits Reflect 'Friends to All, Enemy to None' Policy*. Available online: https://solomons.gov.sb/high-level-visits-reflect-friends-to-all-enemy-to-none-policy/ (Accessed on 24 April 2023)

SPC. (n.d.), *Solomon Islands Statistics. Pacific Community*. Available online: https://sdd.spc.int/sb (Accessed on 5 March 2023)

Surfaid. (2021), *Sexual and reproductive health for women in Solomon Islands*. Available online: https://surfaid.org/surfaid/posts/sexual-and-reproductive-health-for-women-in-solomon-islands (Accessed on 28 May 2023)

Tabe, T. (2011), *A study of the I-Kiribati community in Solomon Islands*. University of Hawaii at Manoa. Available online: https://scholarspace.manoa.hawaii.edu/server/api/core/bitstreams/71c69704-c293-4bba-a258-a33236249612/content (Accessed on 7 March 2023

The Island Sun. (2023), 'Women Leaders Want Security Treaty Cancelled'. *The Island Sun*. Available online: https://theislandsun.com.sb/women-leaders-want-security-treaty-cancelled/ (Accessed on 20 April 2023)

Washington DC. (7 July 2023), 'Solomon Islands Stadium – gift or concessional loan'. [Facebook Post]. *Yumi Tok Tok Forum,* 4 June 2023.

Xinhua. (2021), *China outlines development of women, children*. The State Council of the People's Republic of China. Available online: http://english.www.gov.cn/policies/latestreleases/202109/27/content_WS61516ea9c6d0df57f98e0f0f.html (Accessed on 20 April 2023)

Annex 1. Interview questions

1. What do you know about the China-Solomon Islands Security Agreement? Any regional and international implications?
2. What is your observation of the implementation of this Agreement across government/ by relevant government sectors?
3. Are you aware of any provisions/ activities under the Agreement that supports/ relate to women's peace and security in the country?
4. What are some negative and positive aspects of the Agreement on the women's peace and security in Solomon Islands?
5. What should the government do to encourage positive impact of this Agreement on women, peace, and security?
6. Are you aware of contributions from other development partners to women peace and security in Solomon Islands?v

The Gender Question in China's Soft Power Engagement in the Global South

by Govind Kelkar and Ritu Agarwal

1. Introduction

With China's rise as a major global economic power, there has also been an increased interest in the importance of soft power and its robust role in developing a positive perception of Chinese culture, polity, and economy within the global South. How did China project its socio-cultural values, economic prosperity, and attraction to an environment where others would be more inclined to accept Chinese values and power and less likely to oppose the party-state's foreign policy objectives?

This paper presents an analysis of China's soft power engagement with the global South in an attempt to explore policies and practices on gender equality and women's empowerment. After an initial discursive view of some distinctive characteristics of China's soft power, we underline major instrumentalities in its global South engagement. Throughout the development of these mechanisms or instrumentalities, there has been a missing factor of gender equality and women's empowerment. However, in multilateral platforms such as the United Nations (UN) and world conferences as well as in national planning, some policy attention has been given to the question of gender equality and the empowerment of women. Nevertheless, these policy statements have largely remained statements of policy intentions.

Since the 18th National Congress of the Communist Party of China (CPC), President Xi Jinping and the CPC Central Committee have committed to adhering to the basic national policy of gender equality, "a code of conduct and value standard" for the entire society (China Government Network 2021: 3), and advocated for women's equal rights through strategic measures like laws and policies that would ensure women equal access to economic resources and participation in economic development in the family and society, including 'equal sharing of housework' and family responsibility such as care work (Chinese Government Network 2021:31). Such policy pronouncements raise the question: What is the role of China's leadership in the creation of a cultural and economic soft power platform that has a conceptual current and practices of gender equality and women's empowerment?

Our conceptualization of China's soft power has some limitations, largely driven by the management aspect of this paper. We have not included in our analysis two aspects of soft power: the role of non-state actors such as 'Love in Africa' (a female Chinese migrant network in Zimbabwe), private market players such as Huawei, or, more importantly, the Belt and Road Initiative (BRI) projects in the global South. Admittedly, these have created local aspirations for and attractions to the Chinese way of life. However, they would need an independent comprehensive analysis of public diplomacy.

The data that support our understanding of China's soft power were collected from three channels: 1) our frequent visits to rural China in the past two decades, which helped us to conduct participant observations; 2) our regular engagement with Chinese students and scholars at the Asian Institute of Technology, Thailand, Jawaharlal Nehru University, India, and the Yunnan Academy of Social Sciences, China; and 3) a systematic literature review on the subject, including local reports on feminist activism and geopolitical studies. It is important to note that our access to the fields in China resulted from a careful establishment of interviewee-interviewer trust that respected privacy and anonymity. In writing this paper we carefully analyzed our field notes as well as context analysis and reports by local media. Throughout this study, our major argument is that gender is an important dimension for understanding China's soft power, and this has been a major neglected area in studying China's masculinized knowledge of soft power.

2. Defining China's Soft Power

In his 2011 study, Joseph Nye describes two types of power. Hard power is the ability to get others to act in ways that are contrary to their initial preferences and strategies through coercion, threats, and inducements (Nye, 2011: 11). Unlike hard power, soft power is the ability to get 'others to want the outcomes that you want' and 'to achieve goals through attraction rather than coercion' (Nye, 2004: 5). Nye's writing on soft power shows three key sources of soft power:

culture, values, and foreign policy. China's term for soft power (软实力, ruǎn shílì), however, emphasizes the cultural dimension; it tends to combine traditional culture with ideology, history, morality, and economic governance. Soft power in the Chinese context is different from soft power as explained by Nye. The Chinese concept of soft power sees fluid boundaries between hard power (硬实力, yìng shílì) and soft power, which are symbiotic and mutually empowering. In China, soft power is seen as associated with political stability and social cohesion (Repnikova, 2022: 52). For example, the internationalization of Chinese media and higher educational institutions is associated with the growing new markets and revenue generation for Chinese universities.

The CPC pays sustained attention to how China is seen in the world (Pu, 2019). The CPC has proactive and reactive approaches in its efforts to show a peaceful and non-threatening China while emphasizing its achievements. Reactive efforts include responses to foreign criticism of Chinese policies (Edney, 2014). These messages are communicated by party-state media like Xinhua, its think tanks, institutes, and public relations firms. At times, its messages are coercive; it denies access to and/or silences those who criticize the party-state's policies (Shambaugh, 2015).

2.1 Chinese Scholars' Discussions of China's Soft Power Focus on 'Traditional' Chinese Culture

Wang Huning analyzed that soft power is an element of national power formed by a phenomenon of 'power diffusion'. It comes from intangible resources such as culture. Therefore, culture is not only the background of a country's policy but also a kind of power or strength that can influence the behaviour of other countries (Wang, 1993). A 2006 issue of the English version of *The Guangming Daily*, the official newspaper of CPC, stated:

> As a birthplace of culture with a history of more than 5,000 years of civilization, if China only exports TV sets but not the content played on TV sets, that is, does not export Chinese ideas and concepts, then China will become a hardware processing factory. In fact, culture is an important part of comprehensive national strength, which is what people call soft power, and it has become the focus of competition among countries.[1]

The main idea was that since China is moving to the center stage of world politics, it should control or influence the main discourse on soft power. Daniel Lynch (2020) argued that the concept of soft power is largely controlled by the

West to fulfill their own agenda and, therefore, the Chinese are proposing their own model of soft power, which points to recovering their confidence in their civilization and creating a new turn in world politics towards harmonious and sustainable development.

In 2013, China established the National Research Centre, an affiliate of Chinese Foreign Affairs University, Beijing, to study soft power. In the last few years, the centre has organised workshops and conferences to study soft power in China. In the recently held Conference on Building National Soft Power, the director of the centre emphasised that the development of soft power has been a consistent focus of the CPC, and in the last few years the CPC has consistently proposed enhancing the cultural soft power of China ([国家软实力研究中心, guojia ruanshili yanjiu zhongxin] cfau.edu.cn) to enhance understanding of China and to create more scholarly exchanges for Chinese and foreign scholars, the Chinese Academy of Social Sciences launched the China Social Science Forum in 2010. It aims to build a platform for social science and cultural exchanges between China and foreign countries and enhance the world's understanding of China (hqu.edu.cn). Its focus has been on improving China's national image and making sure that people understand China objectively and comprehensively.

Research shows that China's economic rise will not make China's cultural outreach visible, as its economic rise has been aligned to Western-based market values. Therefore, China must be firmer than before in following its historical values embedded in socialism, its political institutions, and its culture (Wang 2016). Others believe that China's unique historical legacy and values are a civilisational power that has the capacity to challenge Western norms. Therefore, China should not keep a low profile but rather work towards creating its own national image and telling its stories comprehensively to the world (Lynch, 2020: 49). Soft power is central to China's strategic policy that emphasises conscious cultivation of a positive national image to the outside world to project China as a peace-loving, people-based (以人为本 yiren weiben), tolerant, confident, and responsible power (Guo and Hua, 2007).

During the 19th National Congress of the Communist Party of China, Chinese President Xi Jinping clearly stated that:

'文化是一个国家、一个民族的灵魂，文化兴国运兴，文化强民族强'
(wénhuà shì yīgè guójiā, yīgè mínzú de línghún, wénhuà xīng guóyùn xīng, wénhuà qiáng mínzú qiáng) 'Culture is the soul of a country and a nation, culture makes the country prosper, and culture strengthens the nation.'[2]

It should be noted that the construction of cultural soft power in the People's Republic of China (PRC) era is a major strategic task, which as the Chinese phrase puts it, is 'formed at the center' and 'released outwards' ('形于中' 而 '发于外' *xing yu zhong er fa yu wai*). This means that soft power is formulated by the party and government given its cultural history, political system, and socioeconomic development, and this model of China will be used to tell the outside world about Chinese strength embedded in its cultural values, 'intertwining with economics and politics.... ' in the competition for comprehensive national power' (Li, 2008: 2)

2.2 Increasing China's Attractiveness with Poverty Reduction Programmes and Economic Prosperity

China has always been attractive to the countries in the global South as an economic model of prosperity, especially in terms of raising the living standards of its population and lifting them out of poverty. China has contributed significantly to global poverty reduction by lifting 770 millions of its rural population out of poverty to achieve the goal of the UN 2030 agenda for sustainable development. Initially, in its development efforts, China accepted assistance from the World Bank in the field of poverty alleviation, received support in financial input, knowledge transfer, and technical assistance, and collaborated significantly with the international community. However, at present, China has taken an active part in global poverty management, promoted exchanges and cooperation with other countries, and thus created a new model of international exchanges and cooperation on poverty alleviation.

China has launched various international poverty alleviation cooperation projects for other developing countries. In Asia, China and The Association of Southeast Asian Nations (ASEAN) countries have launched a rural poverty alleviation plan and carried out East Asian Poverty Reduction Demonstration Cooperation and technical assistance projects in rural communities of Laos, Cambodia, and Myanmar. In Africa, China has provided aid in building water conservancy infrastructure, vocational and technical schools, government-subsidized housing, and hospitals. In Latin America, China has built agricultural technology demonstration centers to help local people and set up the International Research and Training Centre for Rural Education and other institutions.

China Foundation for Rural Development (CFRD), the former China Foundation for Poverty Alleviation (CFPA),[3] was established in 1989 as one of the largest charity organizations in China in the field of poverty alleviation. It is registered under the Chinese Ministry of Civil Affairs and supervised by the Ministry of Agriculture and Rural Affairs. It has set up international offices in Myanmar, Nepal, and Ethiopia. Besides providing healthcare and nutritious food to vulnerable populations, focusing on mothers and children, it also provides scholarships, infrastructure construction, etc. To support the livelihood of communities, CFPA has projects to promote economic development through tourism, commerce, and microfinance. CFPA (Nepal), through its capacity building program, launched women's occupational support programs such as raising livestock and opening small businesses. In 2019, it also provided loans of 50,000 Nepalese rupees to 158 poor women to improve their livelihood with income-generating activities. [4] Evidently, women were seen as a subset of the poor in the sense that poverty reduction programs would automatically result in extending benefits equally to women and men. However, research showed that this did not happen; men still controlled and owned resources, and they benefitted from such poverty reduction programs while women continued to be economically dependent on men, as in other development programs (Duncan and Li 2001; Kelkar 2016; UN Women and OHCHR 2013). In the case of Nepal, we do not have detailed information on how to ensure that women are benefiting from these programs. This resulted in an exclusionary way of working with women on their right to resources and freedom in making decisions.

3. Factoring Gender in China's Soft Power

To analyze the gender dimension of China's soft power, we need to inquire whether there are gender equality and women's empowerment concerns in the soft power tools that have been used to influence the world about the 'good China story'. We would like to understand what policies or laws to reduce or end women's inequality and address gender relations were formulated at the center (i.e., in domestic policies) and how they were released or conveyed to the outside world. What was their role in the construction of socialist civilizational power and its economic prosperity?

3.1 Women in China's National Revolutionary Agenda

Throughout the history of the PRC, the CPC and government leadership have repeatedly criticized lingering feudal patriarchal social relations and made policy corrections for women's economic and social empowerment with asset rights, freedom from familial control, and employment outside the home or housework. Some of these examples include:

As early as 1948 the CPC Central Committee decreed that when a family is taken as a unit for issuing land deeds, a note must be made to the effect that men and women have equal rights to the land. Following the establishment of the PRC in 1949, new marriage laws reduced the male power in the family by providing for choice of partners, monogamy, and equal partnership in raising children and by changing patterns of inheritance and custody of children in favor of women. The Agrarian Reform Law gave women the right to hold land in their names (for details, see Kelkar, 1990). The implementation of these laws, however, was followed by numerous cases of women suicides and murders.

In The Great Leap Forward in 1958, women were encouraged to join the labor force as part of agricultural collectivization. Stacy (1983, p.214) noted that 'there were estimates of 4,980,000 nurseries and kindergartens and more than 3,600,000 dining halls were set up in rural areas by 1959'. However, these lasted only a few years following local male demands for 'hot and cooked food at home'.

A nationwide campaign in the mid-1970s for 1) more equal work point ratings, including redefining 'equal work' as work of comparable value rather than the same work; 2) men sharing household work and childcare responsibilities; and 3) promotion of matrilocal marriages and questioning patrilocality as a source of gender inequality embedded in traditional marriage practices and family structures (Soong Ching-Ling in *Renmin Ribao*, 1975; Kelkar 1990: 124).

Women experienced rapid progress in gender equality during the decade of the Cultural Revolution (1966-1976), using men as the yardstick: 'whatever men can do, women can do too'. However, there is evidence that women still suffered a low status in the ultra-left movement of the Cultural Revolution (Wang, 1997).

In the mid-1980s, several professional women's organizations, with support from All-China Women's Federation (ACWF) and Women's Committees in All-China Federation of Trade Unions, protested changes brought about by the Household Responsibility System and demanded gender-egalitarian relations in the economic distribution system (Kelkar, 1985; Nolan 1983, Shandong Women's Federation, 1986). Chinese women rejected the policy suggestions that asked them to rearrange their time to attend to both housework and contracted work, whether in agriculture or side-line production. Criticizing the traditional morality that woman should be a virtuous wife and good mother', women suggested to the policymakers that if men assumed more responsibility for housework, women would become more equal within their families as well as in society (Kelkar, 1990: 131).

2005 amended Law on Protecting Women's Rights and Interests stipulated women have equal rights in the Household Responsibility System of land, and that women's access and control over land must be guaranteed irrespective of their civil status (Wang, 2013; Zhang et al., 2015).

3.2 Continuous Commitment at the Global Level

In the initial years of China's revolutionary construction, the party-state formulated policies to strengthen women's position and dismantle the traditional patriarchal structures and the social and political discrimination against women. Did these examples of historical concern for gender-egalitarian relations form part of the PRC's soft power negotiations in constructing multilateral and bilateral relations? At the global level, China signed the UN Convention on Elimination of All Forms of Discrimination Against Women (CEDAW) in 1980 and the Beijing Platform of Action at the UN Fourth World Conference on Women in 1995.

The hosting of the Fourth World Conference on Women in Beijing in 1995, which adopted its outcome document the Beijing Platform for Action, clearly showed China's efforts to seek global commitment to women's empowerment. In preparation for this conference, a few researchers were engaged in writing about women's contributions to building a socialist society and their struggle for equal rights to resources, property, and decision-making. Soon after the 1995 conference, a number of gender-related research programs were introduced in various Chinese universities and think tanks in China in collaboration with international civil society research institutions. Some scholars noted two forces that contributed to the mushrooming of women's studies in many countries and also in China at the provincial and municipal levels: first, women's movements which addressed practical problems related to women's daily lives and, second, the increased number of women academics and professionals who wrote theoretical works on feminism in relation to their context-specific cultural and historical backgrounds (Li Xiaojiang and Li Hui, 2023).

President Xi Jinping pledged $10 million (USD) in 2015 to UN Women for their work on peace and development. Importantly, China has successfully promoted itself through the election of its staff to key roles in the UN and many inter-governmental bodies. This implicit power manifests itself in China's participation and presence in every meeting and at every speech. China's role in multinational and national platforms is consistent with gender equality because PRC leadership sees this 'discourse power' as crucial to its international power (Palmer, 2023). Also, China has signed the UN Sustainable Development Goals (SDGs) including Goal 5 on gender equality and women's access to sexual and reproductive health as well as ensuring equal economic resources.

China has pledged to support women and girls from developing countries in the provision of health care, vocational training, financing for education, and other assistance (Centre for Emerging Worlds, 2018). Reportedly, China Women's University has established a training and research center for women from developing countries. In Nepal, the Women's Federation of Beijing Municipality started various capacity-building programs for women by promoting entrepreneurship and employment generation schemes. As part of this collaboration, the National Women's Association of Nepal started a radio project aimed at enhancing women's capacity building in rural areas.

In his speech in October 2020 at the high-level meeting of the 25th anniversary of the Fourth World Conference on Women (Beijing+25), President Xi Jinping acknowledged the important role of women and announced the need for action: 1) to strive for genuine gender equality and create opportunities for women's participation and decision-making, to eliminate prejudice, discrimination, and violence against women, and to make gender equality a social norm and moral imperative for all; and 2) to enhance global cooperation in advancing women's development to eliminate violence, discrimination, poverty, and other old problems and address new challenges such as bridging the gender digital divide and supporting greater representation of women in the UN system.

More recently, at the 20th National Congress of the CPC in October 2022, President Xi Jinping emphasized:

"We will accelerate the development of China's discourse and narrative system, better tell China stories, make China's voice heard, and present a China that is credible, appealing, and respectable."

"We will remain committed to the fundamental national policy of gender equality and protect the lawful rights and interests of women and children."

As we noted above, China has made commitments at several major international platforms for gender equality and women's rights (e.g., CEDAW, SDGs) and has a comprehensive *Outline for the Development of Chinese Women (2021-2030)* with the party and state guaranteeing 'to adhering to the basic national policy of gender equality' and having a guiding ideology of "gender equality to become a code of conduct and value standard that the whole society follows.... and give full play to the role of 'half the sky' of women in building a socialist modern country" (China Government Network 2021:3). In the following discussion, we intend to explore the commitments to gender equality and women's empowerment in mechanisms of China's soft power.

4. Mechanisms of China's Soft Power

4.1 Confucius Institutes

Confucius Institutes (CIs) are important mechanisms for promoting China's soft power strategy. Confucius Institutes were established to help the world better understand China's history, literature, and culture. The main idea behind establishing these CIs is to attract overseas students to study the Chinese language and related courses and thus promote Chinese culture and create a national image through art, culture, and films. According to official reports of 1 June 2020, there were 541 CIs and 1,170 Confucius Classrooms (CCs) in 162 countries and regions (Repnikova. 2022:11). However, there are different perceptions and interpretations of the roles and functions of these institutes. Some see them as part of cultural diplomacy and cultural exchange, while others perceive them as academic malware, part of power asymmetries and cultural imposition with a political goal embedded in the idea of soft power (Hartig, 2014; Shahlins, 2008). Nevertheless, what is generally accepted is that CIs have effectively promoted people's awareness and understanding of Chinese culture and China's image around the world.

There are, however, questions on the quality of teaching, outdated depictions of China, and ignoring local cultural contexts (Zhan and Lu, 2019). Generally, Confucius Institutes were set up to promote the Chinese language and culture among non-Chinese people of a country. Some of the available information about Confucius Institutes in Asian countries shows that students were taught Chinese language and culture (art, music, and traditional dance) (Qiao, 2024). While we do not have any concrete evidence of how women's roles and gender relations were taught as part of the Chinese culture, we could make an inference that women's rights and concerns for gender equality were not part of these lessons offered by Confucius Institutes. In our feminist analysis, we noted that Confucian culture imbibes social hierarchy and familial obligations for women, likely reflecting traditional gendered contents for women in language and culture courses.

4.2 China's Educational Internationalisation

Higher education has been used as an instrument by China to carve out a sphere of influence both to complete its geopolitical objective of extending its influence in other countries and the economic agenda of ensuring the expansion of global markets for Chinese products (Romi Jain, 2021). It also might help to create a positive image of China by promoting Chinese culture, language, and civilizational values. At the turn of the 2000s, China geared itself to be an attractive international center for knowledge production and training. The number of international students in China increased from 1,236 to 492,200 between 1978 and 2018 (Shi and Hu, 2019). According to the China International Migration Report (2018), China is the world's fourth-largest source of international immigrants. In 2017, China was the world's largest exporter of international students and the world's third most popular destination country for overseas students in Asia.

China has become an important and attractive education destination for South Asian students. In 2016, the number of Bangladeshi students studying in China was 4,900 (three times higher than in India), and the number of Myanmar students studying in China was 17 times higher than in India. Currently, there are more than 6,400 Nepalese students studying in China. In the case of Pakistan, more than 18,000 students were enrolled in Chinese universities and after returning they joined different public and private research and development institutions. At present, to strengthen cultural cooperation, the Chinese government is set to provide 100 government scholarships to Nepalese students.

Interestingly, monetary gains from self-funded international students, including those from the global South, have presented an attractive opportunity to the Ministry of Education and many Chinese universities. Whereas many students and short-term visitors from developing countries returned from China with an appreciation for the country, there were others who questioned China's fusion of cultural and market logic and criticized China's quality of education and racial discrimination (Romi Jain, 2018).

4.3 The Media: China's International Communication Platform

China's external communication has a long history dating back to the Mao era, when print media and some books like *Away from All Pests: An English Surgeon in People's China 1954-1969* by Joshua S. Horn (1914-1975) and *Fanshen: A Documentary of Revolution in a Chinese Village* by William Hinton (1919-2004) played a major role in telling China's story globally. In the 1990s, China's role in the international community underwent major changes. In 1996, the Foreign Languages Publishing Bureau established the China International Publishing Group, which mainly distributes books, periodicals, and multimedia business forms.

China published a series of books, periodicals, and magazines, thus creating a knowledge platform to promote exchanges and understanding about China's soft power. One of the important steps in this direction was the establishment of the Chinese Cultural Soft Power Research Centre in 2009 in Hunan with cultural soft power as its main research object. The center published twenty-four soft power academic monographs such as *Blue Book of Cultural Soft Power Research*, *China Cultural Soft Power Development Report*, *Chinese Cultural Soft Power Research Series*, *Chinese Cultural Soft Power Research Outline*, and 400 journal papers carrying socialist core values and the rising economic strength of China.

The flagship publication of ACWF, *Women of China*, played a significant role in creating a socialist feminist cultural front, a 'site of feminist contention through revealing behind-the-scenes stories' about women's agency that was crucial to understanding feminist struggles in socialist China. The magazine *Women of China* has been noted for its multiple voices in educating Chinese society about women's contributions to the construction of socialist China and the transformation of people's world views on domestic and international political affairs (Wang, 2010).

In early 2012, China's Media Going Global document sought to establish a national strategy to spread Chinese culture and promote international exchanges through the setting up of media channels and newspaper offices like Xinhua News Agency, China's Central Television (CCTV), and *China Daily* abroad. Later, China's broadcast media channels, like China Central Television, opened Arabic and Russian channels to produce and broadcast multi-language television programs (Ren Qi, 2013). By the end of the 20th century, China Xinhua News Network Corporation (CNC) had 101 international bureaux (Jiang and Zhang, 2019) and had launched CNC World News. In 2013, Nepal started the first *China Daily* Asia edition and *Asia Pacific Daily*, which is sponsored by Xinhua News Agency.

In 1981, *China Daily* was established and became the first national English language daily, striving to let the world understand China and let China reach out to the world. Subsequently, Xinhua News Agency, China Radio International, China Central Television's foreign channel, and a growing number of foreign communication websites have gradually formed a system of China's mainstream media 'going global'. From 2011 to 2016, during our several visits to China, we noted young women dressed like dolls were made to stand at ancient royal palaces of the Forbidden City in Beijing and other tourism centers in China. Chinese feminine fashion, showing their bodies and beauty, was worn by young women. Fashion magazines interpreted these as an expression of women's self-confidence in China's modernization period (Xu and Ge, 2016). This brought changes in fashion brands' advertisements and implicit aspirations for beautiful bodies as market commodities.

To accelerate the construction of international communication capabilities, Beijing was chosen as a regional site for the audio-visual global program. Star Times has gradually established a huge network system that can support the operation of tens of millions of users since it launched digital broadcasting and TV services in Africa. Star Times has developed business in more than thirty African countries, has 13 million digital TV users, 27 million Internet video users, and 13 million social media fans, becoming a well-known audio-visual brand in Africa. China succeeded in using its soft power to tell the world about its cultural mix of politics and economics and claim its position in the world.

4.4 Sports and Expo Events

As part of soft power, China has organized a range of spectacles and mega-events such as the 2008 Beijing Olympics and 2010 Shanghai World Expo, as well as frequent regional summits and various BRI events. These summits and trade expos, though involving huge expenses, were aimed at international audiences to promote China's political agenda and gain credibility for its status as a powerful country. For example, the Shanghai Expo was organized to promote China's friendly cooperation with various countries and to demonstrate China's accomplishments over the past sixty years. It is important to note that Chinese authorities used these events as domestic educational platforms, in the sense of conveying to Chinese citizens national self-importance and 'Chinese greatness, past, present and future' (Hubert, 2017: 17). Of course, these mega-events have led foreign journalists and some Chinese youth to criticize the top-down approach in organizing them as well as restrictions on foreign journalists reporting on China's rural reality. At the same time, Chinese state media have attacked Western journalists for 'not understanding the real China' (Latham, 2009:34).

Interestingly, China's soft power also has domestic factors in consideration although these are often subtle. The grandeur and lavishness of expos and sports events have been used as a showcase for Chinese citizens of the power and prosperity of the new China. The appeal of economic development and a showcase of prosperity are seen to strengthen China in both foreign and domestic spheres. As formulated during the Hu Jintao period, the strength of a country can be summed up in three parts: material strength, spiritual strength, and cultural strength. Culture is a force and self-identity, thus having an appeal to the world outside as well as inside the country.

5. Conclusion

Admittedly, China has achieved its soft power objective of creating a positive story of China's economic development, a socialist market economy with Chinese characteristics. Research shows that there is an appreciation of China's emergence as a global power with its own cultural and political characteristics. Chinese soft power strategies have left strong imprints through diplomatic support, investments, higher educational exchanges, and Confucius Institutes in many countries of Asia and Africa. In Nepal and Pakistan, China has become a major destination for students to pursue higher education, including PhD degrees (Hussain and Mehmood, 2018).

Notwithstanding its soft power success, China's experience of socialist construction suggests that it is unrealistic to expect that gender equality will automatically follow the establishment of a socialist system. Rather, it suggests that women struggle to resolve gender-specific subordination and exclusion from decision-making in social, economic, and political development, which is likely to continue if there is a tendency to subsume gender equality in general socio-economic development, including poverty reduction programs. The structural patriarchy at best will allow only a marginal change in the gendered position of women as token evidence of non-discrimination and gender inclusivity.

China's experience further suggests that without a fundamental transformation of power relations within the family, women will be unable to free themselves from domestic confinement, and any attempt at building and narrating a 'good China story' is likely to remain inconclusive. The Confucian tenets of women's responsibility, family harmony, obedience, and care work as major components of China's culture are likely to strengthen traditional patriarchal structures of women's inequality within China and partner countries in the global South. Further research is needed to see if these tenets were changed or replaced by including women's rights to resources and freedom from the traditional familial system of women's subordination and discrimination.

There are two contradictory trends in the Chinese state regarding gender equality: One projects China as a model for gender equality whilst the other is a traditional position for women, with lower social status and trapped in Confucian values. The Women's Federation at different levels in China has promoted the state agenda of building a civilized, safe, and optimally beautiful family. It began by resolving marriage and family conflicts and disputes and striving for a more cooperative family. With the new mix of the Internet, women's organizations, and legal services, China has tried to create a new model of family where women take most of the responsibility of being caregivers at home. In this drive to promote women's social roles, Zhejiang Women's Federation, for example, has promoted the establishment of women's and childcare platforms to make women fulfil their roles and responsibilities. Besides providing basic services such as women's entrepreneurial and employment guidance, the federation has also started training classes to care for children and help special groups, family education courses promoting a harmonious family, and psychological counselling sessions for the management of marital disputes.

According to data, in 2015, the percentage of women who decided not to have children was 6.1 percent, and by 2020 it was expected to rise to 10 percent. This phenomenon has caused policymakers to rethink their strategies for promoting the birth rate in China. To boost the declining birth rate, Sichuan province recently revised its birth regulations by allowing unmarried people to register the births of their newborns. This has triggered widespread discussion. Sichuan authorities subsequently clarified that this was not to encourage non-married couples to have children but to protect the rights and interests of the 'unmarried first pregnancy' group.

Because of its preoccupation with a high economic growth rate, concern for gender equality and the rights of women have been side-lined in the political economy of China. The 2011 3rd Survey on the Status of Chinese Women brought out many details of gender inequalities and discrimination in the workplace in urban China (Fan, 2014). China doesn't have any definition of discrimination against women in accordance with CEDAW. There are no women in the Standing Committee of the Politburo. Among the five state councilors – a rank lower than that of vice-premier but theoretically higher than that of the minister – there is now one woman, Shen Yiqin, who until the fall of 2022 was party secretary in Guizhou province.

The National People's Congress has less than twenty-five percent women, while the global average of women's representation in national parliaments is 25.9 percent. Women earn less than seventy percent of men's earnings and spend twice as much time as men doing household work (All-China Women's Federation, 2021).

Despite the leadership's commitments to gender equality and women's empowerment in its national planning, China fails to carry out its soft power policies and to meet the targets of SDG Five. Gender has been a contested ground in current geopolitics (Cai and Li, 2021). Systemic barriers to gender equality and the elimination of violence against women have been identified such as unjust trade and investment agreements, corporate capture, land and resource grabbing, climate change, all-pervasive patriarchy, and fundamentalism.

Despite these reports of socio-political neglect of gender equality, there have been indications of women's growing agency and awareness of their rights. The ACWF demanded that the party support women's rights to economic resources and that there be strict action against gender violence and the sexual abuse of women (Zing, 2014; Kelkar, 2016).

The recognition of gender equality issues does not find a place in China's foreign policy and trade negotiations. Gender equality issues and any related promotion of the rights of women and girls are seen as an attempt to interfere in the cultures and traditions of sovereign states in conflict with the five principles of peaceful co-existence.[5]

Chinese women academics and feminist groups have argued for comprehensive and consistent gender equality policies in its soft power approaches and trade and aid relations. The women's movement in China and numerous women's professional organizations have made concerted demands for realizing equal rights to resources, decision-making, and the sharing of domestic care work (Amnesty International, 2022).

In the preceding discussion, we noted that PRC policy pronouncements (both on national and multilateral platforms) address women's conditions of inequality and marginality in society. These were hardly followed through, however, due to patriarchal norms and practices that explicitly made the policies null and void. This leads us to conclude that if a fundamental change in perceptions and practices of gender hierarchies is not made, there seems little hope of achieving gender equality and women's empowerment. This fundamental change lies in (1) a departure from considering women's equality as a subset of poverty reduction or economic prosperity; and (2) the creation of an enabling environment with the policy and practice of gender equality as an embedded or explicit aspect of China's cultural and political system and trade negotiations. Of course, this also requires realizing women's equality and dignity as well as freedom from masculine attitudes within the home and in governance structures. The future of a more powerful China with a good story to tell the world lies in the increased agency of women, their unmediated (by the household and its head) rights to resources and political decision-making, and freedom from violence and control in their lives.

Notes

1 Cited in https://epaper.gmw.cn/gmrb/html/2013-07/26/nw.D110000gmrb_20130726_4-15.htm. Accessed 16 February 2024.
2 Cited in https://www.workercn.cn/255/201907/09/190709111352331.shtml. Accessed 16 February 2024.
3 See its website: http://en.cfpa.org.cn.
4 http://en.cfpa.org.cn/index.php?file=article&cmd=show&artid=242
5 The Five Principles of Peaceful Co-Existence are: mutual respect for sovereignty and territorial integrity, mutual non-aggression, non-interference in each other's internal affairs, equality and cooperation for mutual benefit, and peaceful co-existence.

References

All China Women's Federation and National Bureau of Statistics of China. (2021), *Fourth Survey on the social status of women in China*, Available online: https://fegw.sh.gov.cn/type3/20211228/a528ce531dd04f29a842bfd68bb6819c.html. (Accessed on 19 March 2025)

Amnesty International. (2022), *China*. Available online: https://www.amnesty.org/en/location/asia-and-the-pacific/east-asia/china/report-china/ (Accessed on 13 August 2023)

Brazys, S. and Dukalskis, A. (2020), 'China's message machine'. *Journal of Democracy*, 31 (4): 59-73.

Cai, Y. and Li, Y. (2021), Global China from a Gender Lens. *IDEES* Special Issues No. 52. China Before a World in Crisis. Available online: https://revistaidees.cat/en/global-china-from-a-gender-lens/ (Accessed on 20 February 2023)

Chen, L. (2019), *How to enhance cultural soft power in the new era* [陈良斌-新时代如何提升文化软实力] (*Xin shidai ruhe tisheng wenhua ruan shili*). Available online: https://www.workercn.cn/255/201907/09/190709111352331.shtml (Accessed on 3 February 2023)

Chen, E. (2016), 'Power Femininity' and Popular Women's Magazines in China', *International Journal of Communication,* 10: 2831-2852.

China Government Network. (2021), *Program for the Development of Chinese Women, 2021-2030*.

China Social Sciences Forum. (2010), *Soft Power and Sino-Foreign Relations International Symposium will be held at Huaqiao University*. [中国社会科学论坛：" 软实力与中外关系" 国际学术研讨会将在华侨大学举行]. (*Zhongguo shehui kexue luntan: ruanshili yu zhongwai guanxi guoji xueshu yantao hui jiang zai Huaqiao daxue juxing*). Available online: https://www.hqu.edu.cn/info/1212/75690.htm (Accessed on 3 October 2022)

Croll, E. (1978), *Feminism and Socialism in China*, London: Routledge and Kegan Paul.

Duncan, Jennifer and Li Ping. (2001), *Women and land Tenure in China: A study of Women's Land Rights in Dongfeng County, Hainan Province*, Rural Development Institute, Seattle, Washington, USA.

Edney, K., Rosen, S., and Zhu, Y. (eds.). (2020), *Soft Power with Chinese Characteristics: China's Campaign for Hearts and Minds*, London: Routledge, Taylor and Francis.

Edney, K. (2014), *The Globalisation of Chinese Propaganda: International Power and Domestic Political Cohesion*, New York, Palgrave Macmillan.

Guang, Y. (2020), 'China's mainstream media "going out" strategy'. [巩育华-中国主流媒体 "走出去" 之路]. (*zhongguo zhuliu meiti zou chu qu zhi lu*) Available online: https://www.mmzy.org.cn/qunyan/jcwz/dxmb/102480.aspx (Accessed on 1 March 2023)

Guo, S. and Hua, S. (2007), *New Dimensions of Chinese Foreign Policy*, UK: Lexington Books, 2007, p. 112.

Hartig, F. (2014), New Public Diplomacy Meets Old Public Diplomacy: The Case of China and Its Confucius Institutes. *New Global Studies*; Berlin, 8(3) pp. 331-52.

He, Y. and Ren, Y. (2021), *At the end of 2020, more than half of women are not satisfied for the status quo and not optimist for the future*. 27 January 2021. Available online: https://freewechat.com/a/MzI5MDEwNzMwMQ==/2247488733/1 (Accessed 19 March 2025)

He, W. (2021), 'Construct a Closer China-Africa Shared Future in Post-Pandemic Era' [构建后疫情时代更紧密的中非命运共同体], (*gou jian hou yiqing shidai geng jinmi de zhongfei mingyun gongtong ti*) Available online: https://news.gmw.cn/2021-01/03/content_34513185.htm (Assessed on 19 March 2025)

Hu, J. (2019), *Soft Power Research in China: An Examination of the History of Conceptual Evolution* [胡键-软实力研究在中国：一个概念演进史的考察] (*ruan shili yanjiu zai zhongguo: yi ge gainian yanjin shi de kaocha*) Available online: https://www.aisixiang.com/data/119049.html (Accessed on 2 December 2022)

Hubbert, J. (2017), Back to the Future: The Politics of Culture at the Shanghai Expo. *International Journal of Cultural Studies*, 20 (1): 48-64.

Hunan Chinese Cultural Soft Power Research Centre. (2009), *Blue book of China's Cultural Soft Power: Annual Report on China's Cultural Soft Power* (Published in English).

Mehmood, H. and Mehmood, S. (2018), Chinese Soft Power Approaches Towards Pakistan: An Analysis of Social-Economic and Political Impacts, *Malaysian Journal of International Relations*, 6: 47-66.

Jain, R. (2021), 'China's Soft Power and Higher Education in South Asia: Rationale, Strategies, and Implications', *Routledge Studies in Education and Society in Asia*.

Jain, R. (2018), '*China's Soft Power Aims in South Asia: Experiences of Nepalese Students in China's Internationalisation of Higher Education*'. ETD Archive. 1061. Available online: https://engagedscholarship.csuohio.edu/etdarchive/1061 (Accessed on 19 March 2025)

Jiang, F. and Zhang, N. (2019), *Three waves of China's external communication (1978-2019)* [中国对外传播的三次浪潮] (*zhongguo duiwai zhuanbo de sanci langchao*) *Global Media Journal*. Cited in Tiger Sniff Network. Available online: https://m.huxiu.com/article/325011.html (Accessed on 6 March 2023)

Johnson, K. A. (1983), *Women: The Family and Peasant Revolution in China*, The University of Chicago Press, Chicago.

Kelkar, G. (1985), 'Impact of Household Contract System on Women in Rural China', *Economic and Political Weekly*, Vol. XX, Review of Women's Studies, 27 April.

Kelkar, G. (1990), 'The PRC at Forty: Women and the Land Question in China', *China Report*, Vol. 26, No. 2, pp. 113-131.

Kelkar, G. (2016), '*Between Protest and Policy: Women Claim their Rights to Agricultural Land in Rural China and India*', UNRISD, working paper, 2016-10, Geneva.

Ren, Qi. (2013), *"Going Out": The Path and Strategy Analysis of the Chinese Newspaper Industry*. Available online: http://media.people.com.cn/n/2013/0319/c359295-20841439.html (Accessed on 19 March 2025)

Tsinghua University National Conditions Research Centre. (2006), '*Knowing Oneself and Enemy: Strengthening Research on China's Soft Power*' [知己知彼：加强中国软实力研究] (*Zhiji zhibi: jiaqiang zhongguo ruan shili Yanjiu*), *National Reports*. Vol. 9 [国情报告 第九卷]. pp. 238-260.

Latham, K. (2009), Media, the Olympics, and the Search for the Real China: Special Section on the Beijing 2008 Olympics. *China Quarterly*, 197, pp. 25-43.

Li, M. (2008), China Debates Soft Power, *The Chinese Journal of International Politics*, 2 (2): 287-308.

Li, X. and Hui, L. (1989), Women's Studies in China, *NWSA Journal*, The Johns Hopkins University Press, 1 (3): 458-460.

Liang, X. (2019), Factory, family, and industrial frontiers: A socio-economic study of Chinese clothing firms in New Castle, South Africa. *Economic History of Developing Regions*, 34:3, pp. 300-319.

Lynch, D. C. (2020), 'The End of China's rise: Consequences for PRC debates on soft power', Edney, K., Rosen, S. and Zhou, Y. (eds)., *Soft Power with Chinese Characteristics: China's campaign for hearts and minds*, New York: Routledge.

Nolan, P. (1983), Decollectivization of Agriculture in China, 1979-82: A Long-Term Perspective, *Economic and Political Weekly*, August 6.

Nye, J. S. (2004), *Soft power: The Means of Success to World Politics*, New York: Public Affairs.

Nye, J. S. (2011), *The Future of Power*, New York: Public Affairs.

Pu, X. (2019), *Rebranding China: Contested Status Signalling in the Changing Global Order*, Palo Alto, CA, Stanford University Press.

Qiao Peng. (2024), Confucius Institute's Role in Chinese Language Development in Indonesia: A Site Study at State University of Malang, *Open Journal of Social Sciences*, 12 (2): 31-46. doi: 10.4236/jss.2024.122003.

Repnikova, M. (2022), *Chinese Soft Power, Elements in Global China*, Cambridge University Press.

Sahlins, M. (2018), *Confucius Institute: Academic Malware and Cold Warfare*, www.insidehighered.com/views/2018/07/26/confucius-institutes-function-propaganda-arms-chinese-government-opinion

Shambaugh, D. (2015), China's Soft-Power Push: The Search for Respect. *Foreign Affairs* 94 (4). pp. 99-107.

Shandong Women's Federation. (1986), 'The Technological Exploitation of Rural Women in Production', Paper presented at the Seminar on Women in Agricultural and Rural Production, Huangxian, May 1986.

Soong C.-L. (1972), Women's Liberation in China, *Beijing Review*, No. 6, p. 11.

Stacey, J. (1983), *Patriarchy and Socialist Revolution in China*, Berkeley: University of California Press.

UN Women and OHCHR (2013), *Realizing Women's rights to land and other productive resources*, United Nations.

Wang, H. (1993), 'Cultural Soft Power as National Strength' [作为国家实力的文化软权力] (*Zuo Wei Guojia Shili de Wenhua Ruan quanli*), *Fudan Journal of Social Sciences*, No. 3.

Wang, Y. (2016), 'The Paradox of Soft Power and Its Chinese Surpass'. [论软实力悖论及其中国超越]. (*Lun ruan shili bei lun qi zhongguo chao yue*) [文化软实力研究] Wenhua Ruanshili Yanjiu, 1 (2), pp. 9-17.

Wang, Z. (2010), Creating a Socialist Feminist Cultural Front Women on China (1949-1966), *The China Quarterly*, No. 204, pp. 827-849, Cambridge University Press.

Why China needs Soft Power, [为什么中国需要软实力] (*wei shenme zhongguo xuyao ruanshili*) Available online: https://epaper.gmw.cn/gmrb/html/2013-07/26/nw.D110000gmrb_20130726_4-15.htm (Accessed on 18 December 2022.)

Xu, Lei and Mingfu Ge. (2016), Urban Feminine Fashion in China From 1987 to Now, *International Journal of Arts and Commerce*, 5 (7). www.ijac.org.uk.

Xu, S. (2014), 'How do overseas scholars view soft power with Chinese characteristics?' [许少民-海外学者如何看待中国特色的软实力] (*hǎi wài xué zhě rú hé kàn dài zhōng guó tè sè ruǎn shí lì*) Available online https://zhidao.baidu.com/question/1637958846959543980.html (Assessed on 19 March 2025)

Yao, G. (2022), 'Zhejiang Women's Federation promotes high-quality sharing of public services "Women and Children Post Station" allows the masses to enjoy the happiness at home' [姚改改- 浙江妇联推进公共服务优质共享 "妇儿驿站" 让群众享受

家门口的幸福]. Available online: https://www.women.org.cn/art/2022/11/18/art_20_171058.html (Accessed on 13 August 2023)

Zhan, C. and Lu, M. (2019), 'The Predicament and Optimisation of Teaching Chinese to Speakers of Other Languages in Confucius Institute', [孔子学院汉语国际教育的困境与优化分析]. (*Kongzi xueyuan hanyu guoji jiaoyu de kunjing yu youhua fenxi*). *Xiandai Jiaoyu Luncong* [现代教育论丛], 230 (6), pp. 60-68.

8

When Civil Society Contests Global China

Challenges and Opportunities for Gender-Related Civil Society Transnational Action on China-Backed Infrastructure Projects in the Global South

by Laura Trajber Waisbich

1. Introduction

'If China is cancelling 103 coal plants in their country coz of environmental and health concerns then why would we believe that we can have coal plants in Africa and make it work?'[1] This provocative question was posted on *Twitter* (now X), in 2018, by Omar Elmawi, a Kenyan lawyer and campaigner. At the time, Elmawi and his colleagues were waiting for a court ruling to suspend the construction of a China-backed coal power plant in Lamu, Kenya. As the post shows, while challenging the project in Kenyan courts, campaigners like Elmawi were not blind to China's role in it.

The ways in which civil society groups engage with and contest China-backed projects in the Global South remains an understudied dimension of the politics of Global China. Even less is known about how women-led activism and gender considerations fit evolving forms of civil society activism in that regards. This chapter contributes to filling these gaps by revisiting emblematic instances of civil society transnational contestation of China-backed (funded, built, or both) large-scale energy infrastructure projects in other developing countries, citing examples from Southeast Asia and East Africa. The cases revisited are two anti-hydropower campaigns in the Mekong Basin – against the Myitsone dam in Myanmar, and the Cheay Areng dam in Cambodia – and one anti-coal power campaign in Lamu, Kenya. These mobilizations in the 2010s managed to halt projects before actual operations started, with civil society opposition growing out of shared concerns about potential negative impacts on local populations and the environment. These campaigns were chosen due to their characterization in the literature as 'exceptionally positive' and 'successful' instances of civil society transnational mobilization (Kirchherr 2018; Yeophantong 2020; Chheat 2022), having not only achieved their intended goals but also contributed to shift China's policies and business practices related to responsible foreign energy investments since then (Tang 2015). By reconstructing how these campaigns came to be, the main issues prioritized, and how gender considerations featured in them, the chapter not only supplements a growing body of research on the gender, social, and environmental impact of Global China, but also contributes to knowledge-generation and learning about civil society activism regarding Chinese development initiatives in the Global South.

This reconstruction effort relies primarily on desk-based research (document, literature, and media reviews), subsequently triangulated with ten semi-structured and informal interviews, mostly to capture Chinese perspectives. Key informants' purposive sampling targeted representatives of civil society and academia knowledgeable about the campaigns, gender issues, or Chinese overseas development initiatives and investments in these regions. The views of other stakeholders (including governmental and corporate actors) were gathered through media and literature review. Interviews were conducted in person in China, as well as remotely, between 2018 and 2023. Most key informants are Chinese nationals and women. Interview data was anonymized to maintain confidentiality.

The remainder of the chapter is structured as follows. Section one presents the contours of civil society mobilization in the context of Global China. Section two examines the selected mobilization instances, highlighting some crosscutting features. Section three focuses on blind spots of otherwise supposedly successful campaigns, including the invisibility of gender issues. The final section offers some advocacy-relevant concluding thoughts.

2. Monitoring Global China: Social Mobilization on China's Development Cooperation

Much has been said about the rise of China as a global developmental actor amidst the re-emergence of South-South development cooperation (SSC) in the 2000s (Mawdsley 2012; Gu et al. 2016). Heated debates emerged over whether 'Southern providers' (including China, Brazil, India, Mexico, Turkey, and beyond) and their new development cooperation approaches (through technical cooperation, policy and knowledge exchanges, development finance, and investments) could transform existing Northern- and Western-led aid paradigms. While research on SSC expanded quickly, much of the debate was and remains infused with simplistic value-laden narratives on the role of Southern countries in global development (Fourie et al. 2019).

Civil society groups in the Global South, including grassroots and professional advocacy groups, independent scholars, and journalists, are important actors in producing knowledge about as well as engaging with SSC initiatives on the ground (Pomeroy et al. 2016; Shipton and Dauvergne 2021). In the past decade, their engagement has offered grounded, nuanced, and alternative perspectives on the policymaking, practices, and impact of Southern-led development cooperation, defying both the overly positive official accounts put forward by Southern governments of 'win-win' (better-than-aid) relations and the overly dismissive accounts plaguing Western media and policy circles (Waisbich 2021a).

Based both in large Southern providers (such as China, Brazil, and India) and in other developing countries where projects unfold, these SSC monitoring movements, as I call them, expanded during the 2010s (Waisbich 2021b). In recent years, however, much of their attention has turned to monitoring Global China (Shieh 2022; Waisbich 2022). Attention to and concerns with China's footprint respond, first, to China's leading role in large infrastructure building and financing, a development cooperation modality that traditionally galvanises social mobilisation due to its perceived and/or enacted socio-environmental impacts (Waisbich 2021b) and, second, to China's increasingly assertive foreign policy and ever-growing global development role through bilateral cooperation and investment, and multilateral initiatives such as the Belt and Road Initiative (BRI) and the Global Development Initiative (GDI). In the context of these emerging monitoring movements, issues like labour conditions, governance, corruption, and environmental degradation in China's development exchanges with the Global South have been extensively discussed (Mohan 2014; Yeophantong 2020; Amar et al. 2022). Gender issues, however, have been comparatively less examined, both in academia and policy circles, as well as by civil society groups (Cai and Li 2021).

Civil society monitoring of Global China can take multiple forms, from grassroots mobilisation to policy advocacy, project-related campaigns, and independent knowledge production and reporting. Mobilisation can unfold both inside China (led by Chinese or China-based organizations – see section three for a more detailed characterisation of these) as well as outside China, in other developing countries, and in the Global North, home to many traditional development cooperation watchdogs. Often, monitoring relies on transnational activism networks (Keck and Sikkink 1998), bringing together representatives of non-governmental organizations, social movements, academics, and journalists who unite around specific 'principled issues' (Guarnizo and Smith 1998). On the one hand, SSC monitoring movements emulate existing (often Northern-led) networks and resources available for insider-outsider advocacy work related to development cooperation and infrastructure building initiatives (Fox and Brown 1998). On the other, groups monitoring rising powers, including China, also innovate by crafting new mobilization strategies and repertoires suitable to the particularities of Southern-led development cooperation initiatives. Increasingly, decoding China and engaging Chinese actors and institutions on their own terms has become crucial to the success of civil society mobilization to engage with, try to overhaul, and even halt China-backed infrastructure projects (Waisbich 2022).

3. Contesting China-Backed Energy Projects in Southeast Asia and East Africa

China is currently the main bilateral financier of energy infrastructure in the Global South, including hydropower dams, coal power plants, oil and gas pipelines, and renewables like solar and wind plants. Energy infrastructure investments also figure in most BRI projects (Zhou et al. 2022). Large-scale energy projects are important for socio-economic development in developing countries but also traditional sources of discontent due to their unevenly distributed costs and benefits (Tan-Mullins et al. 2017). Local communities disproportionately bear the socio-environmental costs. Large infrastructure projects also affect women differently, impacting on their rights, livelihoods, and health, as well as on gender inequalities and gender-based violence (Castañeda Carney et al. 2020). In recent years, additional pressure has been mounting on international financiers of large energy projects, such as China, to balance economic imperatives with securing fair, just, and sustainable futures in the current planetary triple crisis (climate, biodiversity, and pollution).

This section examines past instances of civil society mobilization to halt China-backed large energy infrastructure projects in Southeast Asia and East Africa. The contentious nature of these overseas projects reveals not only the challenges to making President Xi Jinping's vision of ecological civilization and common prosperity an integral part of what China does abroad but also the multiple disputes over what development is and how it should be pursued.

3.1 Challenging hydropower in the Mekong region: the case of Myitsone and Cheay Areng dams

Between 2006 and 2017, China was involved in forty-one per cent of the large hydroelectric power facilities in Southeast Asia (Middleton 2022). In the Mekong basin, a hydropower dam construction boom (Kirchherr 2018) has unfolded since the 2000s with funding from Southern countries such as China and Korea against the backdrop of receding finance from bilateral donors and multilaterals such as the World Bank (Tan Mullins et al. 2017). Despite the growing asymmetrical interdependence between China and its regional partners, national governments welcomed this alternative source of capital with less strings attached, including weaker socio-environmental constraints on borrowers (Laporte 2017; Gong 2021). Meanwhile, the large dams' construction in the Mekong faced significant civil society opposition both inside the countries and at the regional level (Kirchherr 2018; Yeophantong 2020; The Rupture Project 2022).

The Myitsone dam was announced in 2006 as a bilateral China-Myanmar initiative with Chinese actors serving as funders and contractors. The plant was to be built on Myanmar's longest river, the Ayeyarwady, in the Kachin state (close to China's Yunnan province). Financed by the Export-Import Bank of China (CEXIM), the plant would function through a joint venture, the Upstream Ayeyarwady Confluence Basin Hydropower Co., Ltd. The state-owned China Power Investment (CPI) was set to hold eighty per cent of its shares. Pre-construction work started in 2009 but rapidly faced civil society resistance.

Contestation initially took place locally, led by the Kachin people, through public letters, leaflets, and bombings near the project site. Opposition grew from 2010 and became a national popular mobilization to suspend the dam under the umbrella of the 'Save the Ayeyarwady' campaign, which gathered environmental activists, scientists, historians, and artists. Aung San Suu Kyi, a Myanmar democracy icon at the time, added her voice to the campaign. The key issues of contention revolved around environmental and social impacts on the Kachin people and the downstream community of the Ayeyarwady (including displacement and resettlement of around 12,000 people) alongside wider river-related national cultural and heritage concerns (Chan 2017; Kirchherr 2018). Led by Myanmar organizations, such as the Burma Rivers Network, the anti-dam mobilization also received international attention and support. International non-governmental organizations (NGOs) like International Rivers played a complementary but important role, for instance in foregrounding mismanagement in environmental impact assessment studies (Gong 2021).

In June 2011, a civil war broke out in Kachin, and then-President Thein Sein announced the suspension of the project, against China's will. This led to the Chinese government and CPI boosting efforts to convince the government of Myanmar to resume the project, including through public relations campaigns and invitations to Myanmar non-governmental stakeholders (including civil society organizations, journalists, opposition parties, and Kachin representatives) to visit China (Mogensen 2017; Chan 2017; Gong 2021). People-to-people events in China were held by the China NGO Network for International Exchanges (CNIE), an organization set up by the Central Committee of the Chinese Communist Party (Hsu 2017; MFA/PRC 2012).[2]

The Beijing-based Global Environmental Institute (GEI) also got involved, conducting trainings of Myanmar officials, hosting closed-door meetings with different stakeholders following the project's suspension, and collaborating with the Chinese contractor, CPI, to investigate socio-environmental impacts and management if the dam construction were to have been resumed (GEI 2015; Ji and Zhang 2016; Yeophantong 2020). While both CNIE and GEI played different 'citizen diplomacy' and technical expert advice roles in close dialogue with the Chinese state (Tang 2015; Yeophantong 2020), other Chinese organizations, such as the Yunnan-based environmental group Green Watershed, took a different route. Acting 'to promote sustainable development of China's overseas investment' (Yu 2012), Green Watershed conducted their own study trip to Myanmar to monitor Chinese investment projects *in loco*. Their visit equally sought to connect Chinese and Myanmar actors by generating knowledge on the impact of projects and listening to different stakeholders on the ground. Still, despite Chinese diplomatic and para-diplomatic efforts, the dam construction was never resumed.

As for Cheay Areng, the hydropower plant was planned to be built in a biodiversity-rich area in the protected Cardamom Mountains of Cambodia, mostly inhabited by Chong and Khmer communities. CEXIM secured the project funding and construction passed into the hands of a series of Chinese companies (China Southern Power Grid, China Guodian, and Sinohydro). Construction gained pace around 2013 and was followed by local resistance, as the dam would displace 1,500 people living by farming, fishing, and collecting forest products (Hensengerth 2017). Affected communities rejected compensation and launched a campaign to halt the project. The major issues of contention revolved around environmental harm as well as the impact on traditional livelihoods and the spiritual well-being of local communities. Local resistance was supported by a network of dissident monks organised in the Independent Monks Network for Social Justice, as well as other Cambodian organizations (including the Cambodian Youth Network, the Samreth Law Group, Mother Nature Cambodia, Rivers Coalition in Cambodia, and 3S River Protection Network). International environmental groups (such as International Rivers, Earth Rights International, and Conservation International) also took part (Yeophantong 2020; Chheat 2022).[3] In 2015, the campaigners issued a complaint to the United Nations special rapporteur on the situation of human rights in Cambodia. The complaint mainly focused on the project's environmental risks and violations of indigenous peoples' rights. It also raised social and gender concerns, including a disproportionate impact on women, who are traditionally responsible for activities such as gathering water and growing food.[4] In February 2015, Prime Minister Hun Sen suspended the dam's construction, and, in 2017, the project was put on hold indefinitely. It was never resumed.

These two anti-dam campaigns display commonalities. Both combined what social movement scholarship calls 'environmentalism from the poor' (Martinez-Alier 2014) with NGO-led national and transnational advocacy efforts (introduced earlier). Mobilization was driven by the local disenfranchised, often indigenous, populations standing up for nature preservation against corporations and the state. Their claims revolved around environmental and social justice issues, including recognition, participation, and other human rights considerations. Both in Myanmar and Cambodia community-led mobilization happened because the host country and the Chinese government failed to adopt context-specific socio-environmental and human rights safeguards to prevent disproportional harm to local communities. Local mobilization was then amplified, first nationally and then internationally, with an increasing emphasis on environmental issues.

National politics played a crucial role. The projects were cancelled because activists succeeded in challenging the appropriateness of building large dams in critical habitats, protected areas, and indigenous lands by inserting their claims into already volatile political arenas. In both cases, local struggles escalated to national struggles, moving the contention from the margins to the centre of domestic politics. International actors, starting with regional ones, also played a role by helping national activists (e.g. in legal mobilization) and raising awareness about their claims to external audiences. Regional and international actors that openly joined the campaigns include non-governmental groups from neighbouring countries such as the regional Save the Mekong Coalition and international NGOs (INGOs) such as International Rivers.

In both cases, activists leading the international campaigns did not strongly emphasise the Chinese financier and builder aspect and made little use of China-based arenas in their legal and advocacy mobilization. Such a tactical choice reflects a shared perception of Chinese financiers and contractors as hard to influence (Cheathh 2022; Laporte 2017). Reasons for this include, first, the broad and voluntary nature of China's existing guidelines for companies and the financial sector in overseas investments; second, China's deference to host country systems, coupled with insufficient home country (i.e. China) standards for hydropower impact on local communities; and, third, China's policies focusing on philanthropic efforts rather than conflict resolution, coupled with overall policy implementation gaps on the ground (Garzón 2018 [2014]; Tang 2015; Tan-Mullins et al. 2017; Cai et al. 2017; Gong 2021). Comparatively less attention by campaigners to shaping Chinese actors' behaviour is not unrelated to Chinese organizations (such as CNIE, GEI, or Green Watershed) not openly joining the efforts to halt the projects, despite having engaged with both cases on their own terms.

Lastly, the issue of gender impact did not prominently feature in these transnational anti-dam campaigns, which focused instead on the protection of the environment and marine life and on community rights and displacement. According to interviewees familiar with the region, although gender concerns are neither completely absent from hydropower-related civil society mobilization in the Mekong – nor from governmental and corporate risk assessments, and their impact mitigation actions – they are seldom singled out or dealt with in a comprehensive manner.[5] I will come back to this point later in the chapter.

3.2 Challenging fossil fuels in Kenya: the case of Lamu coal power plant

In September 2021, Xi Jinping announced China would stop funding coal power plants overseas as a sign of country's global commitment to fighting climate change. By April 2022, fifteen overseas coal power projects had been shelved or cancelled. While uncertainties remain regarding projects already in the pre-construction phase, plants being built specifically to power industrial zones, and the retirement of the plants already financed (Clark et al. 2022), state-owned construction firms started to pull out of coal projects and look at expanding investments in renewables (Chen and Shen 2022).

Some years before Xi's pledge, however, China got involved in a controversial coal-related project in East Africa that was halted due to strong civil society opposition. In 2014, the Kenyan government launched a project to build Kenya's first ever coal-powered plant in Lamu county near its border with Somalia. The bid was won by a consortium of Kenyan and Chinese energy companies, led by Amu Power Company. The Industrial Commercial Bank of China (ICBC) would finance sixty per cent of the project, alongside other international financiers, such as the African Development Bank (AfDB). The coal power plant was planned near a United Nations Educational, Scientific and Cultural Organization (UNESCO) World Heritage Site in an ecologically important coastal mangrove forest area. Construction was planned to start in December 2015, but by mid-2016 it was already facing delays and an intense international mobilization. In 2019, the project was suspended following a court ruling.

A group of Lamu-based organizations, namely Save Lamu, Muslims for Human Rights – Muhuri, and the Kwasasi Mvunjeni Farmers Self-Help Group, led the mobilization alongside larger national organizations, such as the Katiba Institute, 350 Kenya, and deCOALonize. Community concerns about the environment and land, as well as livelihoods, culture, and health, were central. Those were brought to the forefront by larger organizations in Kenya and amplified by international actors in Africa and beyond, including regional and international environmental and development INGOs (such as Natural Justice, Greenpeace, Accountability Counsel, and the Heinrich Böll Stiftung) and United Nations entities, namely UNESCO and United Nations Environmental Programme (UNEP). These diverse voices gathered in their common opposition to coal power and the promotion of alternative, just, and sustainable energy and development futures in Kenya and East Africa (UNEP 2018; Zhu 2020).

Accounts from the initial street protests in Lamu highlight the role played by Lamu women in leading the local opposition to the plant and to coal more broadly (Save Lamu 2018; EJAtlas n.d.; Patel 2021). However, attention to gender impact and the participation of women's groups became less and less visible in campaign efforts as the mobilization expanded. The dilution of gender issues in more outward-facing arenas did not prevent Lamu women from mobilizing and raising their specific concerns, for instance through national and regional workshops facilitated by organizations like 350Africa.org and WoMin (350Africa.org 2017). No evidence of Chinese or China-based civil society open engagement in the campaign against this project was found, yet experts interviewed believe certain Chinese and China-based actors did pursue some degree of discreet or covert diplomacy and advocacy efforts. This includes joining forces in drafting letters and other background material behind the scenes to assist in the international advocacy work. Organizations like the World Wildlife Fund (WWF) China, for instance, had already been involved, even if from afar, in monitoring Chinese investments in Lamu, apart from the coal power plant, in what is known as the Lamu Port-South Sudan-Ethiopia Transport Corridor Project (LAPSSET) (Le 2016; Waisbich 2021b).[6] The Lamu controversy also received coverage from independent Chinese journalists and activists in outlets reporting on Global China such as the *China Dialogue* (now *Earth Dialogue*) and the *Panda Paw Dragon Claw* blog.[7]

Campaigners combined policy advocacy and legal strategies targeting the Kenyan government as well as Chinese stakeholders (including the Chinese embassy and ICBC) and other financiers.[8] In 2016, organizations filed a lawsuit with the Kenya's National Environment Tribunal against the Kenyan National Environmental Management Authority and Amu Power for violating environmental and social impact assessment license requirements. In 2019, Kenyan judges revoked Amu Power's license to build the plant and, following growing pressure by environmental groups, AfDB pulled out, bringing the project to a halt. In 2020, ICBC also pulled out. The case is currently under appeal. Campaigners' engagement with the Chinese diplomatic mission in Nairobi was unsuccessful in the early days, but a meeting was secured with the Chinese ambassador after the court's ruling. At the time, the ambassador expressed his personal discomfort with backing a coal project, while campaigners reiterated that they were not 'oppos[ing] development' but rather 'push[ing] for development that is sustainable and doesn't harm the people of Lamu and Kenyans at large' (Save Lamu 2019). They also reiterated that China was welcome to invest in renewable energy options (including wind, solar, and others) (ibid).

Like the campaigns in the Mekong, the mobilization against the Lamu coal power plant managed to stop a China-backed energy infrastructure project. The success in Lamu was mostly due to the role of national actors and institutions in the host country (i.e., Kenya-based campaigners and national courts) in contesting a social-environmentally controversial and risky project and forcing governmental and business actors, some of them Chinese, to reconsider investment plans and policy priorities. The Lamu case also features greater engagement of multilateral actors, including co-financing institutions AfDB and specialised UN agencies. Their involvement provided Kenyan groups with additional pressure points for transnational activism besides China-related ones (Waisbich 2021b). Kenyan activists contested the project primarily on environmental grounds. Campaigners strongly targeted (and found space to act in) national arenas while also seeking to influence the international financier side (including China). Finally, this case illustrates another mobilization that managed to halt a large energy infrastructure project that neither featured a visible gender impact-related advocacy strategy nor openly relied on the participation of Chinese or China-based civil society organizations.

4. Analysing Blind Spots in Otherwise Successful Campaigns

Having revisited emblematic civil society mobilizations across different energy sectors and regions, this section discusses two blind spots in these otherwise successful campaigns: consideration of gender issues and participation of Chinese and China-based organizations. Analysing these blind spots matters for those seeking to end the invisibility of gender-related issues in Global China-related transnational activism, as well as to engage more Chinese voices in future conversations regarding China's participation in large energy infrastructure projects in the Global South.

4.1 Gender blindness

Gender blindness is a common feature in the cases discussed throughout this chapter in spite of the active participation of women activists and organizations in local opposition and mobilization against the proposed projects (a feature also found in indigenous communities' resistance against China-backed extractive projects in Latin America, see Amar et al. 2022). Gender issues were marginal, or even invisible, in the concerns and narratives transnationally articulated by activists regarding the problematic nature of large China-backed energy infrastructure projects. Often, the main galvanizing issue was environmental impact. Certain social and human rights issues, such as culture, livelihoods, and health, were present but less centrally so to how activists framed their opposition to projects. Meanwhile, concerns with gender issues, including the specific and differentiated impact of the proposed projects on women and broader gender inequality considerations, were largely overlooked or underplayed.

Rather than being unique to the aforementioned campaigns, which focused on specific large energy projects and strongly targeted host governments, gender considerations are similarly invisible in transnational advocacy efforts targeting

Chinese stakeholders.[9] An illustration is found in a 2020 letter, signed by over 260 organizations worldwide, calling on China to ensure COVID-19 financial relief be allocated to 'high quality', not 'high risk', BRI projects. When defining risky projects, the signatories emphasize the direct impact on local environments, communities, and livelihoods, as well as the harm and destruction of 'forest, marine, desert, river, or other increasingly fragile and remaining intact ecosystems, and the people who depend upon them'. While concerns with people are certainly there, the letter fails to include specific recommendations related to women and gender. From the list of sixty selected problematic projects, only one (a palm oil initiative in Cameroon) explicitly mentions specific constraints to women's rights and livelihoods.[10]

When juxtaposed, the project-specific campaigns and the policy advocacy efforts reveal a broader mobilization pattern of engaging Chinese stakeholders on environmental issues, appealing to China's growing body of 'soft law'[11] on the matter. This includes commitments, initiatives, financing instruments, policies, and regulations such as the Green BRI and the 2021 Green Development Guidelines for Overseas Investment and Cooperation.[12] Certainly, those mobilizing both outside and inside China strategically rely on (and help enlarge) existing policy space for environmental and climate matters (Waisbich 2022). Yet, while doing so, they unintentionally contribute to the marginalization of social and gender issues. The next paragraphs further discuss this trap by considering the contours of Chinese and China-based groups' mobilization on Global China.

The concept of civil society is a widely debated topic worldwide. Chinese law defines three types of civil society organizations (often referred to as social organizations, *shehui tuanti*): social associations, civic non-enterprise institutions, and foundations. Sociologically, however, one can find other types of organizations that operate in China. These include grassroots groups, government-operated NGOs (GONGOs), think-tanks, and international NGOs with offices in China. In this chapter, I employ the term 'Chinese and China-based organizations' to refer to this diverse group of organizations operating in China and engaging with Global China. Within this broad category, one finds social organizations with not just different areas of expertise and identities but also different legal status in China (i.e., some have been formally registered under the 2016 Charity Law and others not) and thus different relationships to the Chinese Communist Party (CCP) and the state. This diversity subjects them to different forms of state control and gives them varied levels of access and exposure to policy and corporate decision-making.

Existing scholarship depicts most Chinese social organizations as non-political, mostly as service organizations. There are, however, social organizations in China that do policy-related research, mobilization, and advocacy work, many of them on environmental issues (Ho and Edmonds 2008; Tian and Chuang 2022). Despite the increasing pressure on social organizations in the last decade (Deane 2021), environmental issues have been considered somewhat 'safer' for grassroots mobilization, advocacy work, and journalism compared to human rights and gender issues (Repnikova 2022). This is true for mobilization on and reporting on environmental domestic issues such as pollution and conservation, as well as for addressing Global China's environmental footprint (Waisbich 2022).

Both domestically and on Global China-related matters, environmental activism takes place through largely 'non-confrontational', 'constructive', and 'solutions-focused approaches' (Ho and Edmonds 2008; Repnikova 2022). When monitoring Global China, the collaboration-centred work by Chinese environmental organizations manifests through acting alongside government and corporations operating overseas with politically acceptable issues and framings. What appears to be acceptable and accepted revolves around the notion of improvement: improving the socio-environmental performance of Chinese actors on the ground, reducing the financial and reputational risks of overseas projects, and improving China's global image (Waisbich 2022).

Concretely, groups in China seek to influence policymakers and the banking sector to strengthen socio-environmental policies and regulations for overseas investments and cooperation, as well as monitor social-environmental performance on the ground. By doing so, they also 'socialize' Chinese companies in the international standards, best practices, and experiences and support them in enhancing social-environmental policies. To achieve these goals, social organizations make recurrent use of financial-managerial and corporate language regarding risks, reputation, performance, and responsible business. For example, GEI describes its work on the Myitsone Dam as 'help[ing to] establish unofficial communication platform between companies and local government, business association, NGO and communities' (Ji and Zhang 2016, 19). A similar characterization is given by the Beijing-based Social Research Institute (SRI) of its own work in monitoring China's investments in Myanmar as helping to 'promote the socially responsible development of China's OFDI' (Outward Foreign Direct Investment) and assisting Chinese and host country stakeholders in 'realiz[ing] a win-win situation' (Cai et al. 2017: 67). The Asia Foundation, a key funding partner for Chinese organizations monitoring Global China, also adopts a similar approach to 'support China's constructive global engagement' and 'work with Chinese partners to bridge an understanding that encourages environmentally responsible behaviours and improved capacity for compliance' (Asia Foundation 2016).

While this type of embedded activism (Ho and Edmonds 2008) has allowed Chinese and China-based organizations to expand their engagement with Global China, it also comes with its own implications. First, organizations find themselves mostly acting through insider tactics rather than outsider tactics (or through combining both) and, thus, refrain from openly vocalising politically sensitive issues and joining confrontational forms of mobilization, including the campaigns led by civil society groups on the ground (as mentioned before and further discussed below). Second, while there is strategic value in 'finding an acceptable manner to communicate with Chinese government and companies and organising dialogues between companies and stakeholders' (Cai et al. 2017: 5) and thus benefit from a growing openness of Chinese actors to socio-environmental issues, engaging in acceptable critique through improvement-focused language also has consequences. One is to fall into what Li (2007) characterises as de-politicization by rendering issues technical.[13] The other is being co-opted or appropriated by those who wish to carry on with business as usual.

The trade-offs are increasingly visible to those mobilizing in China. In the words of one interviewee, environmental activism remains 'acceptable until you hit some boundaries'.[14] On the one hand, as framed by two interviewees, those inside China try to work and act 'in whatever way they can'[15]. As such, by strategically de-politicizing issues and adopting business-friendly language, civil society actors have managed to include concerns about the local community's well-being and dignity on the agenda (Tang 2015). On the other hand, however, by following a technical and non-confrontational path, organizations end up rendering openly political issues, gender included, invisible in their advocacy strategies and dialogue with Chinese officials and companies, including by self-censoring. In the end, the allegedly more radical – or politically sensitive, in the words of interviewees[16] – dimensions like resettlement, ethnic conflict, and gender end up marginalized or subsumed into broad and vague references to social issues. Because these are seen as more political and thus more challenging to act upon and promote, organizations in China are caught in a pragmatic, or even success-driven, trap to continuously work on the lower-hanging fruits such as environmental degradation, climate change, and decarbonisation precisely because they are seen as less political and sound more technical and non-confrontational.[17]

A contributing factor to the invisibility of gender issues is the limited number of organizations actively monitoring Global China inside China, most of them lacking strong social and gender focus and expertise. Despite the growing number of social organizations doing poverty alleviation work (Ji and Zhang 2016) and monitoring state and corporate behaviour overseas (as seen earlier), few Chinese organizations manage to sustain this international work. Even fewer have sustained advocacy work on China's global development role and footprint, and mostly in Asia. The more active ones (i.e., GEI, Greenovation Hub, Green Watershed, SRI, WWF, Greenpeace, World Resources Institute, Oxfam Hong Kong, and Asia Foundation) seem, moreover, to struggle to combine influencing China's green development finance policies through strategic dialogue with actors in the financial and banking systems with monitoring China's overseas projects on the ground, often prioritising the former over the latter.[18] Combined, these factors result in attention to gender being neither systematic nor comprehensive.

According to interviewees, gender concerns often feature in an *ad hoc* and superficial manner in Global China-related work, sometimes responding to a particular international funding requirement or as the result of individual (rather than institutional) efforts to advance the agenda.[19] Groups in China still engaging with the government and companies on overseas project performance often feel there is a long way to go to including gender in corporate social responsibility parameters[20]. Meanwhile, gender experts working on gender and sexuality issues inside China already feel too overwhelmed by domestic issues and constrained by growing state control and repression to turn to Global China.[21] Tian and Chuang (2022) argue, for instance, that social organizations with gender, social, and rights-based work were subjected to greater political control and repression under the 2016 Charity Law.[22] The new regulations have also targeted INGOs with offices in China. Those who managed to remain open downsized operations and ended up with portfolios that include but do not necessarily bridge Global China and gender. The Ford Foundation is an exception in that regard, with more consistent work connecting both areas (Cai and Li 2021). Oxfam Hong Kong also sought to bridge these areas by mainstreaming gender in the context of the China-led multilateral banks, namely the Asian Infrastructure Development Bank and the New Development Bank, as well as in regional projects to promote more responsible and inclusive China-led value chains and private sector investments (Tobing-David 2019). However, these attempts to include gender considerations in the overall monitoring of China's development cooperation remain modest and require continuous investment in more spaces for organizations and individuals with gender expertise to collaborate with the more active groups in this space, namely environmental organizations, and move this agenda forward in China.

4.2 The missing Chinese allies

This leads to the second blind spot: the uneven presence of Chinese and China-based organizations in the openly critical, and eventually confrontational, transnational campaigns on China-led large infrastructure projects overseas. The panorama depicted here shows civil society groups in China playing comparatively smaller or more discreet roles in past dam-related transnational campaigns in the Mekong and hardly featuring in the coal-related campaign in Kenya. Rather than this being unique to the campaigns discussed here, such limited involvement of organizations in China in the open transnational contestation of China-led and -funded projects in other developing countries seems to be the norm (Waisbich 2022; Shipton and Deauvergne 2022; Shieh 2022).

Acknowledging their marginal role in these campaigns means neither underplaying the challenges, discussed above, for groups in China to mobilize nor undervaluing those who have managed to find acceptable ways to act. Rather than indifference, throughout the last decade organizations in China have managed to actively push the boundaries of what is acceptable to discuss in China about Global China, slowly but steadily expanding existing political space for pointing out and suggesting changes in governmental and corporate behaviour overseas. By travelling to the sites of contention and engaging with local actors, Chinese and China-based organizations have contributed to generating new policy debates in China based on alternative and more critical accounts of China's footprint in the region. Their Chinese gaze on how projects unfolded on the ground helped build knowledge and awareness of Chinese companies' performance and multifaceted impacts, especially in neighbouring regions, such as the Mekong basin. Their credentials, as Chinese as well as experts, moreover, helped bridge Chinese stakeholders (companies and diplomatic missions) and various groups in host countries.

At the same time, their absence or un-sustained engagement with partners on the ground (as in the Lamu case, for instance) and the limited number and diversity of Chinese civil society voices regarding Global China, more broadly, are worth discussing. First, to understand the limits of replicating forms of transnational solidarity networks that rely on the active and vocal participation of groups based in the funding and building country. Second, to help inform alternative models of transnational collaboration involving China-based actors in the years ahead. As was pointed out, historically, transnational networks have been a central piece of how civil society groups in host countries mobilized and challenged large internationally funded infrastructure projects. Likewise, in all cases studied here, transnational networks provided local groups with additional material and symbolic resources to exert pressure and eventually negotiate with companies and governments on the ground. Having China as the main funder and builder of large development projects requires civil society groups based in host countries to adjust and adapt mobilization strategies beyond simply emulating those traditionally adopted to influence multilateral banks and Western-based financiers.

Hence, while is illogical to believe mobilization can or will achieve better outcomes for local communities without engaging all stakeholders involved in the projects, including Chinese actors, it is also impractical to assume that groups in China can or will embrace certain types of resistance repertoires and join campaigns to halt projects as visible partners even when they share similar concerns about the problems on the ground due to the costs and risks of openly contesting official projects. There are different repertoires of radical contestation and, as suggested by one interviewee, many actors in China working in this space 'are being radical in their own way'[23]. There is growing evidence of Chinese organizations and experts reaching out to and being approached by peers in the Global South to help liaise with Chinese business on the ground, influence China's stances in new multilateral organizations, and learn about Chinese policies and regulations (Yu 2012; Cai et al. 2017).[24] While these outreach efforts from both sides might not always translate into sustained forms of collaboration, abundant reporting on Global China and greater policy space for organizations in China to engage on them create new opportunities for bringing more Chinese voices, including those with gender expertise and sensibilities, to the table. Local groups on the ground desperately need Chinese partners to navigate the cultural, organizational, language, and policy specifics of China-backed projects. This demand is likely to grow, mirroring China's appetite for global development.

5. Conclusion

This chapter revisited a collection of emblematic civil society campaigns that managed to halt controversial China-backed (funded and built) energy infrastructure projects in Southeast Asia and East Africa. Through a social mobilization lens, it analysed the main framings, strategies, organizational dynamics, and drivers of their success in stopping projects ahead of actual impact on the ground. Such a cross-regional comparative analysis revealed the leadership of host country organizations in crafting politically salient transnational campaigns revolving mostly around environmental issues and using national venues (including pressure on political leadership and national courts) to halt projects, often despite China's opposition to stopping activities. The cases studied here also show the strategic support of international allies and the role of transnational arenas in leveraging mobilization beyond national borders. In all cases, gender issues were marginal, rendered invisible in the public discursive construction of the stated problem. While women's organizations and their concerns were present, it's important to note that gender issues weren't consistently brought up, discussed, or given priority by the leaders of the transnational campaigns. Another lacking element was the participation of organizations in China in these international networks openly backing these more confrontational campaigns. Again, this is not to say they were completely absent but rather to emphasize their limitations but also their choice to monitor projects with other repertoires and goals in mind.

Altogether, these findings offer important insights for those seeking to raise the visibility of gender issues and empower gender-based activism, notably by women groups, in Global China-related mobilization. The first is to recognize the importance of fostering linkages and investing in building relationships between organizations already monitoring Global China and those with gender focus and expertise in China, in host countries, and between them. More and better South-South connections can allow Chinese and China-based organizations to hear from groups in developing countries about their experiences in dealing with Chinese stakeholders overseas. By flagging problems on the ground and thus shaming China or appealing to its face (*mianzi*), host country organizations help their Chinese and China-based peers in 'renegotiating the parameters of what constitutes "responsible" corporate behaviour and contesting state-led discourses of development' in China (Yeopanthong 2020, 104). Working with local organizations, particularly women's organizations and gender experts, might also help those in China challenge increasingly prevalent conceptions that large energy infrastructure projects do not have a gender impact or that gender concerns are a Western invention.[25]

At the same time, greater collaboration can allow civil society groups based in host countries to decode China and better engage with Chinese stakeholders on the ground. The fact that Chinese organizations are more trusted by Chinese companies (Tang 2015)[26] helps in making the case for their continued role as bridges, including in conflict resolution and negotiation settings. In sum, concerted efforts are key to finding the right pressure points and venues and generating combined pressure from outside and from within, increasing the chances of inducing responsible policy and the institutional and behavioural change of host governments, the Chinese government, and Chinese companies.

The second finding is the recognition that the road to greater collaboration is not an easy one. Building connections might take time and will require outreach, trust-building, and joint strategizing efforts. It requires Chinese and China-based organizations to further develop their will to monitor China abroad and a capacity to act internationally, including knowledge of local languages and local contexts, in both the near abroad (in Asia) and elsewhere. It also requires openness to deal with the 'greater oppositional, conflictual and autonomous forces' (Tang 2015: 22), including from groups affected by projects, and willingness to find ways to integrate local concerns (or their rights-based approaches) into advocacy strategies back in China, finding new acceptable places for all parties. While challenging for all sides, building more diverse networks could prevent the environmental critique from being appropriated and depoliticized in ways that prevent issues, like gender, from being discussed and just and transformative development paradigms from emerging and taking root. Greater diversity might also instigate monitoring movements to critically assess the more technocratic approaches to nature and the environment, widely deployed so far, and keep pushing the boundaries of what more responsible behaviour of government and corporate actors in the context of large energy infrastructure projects means.

Concretely, this might require having civil society groups adopt different framings and language and play different roles, some more visible than others, in transnational project-specific campaigns, as well as jointly engaging in multilateral spaces, like the UN, to raise crosscutting issues related to Global China. While rights-based advocacy might not necessarily find an easy and immediate way into policy advocacy efforts in China, it can certainly help build an enabling space for gender issues to be more visible and present in the years to come.

In conclusion, enhancing civil society transnational activism on gender-related issues requires bolstering cross-country coalitions. For historical, geographical, and organizational reasons, Southeast Asia offers a good starting place to strengthen linkages. This is where more consistent joint civil society engagement on Chinese overseas development initiatives has taken place on hydropower as well as on other large infrastructure projects, extractive industries, and agricultural value chains. Regional (largely environmental-based) activism in Southeast Asia needs to be revitalized alongside renewed dialogue with organizations with greater sensibility of gender-related matters. There is also value in learning from recent promising forms of transnational mobilization on Global China coming from regions like Latin America, which has sensitive territories increasingly affected by Chinese investments in extractive industries and large infrastructure projects (Amar et al. 2022). In past years, local grassroots and advocacy groups, including indigenous and women's groups, with a long tradition of transnational mobilization on large development projects have started to coordinate nationally, regionally, and transnationally (for instance, in UN human rights bodies) to critically engage with the impact of Chinese-backed projects on local communities and the environment.[27] Far removed from primary circles of China geostrategic and geoeconomic concerns, Latin American might offer alternative (and less politically sensitive) venues to foster South-South civil society networks capable of understanding and acting on the gender impact of Global China in the years ahead.

Notes

1 See https://twitter.com/OmarElmawi/status/999690933204672513 (Accessed on 4 February 2025).
2 Founded in 2005, CNIE is an umbrella organization of over 300 Chinese entities and the major focal point in civil society for reaching out to other CSOs around the world on matters of global development. Besides the 'Deep Fraternal Friendship' activities with Myanmar, mentioned here, CNIE also hosted civil society tracks of multilateral processes, including FOCAC, G20, and BRICS. Since 2022, CNIE also leads on reaching to CSOs in other countries to increase popular support to the China-led GDI (CNIE 2022).
3 See International Rivers letter on the Cheay Areng dam. Available online: https://riverresourcehub.org/resources/cheay-areng-dam/ (Accessed on 4 February 2025).
4 See the full submission to the UN. Available online: https://earthrights.org/wp-content/uploads/submission_to_special_rapporteur_on_hydropower.pdf (Accessed 4 February 2025).
5 Interview with a China-based development expert, 2023; Interview with a China-based gender and development expert, 2023.
6 Interview with a China-based gender and development expert, 2023; Interview with a UK-based INGO representative, 2023.

7 See https://pandapawdragonclaw.blog/2020/01/17/how-does-2020-bode-for-chinas-overseas-investment-a-chinese-lawyers-take/ or https://dialogue.earth/en/energy/lamu-kenyan-coal-project-chinese-investors-take-environmental-risks-seriously/ (Accessed on 24 May 2023).
8 See, for example, the letter sent by faith-based groups to GE, at one stage set to acquire a stake in Amu Power, asking it to reconsider its support for the project. Available online: https://www.asyousow.org/letters/joint-letter-to-ge (Accessed on 4 February 2025).
9 An exception has been the mobilization around the China-based new multilateral banks (the Asian Infrastructure Development Bank and the New Development Bank), strongly led by the BRICS Feminist Watch (see Waisbich 2022).
10 The full letter can be found at https://foe.org/blog/chinese-covid-19-relief-to-investments/ (Accessed on 4 February 2025).
11 Interview with a UK-based INGO representative, 2023.
12 This regulation updates the 2013 Guidelines on Environmental Protection and Cooperation, jointly issued by the Ministry of Commerce and the Ministry of Environment and the first-ever to establish criteria for Chinese companies operating overseas. Other regulations on foreign projects and outbound investments have also existed in China at least since 2008.
13 A similar dynamic is found by Tian and Chuang (2022) in the context of grassroots organizations working with sex workers in China.
14 Interview with a China-based INGO representative, 2018.
15 Interview with a China-based INGO representative, 2018; Interview with a UK-based INGO representative, 2023.
16 Interview with China-based NGO representative, 2019.
17 I thank Cai Yiping for her insights on this point, notably on the idea of a downside to the otherwise 'successful' mobilization of environmental groups in China.
18 Interview with a China-based development expert, 2023; Interview with a UK-based INGO representative, 2023.
19 Interview with a China-based gender scholar, 2019.
20 Interview with a China-based INGO representative, 2018.
21 Interview with a China-based gender scholar, 2019; Interview with a China-based gender and development expert, 2023.
22 Interview with a China-based gender and development expert, 2023.
23 Interview with a UK-based INGO representative, 2023.
24 Interview with China-based NGO representative, 2019; Interview with a China-based gender and development expert, 2019.
25 Interview with a China-based INGO representative, 2018; Interview with a China-based development scholar, 2018; Interview with a China-based gender and development expert, 2023.

26 Interview with a China-based development expert, 2023.
27 See, for instance, https://www.business-humanrights.org/en/latest-news/latin-america-14-cases-show-environmental-and-human-rights-violations-by-chinese-companies-report-for-un-says/ (Accessed on 4 February 2025).

References

350Africa.org (2017), *Women for Women: harrowing realities from Kitui coal Basin*, 26 May 2017. Available online: https://350africa.org/women-for-women/ (Accessed on 11 July 2023)

Asia Foundation. (2016), *China*, 23 November 2016. Available online: https://asiafoundation.org/publication/china/ (Accessed on 5 May 2023)

Cai, F., Zhang, J., and Chen, J. (2017), *The Social Responsibility of China's OFDI and NGOs' Engagement Taking the Myanmar Letpaduang Copper Mining Project as an Example*. Beijing: Social Resources Institute.

Cai, Y., and Li, Y. (2021), Global China from a Gender Lens, *Idees*, No 52 China before a world in crisis, 24 July 2021. Available online: https://revistaidees.cat/en/global-china-from-a-gender-lens/ (Accessed on 5 May 2023)

Castañeda Carney, I. et al. (2020), *Gender-based violence and environment linkages: The violence of inequality*. Edited by J. Wen. IUCN, International Union for Conservation of Nature.

Chen, H., and Shen, W. (2022), China's no new coal power overseas pledge, one year on, *China Dialogue*, 22/09/2022. Available online: https://dialogue.earth/en/energy/chinas-no-new-coal-power-overseas-pledge-one-year-on/ (Accessed on 5 May 2023)

Chheat, S. (2022), Contesting China-funded Projects in Cambodia: The Case of Stung Chhay Areng Hydropower, *Asian Studies Review*, 46(1), pp.19-35.

China NGO Network for International Exchanges (CINE). (2022), *International Civil Society Solidarity Conference on the Global Development Initiative*. Concept Paper.

Clark, A., Nedopil, C., and Springer, C. (2022), China and the Prospect of Early Retirement of Coal Plants in the Global South, 12 July 2022, *China Global South Project*. Available online: https://chinaglobalsouth.com/analysis/china-and-the-prospect-of-early-retirement-of-coal-plants-in-the-global-south/ (Accessed on 9 May 2023)

Deane, L. (2021), Will There Be a Civil Society in the Xi Jinping Era? Advocacy and Non-Profit Organising in the New Regime, *Made in China Journal*, 15 July 2021. Available online: https://madeinchinajournal.com/2021/07/15/will-there-be-a-civil-society-in-the-xi-jinping-era-advocacy-and-non-profit-organising-in-the-new-regime/ (Accessed on 9 May 2023)

Environmental Justice Atlas. (n.d.), *Coal Power Plant in Lamu, Kenya*. Available online: https://ejatlas.org/conflict/coal-power-plant-in-lamu-kenya (Accessed on 11 July 2023)

Fourie, E., Nauta, W. and Mawdsley, E. (2019), Introduction, in E. Mawdsley, E. Fourie, and W. Nauta (eds) *Researching South-South Development Cooperation. The Politics of Knowledge Production*. London and New York: Routledge, pp.1-11.

Fox, J. and Brown, L. D. (eds) (1998), *The Struggle for Accountability: The World Bank, NGOs, and Grassroots Movements*. Cambridge, Mass.; London: MIT Press.

Garzón, P. (2018 [2014]), *Handbook on Chinese Environmental and Social Guidelines for Foreign Loans and Investments: A Guide for Local Communities*. Third Edition. Quito: China-Latin America Sustainable Investments Initiative.

Global Environmental Institute (GEI) (2015), Investigating the impact of the Myistone Dam on an immigrant village in Myanmar, 15 July 2015. Available online: http://www.geichina.org/en/investigating-the-impact-of-the-myitsone-dam-on-an-immigrant-village-in-myanmar/ (Accessed on 9 May 2023)

Gu, J., Shankland, A. and Chenoy, A. (2016), *The BRICS in international development*. Basingstoke: Palgrave Macmillan.

Gong, X. (2021), Logics of Appropriateness: Explaining Chinese Financial Institutions' Weak Supervision of Overseas Financing. *World Development* 142 (June): 105465.

Guarnizo, L. E. and Smith, M. P. (1998), 'The Locations of Transnationalism', in M.P. Smith and L.E. Guarnizo (eds) *Transnationalism from Below*. New Brunswick: Transaction Publishers, pp.3-32.

Ho, P. and Edmonds, R. L. (eds) (2008), *China's Embedded Activism: opportunities and constraints of a social movement*. London; New York: Routledge (Routledge studies on China in transition, 30).

Hsu, J. Y. J. (2017), Burmese Civil Society Challenges China's Development Assistance in Myanmar, *Made in China Journal*, 26 March 2017. Available online: https://madeinchinajournal.com/2017/03/26/burmese-civil-society-challenges-chinas-development-assistance-in-myanmar/ (Accessed on 9 May 2023)

Ji, L. and Zhang, J. (2016), *Chinese NGOs "Going Global": Current Situation, Challenges and Policy Recommendations*. Beijing: Global Environmental Institute (GEI), November.

Keck, M. E. and Sikkink, K. (1998), *Activists beyond Borders*. Ithaca, NY: Cornell University Press.

Laporte, C. (2017), Emerging Donors on the Field: A Study Case of China and South Korea in Lao PDR, in I. Bergamaschi, P. Moore, and A. B. Tickner (eds) *South-South Cooperation Beyond the Myths: Rising Donors, New Aid Practices?* London: Palgrave Macmillan UK, pp.197-223.

Le, D. (2016), Environmental and Social Risks of Chinese Official Development Finance in Africa: The Case of the Lamu Port Project, Kenya. *African Review of Economics and Finance* 8, no. 1: 106-29.

Li, T. M. (2007), *The Will to Improve: Governmentality, Development, and the Practice of Politics*. Durham: Duke University Press.

Mawdsley, E. (2012), *From Recipients to Donors: Emerging powers and the Changing Development Landscape*. London: Zed Books.

Ministry of Foreign Affairs, People's Republic of China (MFA/PRC) (2012), *China-Myanmar friendship activities held in Yangon to boost ties*, Embassy of the People's Republic of China in the Republic of Union of Myanmar, 17 May 2012. Available online: http://mm.china-embassy.gov.cn/eng/sgxw/201205/t20120517_1387467.htm (Accessed on 9 May 2023. No longer available online).

Middleton, C. (2022), The political ecology of large hydropower dams in the Mekong Basin: a comprehensive review, *Water Alternatives*, 15(2), pp. 251-289.

Patel, S. (2021), *Why we should involve women in project decisions: the case of Lamu Coal Plant*, DeCOALonize [Blog]. Available online: https://www.decoalonize.org/why-we-should-involve-women-in-project-decisions-the-case-of-lamu-coal-plant/ (Accessed on 11 July 2023. No longer available online).

Pomeroy, M. et al. (2016), Civil Society, BRICS and International Development Cooperation: Perspectives from India, South Africa and Brazil, in J. Gu, A. Shankland, and A. Chenoy (eds.) *The BRICS in International Development*. London: Palgrave Macmillan UK, pp. 169-206.

Repnikova, M. (2022), *Chinese Soft Power*. Cambridge: Cambridge University Press (Elements in Global China).

Save Lamu (2018). Lamu Women Opposing the Proposed Coal Power Plant Project, Discuss on the Effects that will be Caused as a Result of the Project, *Save Lamu*, 12 July 2018. Available online: https://www.savelamu.org/lamu-women-oppose-proposed-coal-power-plant-project/ (Accessed on 9 May 2023)

Save Lamu (2019), Chinese Ambassador to Kenya Wu Peng Invites DeCOALonize Members for a Meeting Tells Them, He Personally does not Support Coal Plants, *Save Lamu*, 1 July 2019. Available online: https://www.savelamu.org/chinese-abassador-to-kenya-wu-peng-invites-decoalonize-members-for-a-meeting-says-he-personally-does-not-support-coal-plants/ (Accessed on 9 May 2023)

Shieh, S. (2022), Civil Society's Multifaceted Response to China's Belt and Road Initiative, *Global China Pulse*, 1(1), pp. 99-109.

Shipton, L. and Dauvergne, P. (2021), The Politics of Transnational Advocacy Against Chinese, Indian, and Brazilian Extractive Projects in the Global South, *The Journal of Environment & Development*, 30(3), pp. 240-264.

Tan-Mullins, M., Urban, F. and Mang, G. (2017), Evaluating the Behaviour of Chinese Stakeholders Engaged in Large Hydropower Projects in Asia and Africa, *The China Quarterly*, 230, pp. 464-488.

Tang, D. (2015), *Socialisation from Below – the Role of Myanmar Civil Society in China's Adoption of the Public Participation Norm*. PhD Dissertation. University of Manchester.

The Rupture Project (2022), Civil society in the Mekong: What can we learn from environmental struggles?, *The Rupture Project*, 16 August 2022. Available online: https://www.newmandala.org/civil-society-in-the-mekong-what-can-we-learn-from-environmental-struggles/ (Accessed on 9 May 2023).

Tian, F. and Chuang, J. (2022), Depoliticizing China's Grassroots NGOs: State and Civil Society as an Institutional Field of Power, *The China Quarterly*. 250, pp. 509-530.

Tobing-David, V. E. (2019), *The Gender Transformative and Responsible Agribusiness Investments in South-East Asia programme: Phase 1 evaluation report*. Oxfam GB.

United Nations Environmental Programme (UNEP) (2018), The Impacts on the Community of the Proposed Coal Plant in Lamu: Who, if Anyone, Benefits from Burning Fossil Fuels? – By DeCOALonize, *Perspectives*, Issue No. 31.

Waisbich, L. T. (2022), 'The Bank We Want': Chinese and Brazilian Activism around and within the BRICS New Development Bank, in P. Amar et al. (eds) *The Tropical Silk Road*. Stanford University Press, pp.190-203.

Waisbich, L. T. (2021a), Participation, Critical Support and Disagreement: Brazil-Africa Relations from the Prism of Civil Society, in M. Alencastro and P. Seabra (eds) *Brazil-Africa Relations in the 21st Century*. Cham: Springer International Publishing, pp.113-132.

Waisbich, L. T. (2021b), *Re-politicising South-South development cooperation: negotiating accountability at home and abroad*. PhD Dissertation. University of Cambridge.

Yeophantong, P. (2020), China and the Accountability Politics of Hydropower Development: How Effective are Transnational Advocacy Networks in the Mekong Region?, *Contemporary Southeast Asia*, 42(1), pp. 85-117.

Yu, X. (2012), Chinese NGOs Travel to Myanmar. *China Development Brief*, No. 53 (Spring 2012). Available online: https://chinadevelopmentbrief.org/reports/chinese-ngos-travel-to-myanmar/ (Accessed on 9 May 2023).

Zhou, L. et al. (2022), *China Overseas Finance Inventory Database*, World Resources Institute [Preprint].

Zhu, A. (2020), *Decoalonisation of Lamu. Interview with Omar Elmawi*, Goethe Institut Kenya, May 2020. Available online: https://www.goethe.de/ins/ke/en/kul/dos/sus/21847312.html (Accessed on 9 May 2023)

Conclusion and Looking forward

By Cai Yiping

The collective production of knowledge on Global China and its gender impact is a process. The first thing that we learned is that collective reflection and analysis do not begin with consensus. Throughout the process, everyone has been open to criticism and self-reflection and has changed their views and positions. It requires us to respect the diversity among researchers and the wide spectrum of expertise they have brought into this research in terms of their disciplinary and knowledge backgrounds. Some are specialised in development studies, some are China experts, and some are from the field of international relations, which is very much Northern dominated in terms of theories and framework. Some have feminist and social movement backgrounds. They are also from different regions of the Global South and with diverse political and cultural backgrounds. We see this as one of the strengths of this project, as it enables all participants to share their insights and analysis from their own unique contexts, experiences, and vantage points on the knowledge realm. Therefore, this diversity does not make their analyses less credible as long as their research methods are appropriate and viable. In fact, the findings of this study debunk the simplicity and generality of the framing of China's global engagement as 'Messiah vs. Monster'. As these case studies illustrate, China's global engagement involves various actors and is a dynamic process. DAWN appreciates the sincere and constructive criticism and critical self-reflection, intellectual integrity, and everyone's contribution in this mutual learning process.

DAWN is fully aware that the subject of this research – Global China – is a moving target, which makes any enquiries on this subject a challenging task. DAWN hopes this research provides food for thought for reimagining South-South relations from a gender perspective to promote positive changes both in China and the Global South. This research project is an example of Southern feminist knowledge building and collaboration through mutual learning, interactive discussion, and candid dialogue.

These empirical case studies challenge the macro-narrative about China's global influence by focusing on the local-global connection and prioritising the bottom-up approach. These papers cover a wide range of relevant topics – China's soft power; women, peace, and security; civil society activism; and investment in mining, infrastructure, and agriculture – and examine the various sectors – from states, the business sector, and financial institutions, to traditional donors and international development agencies, local communities, civil societies, women's organizations, and indigenous groups – while depicting the complexity and interdependency of the process of the development of China's global footprint and the new world these engagements help to create. They put women's agency at the centre rather than seeing women merely as passive victims or a vulnerable group. They juxtapose holding Chinese state and business actors accountable and the capacity building of developing countries to negotiate with China and other development actors. They call on mutual accountability from both China and recipient countries. Therefore, this exploratory research challenges the dominant monolithic image of the rise of China and the victimisation of the South, which is often biased by colonialism, orientalism, and the yellow peril narrative, to explore the possibility of a new South-South relationship. As a new development actor, China's engagement with the Global South should not simply reinforce the donor-recipient dependence syndrome that has traditionally plagued the Global South in development partnerships. Gender equality and women's development are achievable goals and should be put high on the agenda in China's development cooperation, with appropriate operational guidelines and adequate financial resources. This should not be regarded as contradicting China's non-interference and non-conditionality principle in foreign policy. These case studies suggest that recipient countries as active agents are responsible for promoting their own gender agenda in development cooperation projects executed with China and any other development partners. Only in this way does reimagining a South-South relationship and a meaningful transnational feminist dialogue become possible.

To achieve this goal, internal advocacy on all sides is necessary, which requires South-South feminist collaboration. Utilising UN forums and mechanisms, such as the momentum of Beijing+30 and the CEDAW review, could be a possible way forward for advocacy.

Due to time constraints and other barriers, limited mobility during the COVID-19 pandemic, for instance, this project could not comprehensively examine all the interesting topics regarding Global China and its engagement in the Global South, such as the inexorable role that China plays in the global capitalist system (production and consumption) and global value chain, especially given Chinese investments in the extraction of raw materials. What is the peculiarity of Chinese state capital? What are the differences between Chinese capital oriented towards profit-optimisation and traditional private capital that maximises profit in terms of their impacts on women? What mechanisms can be created to facilitate and sustain Global South feminist long-term exchange, movement-building, and policy advocacy? Many questions are yet to be explored. DAWN hopes that the genuine interest generated from this Southern feminist collaboration and the feminist critical analysis of gender and development with regards to Chinese international cooperation born out of this process will continue to grow and that this endeavour will lead to meaningful and strategic engagement with Chinese and other actors.

After two decades of the rapid expansion of its global engagement, China is facing encirclement by the West, led by the US, and growing resistance from people in the Global South, and acceptances as well, especially in the global context when the US and its western allies withdraw from the international aid and explicitly declare to prioritize their own national interests over the development cooperation. Meanwhile, China is also competing with the other emerging powers than the traditional donors from the developed North in the field of international development cooperation. Thus, the blunt question for Southern feminists to answer is: Can South-South feminist dialogue and solidarity detoxify misogyny, patriarchy, militarism, nationalism, imperialism, colonialism, and neo-liberal capitalism and enable us to re-imagine a feminist agenda that puts human rights, dignity, and self-determination, as well as gender, economic, and ecological justice, at the centre? DAWN invites Southern feminist scholars and activists to work and think and act together.

Index

Note: References followed by "n" refer to notes.

ABP. *See* Anchor Borrowers' Programme
Acción Ecológica 28
ACWF. *See* All-China Women's Federation
ADB. *See* Asia Development Bank
Addis Ababa Action Plan 317
AfDB. *See* African Development Bank
Africa Institute of Environmental Law (AIEL) 118–19
African Development Bank (AfDB) 215, 216
African Mineral Development Centre (AMDC) 119
Afuga, B. 171
Agarwal, Ritu 20
agriculture technology demonstration centers (ATDC) 137, 138, 154
AIEL. *See* Africa Institute of Environmental Law
AIIB. *See* Asia Infrastructure Investment Bank
All-China Women's Federation (ACWF) 28, 191, 196, 199, 200
Aluminium Corporation of China 89
AMDC. *See* African Mineral Development Centre
AMV. *See* minerals value chain
Anchor Borrowers' Programme (ABP) 145
Anderson, Katrina 88
anti-coal power campaign in Lamu, Kenya 21, 207–8, 214–17
anti-hydropower campaigns in Mekong Basin 207
  Cheay Areng dam in Cambodia 207–8, 212–14
  Myitsone dam in Myanmar 207–8, 211–12, 213–14
anti-state state 114
Arcadia mining 118

ASEAN. *See* Association of Southeast Asian Nations, The
Asia Development Bank (ADB) 63, 78, 79
Asia Foundation 219–20
Asia Infrastructure Investment Bank (AIIB) 3, 7
Asian Infrastructure Development Bank 221
Association of Southeast Asian Nations, The (ASEAN) 189
ATDC. *See* agriculture technology demonstration centers
AUKUS. *See* United States, United Kingdom, and Australia
Aung San Suu Kyi 211
Australia
  as donor of Solomon Islands 165
  commitments to women's development in Solomon Islands 176–7
  gender equality in Indo-Pacific region 174
  in geopolitical competition 68
  'Pacific Step Up' initiative 66
  partnership with PICs 66
  sanctions on Zimbabwe 111
  security agreement with Solomon Islands 167, 170
  'strategic denial' policy 63
  WPS NAP 2022–2031, 174–5
Away from All Pests: An English Surgeon in People's China 1954–1969 (Horn) 195

B3W initiative. *See* Build Back Better World initiative
Bakare, M. 140
Bandung Conference (1955) 22
BAPA. *See* Buenos Aires Plan of Action
Barriteau, Eudine 44

BCEG. *See* Beijing Construction Engineering Group
Beijing +25 national review report 70, 71–2
Beijing Construction Engineering Group (BCEG) 49, 50, 51
Beijing Declaration and Platform for Action. *See* Beijing Platform for Action (BPfA)
Beijing Platform for Action (BPfA) 8, 9, 68
    Fourth World Conference on Women in Beijing document 192
    Solomon Islands participation in 168
    Tonga's signing of 70
    Vanuatu's signing of 71
Belt and Road Initiative (BRI) 1, 3, 5, 63, 155, 209
    energy infrastructure investments of China 210
    gender equality policies and implementation 79, 80
    Global South projects 186
    human rights and gender, incorporation of 64
    role in China's international development cooperation policy 53
    Tonga, infrastructure projects in 18, 64–5, 69–76
    Vanuatu, infrastructure projects in 18, 64–5, 69–73, 76–8
Bikita. *See* extractivism in Bikita, Zimbabwe; lithium mining in Bikita, Zimbabwe
BPfA. *See* Beijing Platform for Action
BRI. *See* Belt and Road Initiative
BRICS Bank 3
Buenos Aires Plan of Action (BAPA) 22
Build Back Better World initiative (B3W initiative) 5
Business & Human Rights Resource Centre 122
Business and Human Rights Information Centre 89
Byrne, Deirdre C. 15

Cajas National Park, Ecuador 99
Cambodia. *See* Cheay Areng dam in Cambodia
Caribbean, Chinese development cooperation in 39–40
    Couva Hospital project 43, 46, 47–8
    development approaches 40–1
    donor-recipient dependent syndrome 54
    e TecK Phoenix Industrial Park 43, 46, 49–51
    factors to consider in project design 54–5
    framing gender and women's agency in 43–6
    gender mainstreaming 52–3
    using interpretivist philosophy 46
    positionality on gender 41–3
Caribbean-China Economic and Trade Cooperation Forum 40, 45–6
Caribbean Community (CARICOM) 39
CARICOM. *See* Caribbean Community
Carter, Jimmy 26
Castro, Ana Gabriela 93, 101
CCCMC. *See* China Chamber of Commerce of Metals, Minerals and Chemicals Importers and Exporters
CEDAW. *See* Convention on the Elimination of All Forms of Discrimination Against Women
Cevallos, Steven 101
CEXIM. *See* Export-Import Bank of China
CFRD. *See* China Foundation for Rural Development
CGCOC Group Co., Ltd. 145
CGC Overseas Construction Group Co., Limited. *See* CGCOC Group Co., Ltd.
Chambers, Robert 142
Charity Law (2016) 221
Cheay Areng dam in Cambodia
    anti-hydropower campaign against 207–8, 213–14
    hydropower plant initiation and construction 212
    local contestation against 212–13
Chengxin Lithium Group 118
Chicñawi community 96, 106n3
China-Africa agricultural cooperation 140–1
    China's engagement in agriculture investment 138
    modalities for 137–8

China-Solomon Islands security agreement 25, 64, 67, 163, 169. *See also* Solomon Islands
  benefiting from geopolitical situation 177–8, 179
  comparison with Australia's WPS NAP 174–5
  implications for WPS NAP 171–4
  inclusion of women in security agreement discussions 176, 178
  opportunities for advancing WPS 175–6
  perceptions and implementation 169–71
  relationship with China to enhance women's development 176–7
  strengthening implementation of security policies 178
China-Solomon Islands Video Dialogue on Women and Poverty Reduction 69
China Central Television 196
China Chamber of Commerce of Metals, Minerals and Chemicals Importers and Exporters (CCCMC) 90, **91–2**, 93, 114
China Daily 196
China Daily Online 76
China Foundation for Poverty Alleviation (CFPA). See China Foundation for Rural Development (CFRD)
China Foundation for Rural Development (CFRD) 189–90
China International Development Cooperation Agency (CIDCA) 6, 28
China Mineral Resources 118
China Minmetals Corporation (MMG) 87, 89, 93–5, 97
China NGO Network for International Exchanges (CNIE) 212, 226n2
China Power Investment (CPI) 211, 212
China Radio International 196
China's International Development Cooperation in the New Era 1, 9, 11, 29, 42, 69, 78
China Social Science Forum 188
China Women's University 193
China Xinhua News Network Corporation (CNC) 196
Chinese-invested power plant in Kenya, campaign against 20

Chinese People's Political Consultative Conference (CPPCC) 42
Chuang, J. 221, 227n13
CICDHA. *See* Collective on Chinese Finance and Investment, Human Rights and the Environment
CIDCA. *See* China International Development Cooperation Agency
CIs. *See* Confucius Institutes
Civil Society Forum of Tonga (CSFT) 75
civil society organizations (CSOs) 21, 65, 75, 115, 177, 218–19
civil society transnational action 207, 223–4
  Cheay Areng dam in Cambodia, campaign against 207–8, 212–14
  contestation in Southeast Asia and East Africa 210–11
  enhancement on gender-related issues 225–6
  gender blindness 20, 217–22, 224
  Lamu coal power plant, campaign against 207–8, 214–17
  missing Chinese allies 222–3
  Myitsone dam in Myanmar, campaign against 207–8, 211–12, 213–14
  social mobilization on development cooperation 208–10
  use of collaboration with host countries 224–5
CNC. *See* China Xinhua News Network Corporation
CNIE. *See* China NGO Network for International Exchanges
Collective on Chinese Finance and Investment, Human Rights and the Environment (CICDHA) 89–90
Communist Party of China (CPC) 185
  criticizing lingering feudal patriarchal social relations 190–1
  enhancing cultural soft power of China 188
  international image management 187
  national policy of gender equality and women's empowerment 185–6
Comprehensive Nuclear Test Ban Treaty (CTBT) 178
Conference on Commemorating the Tenth Anniversary of the Fourth World Conference on Women 69

Confucius Classrooms (CCs) 194
Confucius Institutes (CIs) 194, 198
Convention on the Elimination of All
  Forms of Discrimination Against
  Women (CEDAW) 10, 42, 68, 192
  General Recommendation 168–9
  public opposition to Tonga's ratification 71
  review for South-South feminist solidarity and advocacy 28–9
  Solomon Islands as part of 168
Convention on the Rights of Persons with Disabilities (CRPD) 10
Conway, Gordon 142
CooperAcción 28
corporate social responsibility (CSR) 12, 113, 145
Couva Children's Hospital. *See* Couva Hospital project
Couva Hospital project 19, 43, 46, 47–8, 51–2
CPC. *See* Communist Party of China
CPI. *See* China Power Investment
CPPCC. *See* Chinese People's Political Consultative Conference
criminalization 96–7
CRPD. *See* Convention on the Rights of Persons with Disabilities
CSFT. *See* Civil Society Forum of Tonga
CSOs. *See* civil society organizations
CSR. *See* corporate social responsibility
CTBT. *See* Comprehensive Nuclear Test Ban Treaty

Das, S. 141
DAWN. *See* Development Alternatives with Women for a New Era
De la Puente, L. 95
Department of Foreign Affairs and Trade of Australia (DFAT) 75, 78, 79, 165
Department of Women's Affairs of Vanuatu (DWA) 72
Development Alternatives with Women for a New Era (DAWN) 1–13, 16, 233, 235
DFAT. *See* Department of Foreign Affairs and Trade of Australia
donor-recipient dependent syndrome 54
Due Diligence Guidelines for Responsible Mineral Supply of China 114–15

Dussel, Enrique 88
DWA. *See* Department of Women's Affairs of Vanuatu

Ecuador. *See* Río Blanco (Ecuador), Chinese mining project in
Ecuagoldmining South America S. A. 99
Elimination of Violence Against Women and Girls policies (EVAWG policies) 168
Elmawi, Omar 207
EMA. *See* Environmental Management Authority
energy infrastructure investments of China 207, 210, 217
Enlai, Zhou 22
environmental activism 219, 220
Environmental Management Authority (EMA) 49, 50
e TecK Phoenix Industrial Park 19, 43, 46, 49
  general public, consultation with 49–50
  operational agreement 50–1
  women's empowerment and opportunity 51–2
EVAWG policies. *See* Elimination of Violence Against Women and Girls policies
Exchange and Training Base for Global Women's Development Cooperation 28
Export-Import Bank of China (CEXIM) 47, 49, 73
  Cheay Areng dam in Cambodia 212
  Myitsone dam project in Myanmar 211
extractivism in Bikita, Zimbabwe 112. *See also* lithium mining in Bikita, Zimbabwe
  Chinese investment 113–14, 118–19
  community share ownership schemes 128
  and corporate accountability frameworks 112–13
  economic crisis and 116–17
  environmental cost and gendered nature 120
  framework for accountability 114–15
  mining reforms 117–18, 119–20
  securitization and militarization issues 128

shifts in indigenisation policies 111, 115, 119–20, 127
social reproduction 128–9

fahu system 71, 84n30
Fanshen: A Documentary of Revolution in a Chinese Village (Hinton) 195–6
Farnworth, C. R. 152
Fast Track Land Reform (FTLR) 117, 121
feminist foreign policy 26–7
  of US 27
financial capital 143, 153
Five Principles of Peaceful Co-existence of China 22
FOCAC. *See* Forum for China-Africa Cooperation
Ford Foundation 221
Forum for China-Africa Cooperation (FOCAC) 137
  Beijing Action Plan 9, 11
  Dakar Action Plan 11
FTLR. *See* Fast Track Land Reform

GAWAL. *See* Green Agriculture West Africa Limited
GDI. *See* Global Development Initiative
GEEJ framework. *See* gender, economic and ecological justice framework
GEI. *See* Global Environmental Institute
Gender and Equality and Women's Development (GEWD) 168
gender blindness 20, 217–24
gender, economic and ecological justice framework (GEEJ framework) 142
gender equality 1, 7–8
  China-Solomon Island bilateral security cooperation 19–20
  China's positionality on gender 9, 12, 41–3
  consideration of enforcement of security measures 54–5
  contradictory trends in Chinese state 199
  CPC's national policy of 185–6
  demands for equal rights 200
  in Forum on China-Africa Cooperation Beijing Action Plan 9
  fundamental change in perceptions and practices 200–1

gender analysis of China's BRI infrastructure 69–78
gender and women's agency in development cooperation 43–6
gender impact of investments and trade in Global South 11–12, 14
  in PICs 68–9, 80–1
  in Solomon Islands 167–8
  Southern feminist collaboration and solidarity for 27–9
  SSC's role 10–11, 23–4, 28
gender mainstreaming of China 25–6, 52–4, 79, 81, 140
GES scheme. *See* Growth Enhancement Support scheme
GEWD. *See* Gender and Equality and Women's Development
Gilmore, Ruth Wilson 113
Global China concept 12–13, 233
  engagement of China-based organizations 220
  improvement of socio-environmental performance 219
  requiring feminist collective analyses 17
  transnational mobilization on 226
Global Development Initiative (GDI) 4, 77, 209
Global Environmental Institute (GEI) 212
González-Vicente, Rubén 89
Gopee-Scoon, Paula 50
governance vacuum 114, 115
Great Leap Forward, The 191
Green Agriculture West Africa Limited (GAWAL) 139–40, 141
  agricultural development activities 145
  agricultural training for Nigerian smallholders 146–8, 154, 155n8, 160–1
  implementation of Chinese aid projects in Nigeria 145
  smallholder participation in outgrower scheme 149
Green Watershed 212
Growth Enhancement Support scheme (GES scheme) 145
Guangming Daily, The 187
Guidelines on Environmental Protection and Cooperation (2013) 227n12
Gu, J. 140

Hinton, William 195–6
Horn, Joshua S. 195
human capital 143
human rights of women 43, 112
　Chinese position on 9–10
　Third World feminism 43–4
Hun Sen 213

ICBC. *See* Industrial Commercial Bank of China
ICESCR. *See* International Covenant on Economic, Social and Cultural Rights
ICRW. *See* International Centre for Research on Women
IFAD. *See* International Fund for Agricultural Development
IMF. *See* International Monetary Fund
Imma, Z'étoile 15
Industrial Commercial Bank of China (ICBC) 93, 215, 216
information capital 143, 152
information-sharing process 152–3
International Centre for Research on Women (ICRW) 26
international Chinese operations, gender and Chinese guidelines for 90, 91–2, 93
international communication platform of China 195–7
International Covenant on Economic, Social and Cultural Rights (ICESCR) 10
International Forum on Women and Sustainable Development 69
International Fund for Agricultural Development (IFAD) 143
International Monetary Fund (IMF) 24
international NGOs (INGOs) 214, 215, 221
International Organization for Mediation (IOMed) 6
international poverty alleviation cooperation projects of China 189
International Rivers 212, 214
International Women's Development Agency (IWDA) 26
interpretivist philosophy 46
IOMed. *See* International Organization for Mediation
IWDA. *See* International Women's Development Agency

Jiangxi Copper 89
Jiao, Y. 140
Junefield Mineral Resources 89, 99

Kari, Hilda 168
Kastam practices 72, 84n33
Kelkar, Govind 20
Kenya. *See* Lamu coal power plant in Kenya
key observers in PCIs 65, 81n3
　Tongan observer 71, 74–5, 79
　Vanuatu observer 77–8, 79

LAC framework. *See* Latin American and the Caribbean framework
Lamu coal power plant in Kenya 21
　anti-coal power campaign against 207, 215–17
　project initiation and 214–15
Lamu Port-South Sudan-Ethiopia Transport Corridor Project (LAPSSET) 216
LAPSSET. *See* Lamu Port-South Sudan-Ethiopia Transport Corridor Project
Las Bambas (Peru), Chinese mining project in 20, 28, 88, 93–4. *See also* Río Blanco (Ecuador), Chinese mining project in
　economic impacts on women 94–5, 103
　environmental impacts on women 95–6, 103
　impacts and resistance 103–5, 104–5
　political impacts on women 96–7, 103–4
　role of women's agency 98
　socio-cultural impacts on women 97–8, 104
Latin America. *See* mining projects of China in Latin America
Latin American and the Caribbean framework (LAC framework) 39
Lavame'a Ta'e'iloa Disabled Peoples Association 75
Law on Protecting Women's Rights and Interests 192
lithium mining in Bikita, Zimbabwe 111, 121
　Bikita mine history timeline *122*
　Chinese investments 118

and economic crisis 120–1
economic, social, and ecological
   impacts 127–8
employment gender discrimination
   123–4
environmental impacts 121–2, 124
impact on women's rights 111–12, 116,
   124–5
violation of labor rights 123, 126
Lynch, Daniel 187

Mafeje, Archie 114
Mamani, Yovana 93
Maritime Silk Road Initiative 63
Massiah, Joycelin 45, 55nn1–2
Media Going Global document 196
Micronesians in Solomon Islands 164,
   179n2
mining projects of China in Latin America
   19, 87–8
   context and characteristics 88–90
   economic impact on women 103
   emergence of women's social
      movements 104, 105
   environmental impact on women 103
   human rights abuses linked to Chinese
      business 89–90
   Las Bambas project in Peru 20, 93–8,
      104–5, 28 88
   political impact on women 103–4
   Río Blanco project in Ecuador 20, 28,
      88, 99–102, 104–5
   socio-cultural impact on women 104
MMG. See China Minmetals Corporation
Mnangagwa, Emmerson 117
Molleturo community in Ecuador 99
Montoute, Annita 28
Mujeres en Resistencia Sinchi Warmi 101
Myitsone dam in Myanmar
   anti-hydropower campaign against
      207–8, 213–14
   Chinese engagement in hydropower
      plant construction 211
   GEI's work in 219
   local contestation against 211–12
   SRI's work in 219

National Council of Women (NCW) 168,
   172
National Research Centre of China 188

National Security Strategy of Solomon
   Islands (NSS) 171, 176–8
National Sustainable Development Plan of
   Vanuatu (NSDP) 76–7
National Women and Girls Economic
   Empowerment Strategy (NWGEES)
   168
National Women's Association of Nepal
   193
natural capital 143
Nepal
   CFPA in 190
   National Women's Association of Nepal
      193
New Development Bank (NDB) 3, 7, 221
New International Economic Order
   (NIEO) 3
New Zealand
   in geopolitical competition 68
   multisectoral support to Solomon
      Islands 177
   'Pacific Reset' strategy 66
   'strategic denial' policy 63
Nigeria, agricultural cooperation with
   China 19, 138, 140–1
   Chinese agricultural aid on female
      farmers 141
   examining on gender perspective 144–5
   GAWAL's role 139–40, 141, 145–8, 154
   GEEJ framework 142
   impacts on female smallholders' income
      and livelihood 143–4, 148–51, 154
   recommendations 154–5
   role of state, industries and universities
      in 138–9
   shifting gender norms through capital
      acquisition 151–3
   sustainable livelihood framework
      142–3, 151
NIEO. See New International Economic
   Order
Nye, Joseph 186

Occupational Safety and Health Agency
   (OSHA) 50
Odero, K. K. 142
OFDI. See Outward Foreign Direct
   Investment
Olasehinde, T. S. 148, 153
One China Policy 41

'One Province, One Country' cooperation model 138
Organization of Women in Resistance Sinchi Warmi 102
organized violence 115
OSHA. *See* Occupational Safety and Health Agency
Outline for the Development of Chinese Women (2021-2030) 193
Outward Foreign Direct Investment (OFDI) 219
Oxfam Hong Kong 221

Pacific Island Countries (PICs) 63
   gender analysis of China's BRI infrastructure in 69-78, 81
   gender equality in 68-9, 80-1
   and international development cooperation of China 65-8
Pacific Islands Forum Secretariat (PIFS) 66, 68
Pacific Leaders Gender Equality Declaration (PLGED) 68, 71, 72
Pacific Platform for Action (PPA) 68
'Pacific Reset' strategy of New Zealand 66
'Pacific Step Up' initiative of Australia 66
Panuelo, David 67
Partnership for Global Infrastructure and Investment 5
Pérez, L. 95
Persad-Bissessar, Kamla 47
Peru. *See* Las Bambas (Peru), Chinese mining project in
physical capital 143
PICs. *See* Pacific Island Countries
PIFS. *See* Pacific Islands Forum Secretariat
PLGED. *See* Pacific Leaders Gender Equality Declaration
PPA. *See* Pacific Platform for Action

Qi Ren 140
QUAD. *See* Quadrilateral Security Dialogue
Quadrilateral Security Dialogue (QUAD) 179n3

RAMSI. *See* Regional Assistance Mission to Solomon Islands
Rape Survivors Network in Zimbabwe 127, 128

Rarotonga Treaty on South Pacific Nuclear Free Zone 178
Raymond, Afra 41
RDCF. *See* Rural Constituency Development Fund
Red Cross Society of China (RCSC) 70
regional activism in Southeast Asia 226
Regional Assistance Mission to Solomon Islands (RAMSI) 166-7, 168
right to development (RtD) 9
Río Blanco (Ecuador), Chinese mining project in 20, 28, 88, 99. *See also* Las Bambas (Peru), Chinese mining project in
   economic impacts on gender issues 99-100, 103
   environmental impacts on gender issues 100, 103
   impacts and resistance 104-5
   political impacts on gender issues 100-1, 103-4
   role of women's agency 102
   socio-cultural impacts on gender issues 101-2, 104
Royal Solomon Islands Police Force (RSIPF) 172, 173
RSIPF. *See* Royal Solomon Islands Police Force
Rural Constituency Development Fund (RDCF) 166

'Save the Ayeyarwady' campaign 211
SCG. *See* Shanghai Construction (Caribbean) Group
S.C.G. Caribbean Group Ltd. 55n3
Scoones, I. 142, 151
SDGs. *See* Sustainable Development Goals
Security Treaty (2017) 167
sexual orientation and gender identity (SOGI) 8
Shanghai Construction (Caribbean) Group (SCG) 47, 48, 55n3, 74
Shanghai World Expo (2010) 197
Shougang Corporation 89
Sinchi Warmi 102, 106n6
Sinomine Resource Group in Bikita, Zimbabwe 118
   employment gender discrimination 123-4

impact on women's rights 124–7
violation of labor rights 123, 126
'small but beautiful' model 155
social capital 143
social organizations. *See* civil society organizations (CSOs)
soft power of China 185. *See also* gender equality
　components of China's culture 198–9
　Confucius Institutes 194, 198
　definition of 186–7
　economic prosperity 189
　educational internationalisation 195
　failure in meeting targets of SDG Five 200
　gender inequalities and discrimination 199
　global level commitment on women's empowerment 192–4
　international communication platform 195–7
　limitations 186
　poverty reduction programmes 189–90
　scholars' discussions on traditional culture 187–9
　socialist construction 198
　sources of data collection 186
　sports and expo events 197–8
　women in national revolutionary agenda 190–2
Sogavare, Manasseh 166, 167, 173
SOGI. *See* sexual orientation and gender identity
Solomon Islands. *See also* China-Solomon Islands security agreement
　diplomatic switch from Taiwan to China 163, 165–6
　economic dependency 165
　gender equality in 167–8
　geography and population 164–5
　Micronesians in 164, 179n2
　National Peace Building Policy 168
　Pijin language 179n1
　political instability 166
　security agreement with Australia 167
　violence in Honiara 166–7
　WPC in 168–9
South-South cooperation (SSC)
　BAPA+40, 22–3

CEDAW review 28–9
China's relationship with PICs through 66
China's role in promotion in 10–11, 28
hybrid model of China's agricultural engagements 139, 141, 145
rethinking from gender perspective 23–4
social mobilization on 208–10
South-South feminist collaboration 234
Southern feminist
　collaboration of China 14–15, 16, 27–9
　perspectives and inquiry of China 14–15
Southern providers 208, 209
step-down programme 152, 155n8
'strategic denial' policy 63
Sun, H. L. 138
Sustainable Development Goals (SDGs) 4, 200
sustainable livelihood framework 142–3, 151

Taiwan 67
　diplomatic relationship with Solomon Islands 165–6
　as 'renegade province' in China's view 165
Tanna and Malakula Road Rehabilitation Project 76
Ten Principles of Bandung 22
Third World 2–3
　feminism 43–4
　Three Worlds Theory 3
Tian, F. 221, 227n13
Tianqi Lithium 89
Tonga, China's engagements in
　infrastructure projects in 64, 69–70
　challenges and recommendations 64–5
　gender equality and women's issues in 70–2
　gender equality awareness programmes 25
　impacts of infrastructure projects 74–6
　infrastructural projects to women's development 72–3
　partners with Chinese BRI projects 18
　research questions on gender impacts 64
Tongling NonFerrous Metals Group 89

Traditional Leaders Act (1998) 125
transnational solidarity networks 222–3
Transparency Solomon Islands (TSI) 172
'trickle down' strategy 18–19
Trinidad and Tobago 42–3
   Chinese investments in construction sector 45–6
   Couva Hospital project 19, 43, 46, 47–8, 51–2
   e TecK Phoenix Industrial Park 43, 46, 49–51
   Raymond's criticism on China's development cooperation in 41
Trump, Donald
   and 'American First' foreign policy 17
   shift in US foreign aid policy under 5–6
TSI. See Transparency Solomon Islands

UDeCOTT. See Urban Development Corporation of Trinidad and Tobago
Ugarte, D. 95
Umaru Baba, S. 153
UNEP. See United Nations Environmental Programme
UNESCO. See United Nations Educational, Scientific and Cultural Organization
UNFAO-SSC. See United Nations Food Agriculture Organization South-South Cooperation Programme
UNFAO. See United Nations Food Agriculture Organization
UN Guiding Principles for Human Rights 114
United Kingdom (UK) 165
   bilateral cooperation with Solomon Islands 177
   sanctions on Zimbabwe 111
United Nations (UN)
   China's participation in UN system 4–5
   CSW59, 8
   Declaration on the Right to Development 42
   General Assembly Resolution 2758, 4
United Nations Educational, Scientific and Cultural Organization (UNESCO) 215
United Nations Environmental Programme (UNEP) 215
United Nations Food Agriculture Organization (UNFAO) 137
United Nations Food Agriculture Organization South-South Cooperation Programme (UNFAO-SSC) 138
United States (US)
   domination in Pacific geopolitics 63
   in geopolitical competition 68
   and QUAD 179n3
   reestablishment of relationship with Solomon Islands 170
   sanctions on Zimbabwe 111
   'strategic denial' policy 63
   USAID programmes in Pacific 66
United States Agency for International Development (USAID) 66
   Executive Order 14169 impact in 6
United States, United Kingdom, and Australia (AUKUS) 170, 178
University of the West Indies (UWI) 47
Urban Development Corporation of Trinidad and Tobago (UDeCOTT) 47, 48, 55n4
USAID. See United States Agency for International Development
UWI. See University of the West Indies

Van der Horst, D. 153
Vanuatu, China's engagements in
   infrastructure projects in 64, 69–70
   approaches in gender equality and women's empowerment 64–5
   gender equality and women's issues in 70–2
   impacts of infrastructure projects 76–8
   partners with Chinese BRI projects 18
   research questions on gender impacts 64
   to women's development 72–3
Veliu, A. 141

WAGED. See Women's Affairs and Gender Equality Division
Waisbich, Laura Trajber 20
Wang Huning 187
Wang Yang 67
Wang Yi 68
'Warmi Muyu' community art project 102
WB. See World Bank
WICP. See Women in the Caribbean Project

women. *See also* gender equality
  Caribbean women's role in political economy 44–6
  in China's national revolutionary agenda 190–2
  China's promotion of gender mainstreaming 52–3
  in Chinese state's development discourse 9–10
  Couva Hospital project, impact of 48, 51–2
  GAWAL's agricultural training in Nigeria 146–8, 154, 155n8, 160–1
  human rights of 43
  instrumentalisation in Global South 14–15
  land acquisition in Nigeria 156n9
  Las Bambas project impacts 94–8
  Phoenix Industrial Park, impact of 50–1, 52
  Río Blanco project impacts 99–102
  struggle against Chinese projects 20
  Zimbabwe's lithium mining impact on rights of 111–12, 116, 119–20, 124–7
Women in Resistance Sinchi Warmi. *See Mujeres en Resistencia Sinchi Warmi*
Women in the Caribbean Project (WICP) 45, 55n1
Women of China 196
Women, Peace, and Security agenda (WPS agenda) 19, 27
Women, Peace, and Security National Action Plan (WPS NAP) 168
  Australia (2022–2031) 174–5
  implications of China-Solomon Islands security agreement 171–4
  opportunities for advancement 175–8
  Solomon Islands (2017–2021) 168, 169, 178
Women's Affairs and Gender Equality Division (WAGED) 71
Women's Committees in All-China Federation of Trade Unions 191

World Bank (WB) 63
  aid projects 24
  development projects in PICs 78
  poverty alleviation assistance to China 189
WPS agenda. *See* Women, Peace, and Security agenda
WPS NAP. *See* Women, Peace, and Security National Action Plan

Xi Jinping
  financial aid to UN Women 192
  national policy of gender equality 185
  speech at high-level meeting of the 25th anniversary of the Fourth World Conference on Women (Beijing+25) 193
  statement on traditional Chinese culture 188
  withholding overseas coal power plants funding 214
Xinhua News Agency 187, 196

Yanjan Group 77
Yumi Tok Tok Forum 171
Yu, Y. 64

ZANU-PF. *See* Zimbabwe African National Union-Patriotic Front
ZELA. *See* Zimbabwe Environmental Law Association
Zhangliang, Hu 6
Zhejiang Huayou Cobalt 118
Zibechi, Raúl 103
Zijin Mining Group 89
Zimbabwe. *See* extractivism in Bikita, Zimbabwe; lithium mining in Bikita, Zimbabwe
Zimbabwe African National Union-Patriotic Front (ZANU-PF) 117
Zimbabwe Environmental Law Association (ZELA) 118–19